EUROPEAN TRAVELER-ARTISTS

IN NINETEENTH-CENTURY MEXICO

EUROPEAN TRAVELER-ARTISTS

IN NINETEENTH-CENTURY MEXICO

   Fomento Cultural Banamex, A. C.

COMISIÓN EUROPEA

With the support of
aeromexico

The organizers of the exhibition wish to thank the Instituto Goethe de México
for its help in arrangements made in France, Austria and Germany.

Cover. Pedro Gualdi, *View of Mexico City* (detail)
Page 2. Daniel Thomas Egerton, *Valley of Mexico* (detail) [1]
Page 4. Johann Moritz Rugendas, *View of the Valley of Mexico* (detail) [2]
Pages 10-11. Juan Patricio Morlete Ruiz, *View of the Plaza del Volador* [3]
Page 12. Hubert Sattler, *Tulum* [4]
Page 14. Pelegrín Clavé, *Day in the Country* [5]
Page 16. Paul Fischer, *The Plaza of Cortés with Popocatépetl and Iztaccíhuatl in the Background* [6]
Pages 20-21. Johann Salomon Hegi, *Mexico City* [7]
Page 22. Atanasio Echeverría, *Ascensión al volcán de San Andrés Tuxtla* (detail) [8]

© 1996 Fomento Cultural Banamex, A.C.
  Madero 17, Colonia Centro, México 06000, D.F.
  ISBN 968-7009-51-9

CONTENTS

Vista de la Plaza del Volador, por la parte del Sur construida desde lo alto del R.ᵉ Palacio, de la Ciu.ᵈ del Mex. con los Templos que se peciven, de Colex. Comv. de Religiosos y de Monjas,

1. N.ᵃ S.ᵃ de la Merced,
2. La Real Vniversidad.
3. Colegio de S. Pablo.
4. N.ᵃ S.ᵃ de Balvanera.
5. S.ᵗ Joseph de Gracia.
6. S.ᵗᵃ Cruz Acatlan.
7. Colᵉ
8. Parrᵒ

PRESENTATION

The task of rescuing the testimony related to the formation of the image of Mexico during the previous century is one of the most satisfying activities for those who, by vocation, are interested in the history of their country and are convinced of the need to make it known to both the Mexican and international public.

Such conviction has guided the activities of the Banco Nacional de México with regard to the support it provides Mexican culture through the undertaking of diverse projects, among the most outstanding of which is the exhibition "European Traveler-Artists in Nineteenth-Century Mexico," an endeavor which permits us to augment the existing awareness regarding the importance of Mexican history and of the relationships maintained with other peoples of the world since the beginnings of Mexico's life as an independent nation.

As such, Banamex welcomed with approval the proposal by the Delegation of the European Community Commission to jointly support the research and organization of this exhibition that will for the first time be viewed by the Mexican as well as the European public, thus providing a greater mutual understanding at a time when important political and economic links are being strengthened between Europe and Mexico.

The exhibition that Fomento Culural Banamex, A.C. has prepared is a truly significant and revealing testimony to the importance that Mexico held for the European travelers and, consequently, for the Europe from which they came, as well as to the value of the works by these traveler-artists in the formation of an aesthetic consciousness of the Mexican essence.

There are many lessons of both a historical and an aesthetic character that can be drawn from the contemplation of the works that have been brought together thanks to the enthusiastic collaboration involving museums and collectors in various European countries as well as in Mexico. Not least among these lessons is that which, beyond the accounts with which we are familiar regarding the complexities and difficulties faced during Mexico's first decades as an independent nation, exists within this testimony as to the cultural and natural richness of a country that, since its very beginning, contributed to the world an enormous cultural originality that was duly appreciated and expressed by this group of travelers who, throughout the century, made known the essence of Mexico in their own nations.

We congratulate ourselves in that this collaborative effort, which in addition to the Delegation of the European Community Commission has included the participation of such companies as Aeroméxico and Grupo Modelo, has yielded a result that will surely serve its purpose in contributing to the strengthening of the relationships between Mexico and Europe.

ALFREDO HARP HELÚ
Chairman of the Board of Directors
Grupo Financiero Banamex-Accival, S.A. de C.V.

ROBERTO HERNÁNDEZ RAMÍREZ
Chairman of the Board of Directors
Banco Nacional de México, S.A.

PRESENTATION

The exhibition "European Traveler-Artists in Nineteenth-Century Mexico," whose organizational initiative was undertaken by the European Community Commission in Mexico and by Fomento Cultural Banamex, A.C., who have in turn been joined by important European and Mexican companies in making it a reality, provides us the perfect occasion to remember the extraordinary richness of the relationship that, throughout more than five centuries, has been enjoyed between the various countries that form the European Union and this great nation of the Americas.

The images reproduced in this catalog are a faithful transcription of the passionate history that explains the European presence in Mexico during the previous century. Now that the epoch in which history was written according to Euro-centric criteria has been surpassed, the works exhibited here permit us to evaluate the complexity of the relationships between the two worlds throughout this span of one hundred years during which the European traveler-artists rediscovered the beauty and importance of the landscapes and the history, customs and humanity of the nascent Mexican society.

At the same time, they were strongly influenced by the coloring and character of the country and its inhabitants, then exotic to a certain degree but which, thanks to the diffusion of that which was Mexican throughout the Old World, were being converted into images that were accessible to the European spectator of those years.

The critical, analytical and sentient contemplation of the works that comprise this exhibition lead us to reflect equally on the importance of the cultural contacts made during that century and on the necessity of continuing to promote such cultural crossovers as an integral part of the multiple interchanges that are today going on between Mexico and Europe and that surely offer a potential greater than that of their rich history.

MANUEL MARÍN GONZÁLEZ
Vice-president of the
European Commission

PRESENTATION

The exhibition "European Traveler-Artists in Nineteenth-Century Mexico" is the result of a joint effort on the part of the Delegation of the European Community Commission and Fomento Cultural Banamex, A.C. which was initiated nearly two years ago when both parties forged an agreement to collaborate in the cultural arena with the aim of contributing to the strengthening of the relationship between Europe and Mexico within the broader, current atmosphere of cooperation between them.

The travelers who visited the nascent Mexican republic have been a subject of study in recent decades and, in Mexico, various publications and monographic exhibitions have been undertaken with regard to this theme, endowing it with the importance it holds as to the discovery and reevaluation of the Mexico's aesthetic treasures carried out by these personalities, from the scientific expeditions of the eighteenth century—especially the voyage by Alexander von Humboldt—to the dawning of the nineteenth century, initiating, in the fullest sense of the word, Europeans as well as the colony's residents into a complete knowledge of the magnitude and variety of the riches of what was then New Spain.

However, the initiative of the Delegation of the European Community Commission—which since its establishment in Mexico in 1989 had not participated in a cultural project as ambitious as this exhibition—and Fomento Cultural Banamex, went beyond that which had been achieved to date by proposing the need for a profound research effort in Europe in order to locate the works that these travelers had taken back with them, or that they had produced after their return to the Old World, which had remained in Europe and were now in the hands of public and private institutions, as well as in private collections.

The total of what was uncovered in Europe combined with that which exists in Mexico provides a more exact and complete vision of the true experience of the voyage and the different artistic motifs, abilities and styles of those who visited Mexico and left us aesthetic testimony of their travels through the country.

The investigative effort regarding this subject is without precedent as to the breadth of what has been researched and compiled in terms of the different nationalities of the artists whose work is being exhibited, as well as the diversity of the motives, duration and consequences of their voyages, in addition to the different levels of artistic training that can be observed among them and the use of techniques as diverse as drawing, oils, watercolor, photography and motion pictures, among others.

The works produced by the European traveler-artists in Mexico have one foot in the Old World and the other on the American continent. They offer us a taste of Europe's eagerness to expand its material and cultural horizons, provide a glimpse into the spiritual world of the traveler, and speak to us of how Mexico was and of how it appeared to the Europeans. The works of art and literature created by these travelers are, therefore, the manifestation of a link between two continents, and two lifestyles, very different yet united by a long history of interchanges.

Beginning with the research done by Fomento Cultural Banamex, and based on earlier studies, the exhibition asserts that the work of the traveler-artists in nineteenth-century Mexico forms part of the tradition of European expeditions throughout the length and breadth of the world, begun centuries earlier and that found renewed meaning from the Enlightenment, that marked routes and fixed points of interest and that decisively influenced the view of the traveler-artists.

The initial curiosity included the participation of various non-European artists such as Patricio Morlete and Pedro Calvo, whose works made the voyage in reverse and are now found in Europe, forming part of the same world view that explains the presence of the European artists in Mexico. All of them are heirs to the Enlightened expeditions such as that by Alessandro Malaspina or that by von Humboldt, whose iconography nourished the imagination of travelers throughout the century.

The natural riches of the newly independent nation were by then known to numerous Europeans who found in them the motivation for visiting, interested as much in the economic as the scientific possibilities. Others were attracted by commercial or industrial concerns, or participated in military or political adventures, or were simply attracted by what, for them, represented something exotic when compared to their everyday customs and aesthetics.

With this diversity of interests, these romantic artists, academic masters and amateur painters crossed the ocean, all of them seduced by the nature and customs of the new overseas republic. Each of them recreated the image of Mexico in his own way and transmitted it to his contemporaries through different means, and throughout the century the European vision of the landscape and people of Mexico began to crystallize, after having been jealously guarded for centuries by the Spanish Crown.

Indicative of the modern character of these personalities is the fact that, in their anxiety to discover and record their impressions in a precise and lasting manner, the travelers were, in general, eager to appropriate the inventions that were made available to them during the course of the century, whether they be traditional drawing instruments such as the camera obscura or a more recent innovation such as the camera lucida—more easily transported—or the impression of images onto light-sensitive paper, later to be known as photography, or finally, at the end of the century, the invention of motion pictures. Thus, the art of the travelers presents us with the complete range of technical resources from a period that was clearly characterized by the use of invention as a basic cultural form with which to confront reality and its problems.

The exhibition attempts to do justice also to the various methods which the traveler-artists utilized in the conservation and diffusion of their works, from the personal travel journal and the intimate character of small albums, perhaps elaborated with the intention of being shared only with family and friends, to the opposite extreme encountered in the sensational exhibition of spectacular panoramas that, in the first half of the past century, attracted thousands of spectators who for the first time viewed images made "from life" in the Americas.

The catalog that accompanies the exhibition attempts, for its part, to describe and explain, via the masterful essays by recognized specialists in art history and history in general, both European and Mexican, the complexity and richness of the subject of the travelers, providing detailed information on the most significant aspects of the lives and works of these singular personalities who, as part of a legion of travelers throughout the century, dedicated a part of their lives to the understanding, description, explanation and diffusion of the novel Mexican world of the past century.

The works exhibited and the accompanying catalog/book represent not only a description of nineteenth-century Mexico, in terms of the substantial amount of information they provide to the understanding of how the image of a nation was created over the span of a century, but at the same time offer us a fascinating portrait of a period whose omnipresent subject is, doubtless, the immense diversity which is Mexico, and in which we can also recognize the image of the traveler-artist who was, in some way, inseparably integrated into the world he expressed in his work.

This provides us with a double perspective on the profound meaning of this exhibition in that although the image of Mexico stands out as the singular theme among all of the travelers represented here, it can also truthfully be said that the majority of these works might be titled "Cultural Portrait of a European Traveler-Artist with Mexico as a Backdrop."

The organization of such an exhibition is truly complex because it entails the collaboration of innumerable individuals and institutions, without whose support it would not have been possible to achieve the goal of exhibiting works that normally are not available for public viewing. In this sense, the participation of a hardworking team has been essential in solving the complicated problems relative to the locating of works, arrangements for their loan, insurance and transportation issues, etc., as well as the good will shown by individuals and institutions, both in Mexico and in Europe, who have granted the loan of their property for this particular public showing.

The Delegation of the European Community Commission and Fomento Cultural Banamex wish to express their satisfaction at having been able to achieve this collaborative cultural undertaking, and the hope that the spectator finds in it a solid contribution to the better understanding of the long and rich past that unites both shores of the Atlantic.

FOMENTO CULTURAL BANAMEX, A.C. THE DELEGATION OF THE
EUROPEAN COMMUNITY COMMISSION IN MEXICO

INTRODUCTION

ELÍAS TRABULSE

At the beginning of the nineteenth century, in summing up the scientific work that had been achieved in the Americas by the Spanish, Baron Alexander von Humboldt wrote:

Since the final years of the reign of Charles III, and during that of Charles IV, the study of the natural sciences has made great progress not only in Mexico, but in all of the Spanish colonies. No European government has sacrificed sums as considerable as the Spanish in the dissemination of the knowledge of vegetables. Three botanical expeditions—those in Peru, New Granada and New Spain—directed by Mr. Ruíz and Mr. Pavón, don José Celestino Mutis, and Mr. Sessé and Mr. Mociño, have cost the State nearly 400,000 pesos. In addition, botanical gardens have been established in Manila and on the Canary Islands. The commission established to draw up the plans for the Güines Canal was also charged with examining the vegetable production on the island of Cuba. All of this research, conducted within the space of twenty years in the most fertile regions of the New Continent, has not only enriched the realm of science with more than four thousand new species of plants, but has also contributed much to the propagation of a sense of pleasure in natural history among the inhabitants of the country.

Since the middle of the eighteenth century, the winds of the Enlightenment in Europe had been felt on the Iberian Peninsula and in its colonies across the ocean. The positions taken by the monarchs mentioned by von Humboldt must be seen within the context of a vigorous momentum of renewal that was most apparent during the period which covers the end of one reign and the beginning of the next, that is, the last third of the century. It was during these years when Spain embarked on a series of political, administrative, economic and cultural reforms that would, in the end, promote material and intellectual progress in its colonies. The basic objective of these measures was to achieve optimum knowledge of the colonies in order to facilitate the most effective control over them, as well as to best exploit their wealth. New Spain, the richest possession of the Spanish empire, began to feel the winds of change in 1765 with the arrival of José de Gálvez, one of the most energetic officials sent by the Crown to the American territories. During his administrative term, reforms were carried out in the areas of public finance, mining and commerce. Additionally, a regular army was created and the defense of the northern citadels of the colony was structured. With his trip to the Californias he made clear the Crown's desires to reconnoiter the northern coastline of the Pacific Ocean.

Parallel to these types of economic and political reforms were those carried out in the area of the sciences. The Spanish government, sharing in the ideas being developed during the Enlightenment, had understood that scientific knowledge stood in direct relationship to material progress. In effect, the Crown's determination to diffuse scientific knowledge was echoed in the Americas, the most learned of the colony's subjects showing themselves to be receptive to the new currents. By soliciting information about natural history, astronomical and geographical data, as well as specimens of plants, animals and minerals for the museums and laboratories in Spain, and by facilitating the diffusion of gazettes and scientific periodicals, the Spanish government fed the development of the sciences in Mexico. The new

taxonomic theories in botany and zoology were disseminated, as well as the new chemical nomenclature. The process of the extraction of silver was interpreted from a purely chemical point of view. Numerous botanical, geodesic, astronomical, meteorological, geographical and statistical studies were carried out. In addition, important scientific institutions were founded: the Real Escuela de Cirugía (Royal School of Surgery), in 1768; the Jardín Botánico (Botanical Garden), in 1788; and the Real Seminario de Minería (Royal Mining Seminary), in 1792. The large Creole and European scientific community that worked in this atmosphere of renewal included such figures as Moziño, Sessé,

Alzate, Roxo, Bartolache, Gamboa, León y Gama, Rotea, Elhuyar, Lidner, Del Río, Bataller, Sonneschmidt, Cervantes, Oteyza, Rangel, Montaña, Barco, Clavigero, Guevara, Lozano, Guadalajara, Barquera, Zúñiga y Ontiveros, and Velázquez de León, among many others.

An interesting facet of this scientific impetus was the number of expeditions recorded by von Humboldt. The Crown's enlightened preoccupation for knowing the natural production of its vast overseas dominion found one of its first formal manifestations in the 1776 issuing of a royal decree which was printed under the title, *Instrucción hecha de orden del rey N.S. para que*

los virreyes, gobernadores, corregidores, alcaldes, intendentes de provincias en todos los dominios de S.M. puedan hacer escoger, preparar y enviar a Madrid todas las producciones curiosas de naturaleza (loosely, "Instructions, by Order of the King, to [all colonial officials] in all the dominions of His Majesty, as to the Collecting, Preparation and Shipment to Madrid of all Nature's Curious Products"), which was sent to the various Spanish colonies. Eleven years later, on March 20, 1787, a royal decree was issued which created a botanical expedition to New Spain and named Martín Sessé as its director. At the same time the chair in botany was established, the first Chairman of which was to be Vicente

Cervantes. The courses were opened in May of 1788 with a brilliant speech by Cervantes, a custom that was to be followed in subsequent years. In the aforementioned inaugural lessons he lectured on, among other subjects, the medicinal plants to be found in the environs of Mexico, the characteristics of the rubber plant, and the classification and properties of the ipecacuanha plant. His celebrated speech on the rubber plant, or *castilloa elastica*, so stirred Alzate that he printed it in one of his *Gacetas de Literatura*. Alzate also printed, in this same gazette, the notable speech given on the opening of the botany courses in 1793, written by Cervantes himself, and in which he eulogized Lin-

its part, the fruits of the botanical expedition were excellent. The work ran from 1787 to 1803, years in which herbs were gathered during tours of a good part of the colonial territory that stretched from California to Guatemala, and in which was achieved the classification of 4000 specimens, accompanied by more than 1400 drawings made by the young Creole artist Atanasio Echeverría and other notable artists. The select group of naturalists that made up this expedition were, in addition to Sessé, Juan Diego del Castillo, José Longinos Martínez, Jaime Senseve and, from 1789, José Moziño. The works *Flora mexicana* and *Plantae novae hispaniae*, products of a joint labor by Sessé and Moziño, were not published until well into the nineteenth century. By their character, these works can be considered alongside the monumental work of Baron Alexander von Humboldt, *Essai sur la géographie des plantes* (Essay on the Geography of Plants), published in 1805, a work in which the author proposed executing not only a taxonomic study, but also to demonstrate the evolution which the various species had undergone in arriving at their current form.

A relevant figure among this group of botanists is the previously-mentioned José Moziño, meticulous researcher, virulent polemicist and untiring traveler. He toured, with his fellow botanists, the north and west of the country and embarked on the expedition with Francisco de la Bodega which reached the coast of Nootka in 1792. The following year, under orders of the viceroy, he toured the Mixteca and Tuxtla regions of the colony. It was on this trip, dated November of the same year, when he produced his *Descripción del volcán de Tuxtla* (Description of the Tuxtla Volcano). We are also indebted to his pen for the charming description of the northern regions of the Pacific coast which he visited, recorded in *Noticias de Nutka* (News From Nootka), in which he included a dictionary of the language of the indigenous Nootkas.

In 1801, he gave an address to mark the opening of botany courses in which he spoke about the relationship between botany and medicine, which was later deemed worthy of publishing in the gazette *Gacetas de México* and subsequently reproduced in the *Anuales de Ciencias Naturales de Madrid*. In his address, he referred in the following terms to the therapeutic riches that lay in the various plants native to Mexico:

There is no medicinal drug, with the exception of three or four, that is not abundantly supplied by our soil, that produces

naeus, utilizing his nomenclature and making a physical-chemical and physiological study of some products obtained from plants. The class of 1789 was particularly brilliant, including among its number José Moziño, Justo Pastor Torres and José Maldonado who, under the direction of Cervantes, carried out within the University, in November of the same year, experiments that were deservingly published as *Ejercicios públicos de botánica* (Public Practices of Botany), making manifest the degree of modernity of the classes conducted by Cervantes. As to the Botanical Garden, its well-managed operation achieved the uniting of 6000 specimens of Mexican flora, inspiring the then-retired Cervantes to write various scientific works which, regrettably, remain unpublished although the naturalist Pablo de la Llave published some of the works between 1824 and 1825. We are also in debt to Cervantes for *Ensayo para la materia médica vegetal de México* (Essay on the Vegetal Medical Material of Mexico), widely used by the authors of the work entitled *Materia médica mexicana*, the first of its type elaborated in Mexico. For

either the same species exactly or others equivalent or maybe of greater efficacy, and all that remains is for the doctors who wish to make use of them with discernment do so, so that Mexico may glory in having its own medical material, constituted only of remedies of indisputable virtue.

In 1803, Sessé returned to Spain in the company of Moziño, taking with them the materials collected and the beautifully executed drawings which, during the political upheavals of the nineteenth century, were unfortunately scattered or lost. Some contemporary copies do, however, exist in various European repositories.

Of paramount importance among scientific studies were the maritime expeditions and the cartographic works that were derived from them. In the area of exploratory voyages of this type, those made by Spanish navigators are outstanding in that they undertook, in evident continuity with their voyages of the sixteenth and seventeenth centuries, explorations of the Pacific coast of North America. In the sixth and seventh decades of the eighteenth century, before any other European nation with the exception of Russia, sailors from Spain and New Spain had reached the northwest coast of the American continent, completing a series of voyages to latitudes which no others had before reached. If the expeditions of the previous two centuries had barely reached a latitude of 42° north, undoubtedly those of the eighteenth century far surpassed this limit, exploring from the northern coast of California to the Russian province of Alaska. One of the principal motives that drove the Crown to finance the undertaking of these expeditions along Pacific coast was news of the existence of Russian outposts, dedicated to the trading of furs, that had been established on land that Spain considered hers. The fear of losing any such northern districts of the badly demarcated colonies propelled the work of reconnaissance and exploration. Another factor that entered into the equation was an interest in participating in the lucrative trading of furs, as well as the established motives that had stimulated Spanish expansion in the previous two centuries which were, principally, the conversion of the indigenous peoples, the search for the mythical interoceanic passage of Anián, the establishment of trading posts and safe ports on the northern Pacific coast that would facilitate the growth of commercial trade with the Philippines and the Orient and, lastly, to prevent any foreign colonization of these territories. All of these factors combined in the Spanish government's determination to establish

Oriolus Castaneus.
Carouge de Cayenne? Buf. au. 3. t. 607.

itself in the Californias and to penetrate and settle areas in opposition to the advancing commercial ambitions of the Russians. To this end, beginning in 1768, Jesuit missions, left by the order after their expulsion from Spanish territory, began to be reorganized in these regions. Thanks to the initiatives by the visiting Spaniard, José de Gálvez, important expeditions were launched this same year that were to, by land and sea, reach the ports of San Diego and Monterrey. The descriptive works by two of the principal members of the expeditions, the engineer Miguel Costanzó and the missionary Friar Juan Crespí, permit us to determine the route followed by each contingent thanks to the information as to the geographic positions, determined astronomically, of the points they referred to. At any rate, New Spain's maritime expansion toward the Pacific north was not consolidated until the year 1773 in which, by order of Viceroy Bucareli, the port of San Blas was reorganized such that in the following year a navy ensign named Juan Pérez headed the first reconnaissance expedition to attempt to reach 60° north lati-

ANONYMOUS

SPIRANTHERA - PLATE 25 [12]

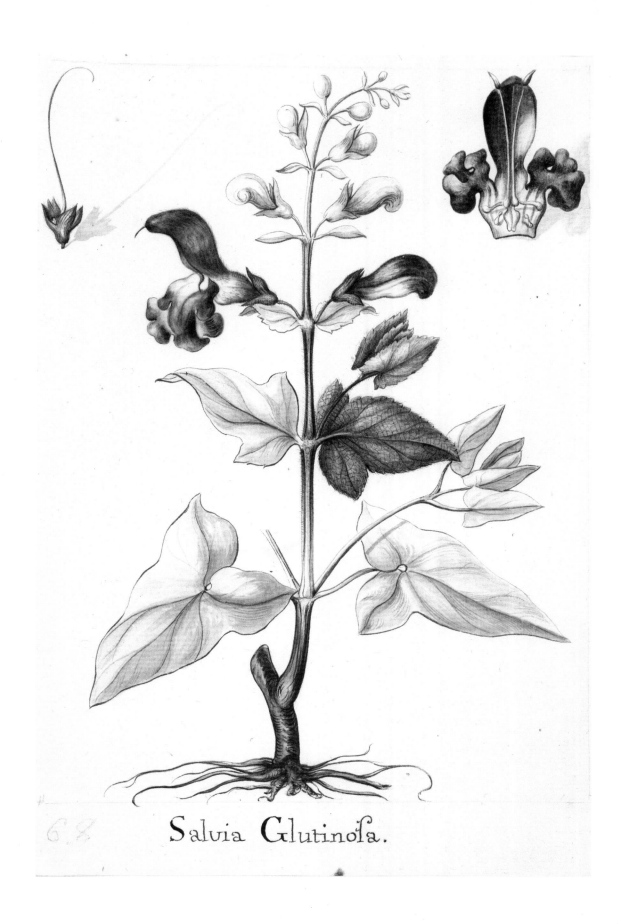

68 Salvia Glutinofa.

ANONYMOUS
SALVIA GLUTINOSA - PLATE 18 [13]

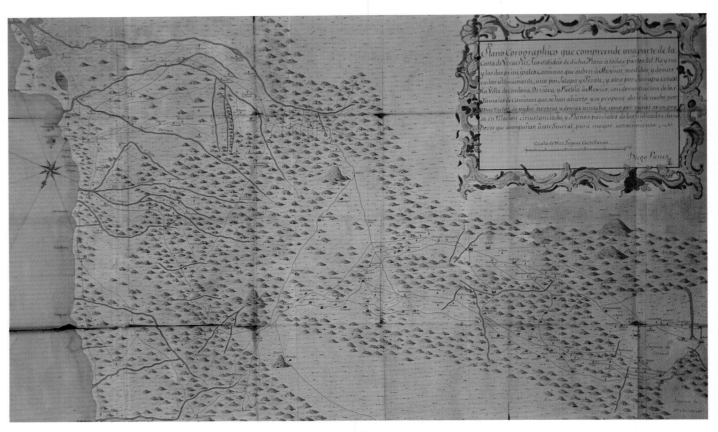

tude. On board the frigate *Santiago*, the explorers marked the location 53°53' as where they noted the mountains of Cabo (Cape) San Cristóbal. After reaching a latitude of 55°49' they turned back. In August of 1774, the *Santiago* dropped anchor in the bay at Nootka, at 49°30' north latitude. A few days later they anchored at the Californian port of Monterrey. This first expedition had reached latitudes never before seen and had brought back the first descriptions of the natives who inhabited these regions. Viceroy Revillagigedo summed up, some twenty years later, the impact of this naval exploit, affirming that its achievements facilitated the successive explorations that followed from that point on. After the return of the *Santiago* to San Blas, a second expedition was immediately ordered. Bruno de Ezeta was named commander and Juan Pérez as assistant. The frigate *Santiago* was reconditioned and left port in the company of the schooner *Sonora*, under the command of Juan Francisco de la Bodega y Cuadra, along with Antonio Maurelle as navigator. In March of 1775, the two ships set sail from San Blas. This expedition visited the port of Sitka, the Bay of Bucareli and the mouth of the Columbia River. On its return to San Blas, in November of the same year, the expedition had surveyed the territories lying between 42° and 55° north latitude. Thus, this vast northern portion of the Americas had been linked, by sea, to the remotest confines of the colony of New Spain.

The success of this expedition prompted the Crown to order, in 1776, a new exploratory voyage which was, for various reasons, to be postponed until early 1779, when the vessels *Princesa* and *Favorita*, under the commands of Ignacio Arteaga and Bodega y Cuadra, set sail from San Blas. The voyage's goal was to reach 70° north latitude. In April, they crossed the 54th parallel and, a few days later, dropped anchor in the Bay of Bucareli. In July, they embarked again, reconnoitering Mt. San Elías, the Isla del Carmen, and the port of Santiago. From there a boat was sent to determine the existence of the elusive and mythical Strait of Anián, the passage between the Pacific and Atlantic Oceans. With his arrival in this port, Arteaga had preceded by fourteen years the discoveries made by Vancouver, although a few months earlier, the English explorer Cook had visited. After

IGNACIO CASTERA
PLAN IGNOGRÁFICO DE LA HACIENDA DE MAZAPA; TEXCOCO [15]

having reached 59°08' latitude, at the inlet known as Nuestra Señora de Regla, the expedition returned to San Blas. The information they brought back helped to consolidate earlier discoveries in such a way that Spain was able to affirm that its territories extended to 58° north latitude and that these possessions had been secured and guaranteed by the surveying undertaken by the voyages of 1774, 1775 and 1779.

For a decade, Spain enjoyed relative tranquillity with respect to the territories that its bold sailors had secured. However, during the 1780's, the danger of losing lands due to the continuous advances being made by other nations once more compelled the Crown to decide on a plan of action in order to preserve its claim, openly defying these threats. One of the first steps taken was the occupation of the port at Nootka and the undertaking of reconnaissance of the outposts established by the Russians. With this plan, the ships *Princesa* and *San Carlos* set sail from San Blas in March of 1788, under the command of Ensign Esteban José Martínez, with Gonzalo López de Haro as navigator.

The ships passed by Nootka and went on as far as 61° latitude, reconnoitering the four outposts that the Russians had established in Onalaska. Two later explorations, under the commands of Salvador Fidalgo (1790) and Manuel Quimper and Francisco Eliza (1790-92), again made contact with the Russians in the area of 60° north latitude, as well as consolidated, for a time, Spain's strategic occupation of Nootka. Another spectacular naval feat followed that concluded the Spanish exploration of the northern Pacific during the eighteenth century. This voyage was captained by Dionisio Alcalá Galiano and Cayetano Valdes, aboard the schooners *Sutil* and *Mexicana*, which left the port of Acapulco in March of 1792. Their mission was to verify the existence of the famous, though imaginary, northern passage which would connect the Pacific Ocean with the Hudson and Baffin bays. Their search established the nonexistence of such a passage and, with their return, this long held supposition, which for many years the most exacting geographers had hoped to reveal, was completely discarded.

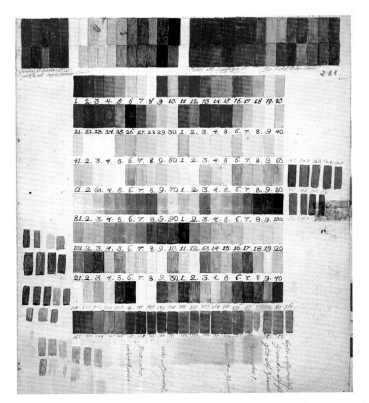

As one might expect, the cartography from the eighteenth century culled from the voyages to the Pacific north was so abundant that hardly any point visited by the various naval expeditions was not the subject of a survey, data from which was later used to create more general maps. In fact, the maps drawn between 1768 and the early part of the eighteenth century achieved an inarguably precise profile of the entire Pacific coast from 21° to 60° north latitude. With the establishment of the port at San Blas began the elaboration of many plans of this strategic departure point for expeditions. One of the first plans, representing the distribution of lots for the early settlers, was drawn up in 1769. In 1777, Francisco Maurelle delineated another map, followed by two more, in 1778 and 1784, by the navigator José Camacho. One of those by Camacho marked the voyage from San Blas to the port of Roca Partida, in Colima, and the other depicted the port at Roca Partida, as well as its arsenal and villa. Finally, fruit of the Bodega y Cuadra expedition of 1792, there exists a magnificent Plan of the Port of San Blas, dated 1793, which formed part of the private collection of Revilla-gigedo. In spite of the fact that some of these expeditions relied on modern, precision instruments, at times the determination of positions of latitude and longitude were made by astronomical methods of doubtful accuracy, thus the variety of results (the orientations of the coastlines having been made by azimuth observations). On the other hand, profiles of the coast as observed from ships were delineated with great care, resulting in a degree of accuracy that permitted easy recognition by later voyagers. Additionally, from a strategic point of view, these surveys were invaluable in justifying the primacy of discoveries and subsequent possession of territories when conflicts arose with other nations. This backdrop aids in our understanding of the great number of drawings of coastlines, islands and ports that were created between 1772 and 1778, years in which Spain felt that its territories in the Pacific north were being threatened by the expansion on the part of the Russians. In 1772, the navigator José de Cañizares made drawings of the islands of Socorro, Santa Catalina, Santa Bárbara and Guadalupe, located along the California coast. Five years later, the previously-mentioned commander, José Camacho, delineated maps of the islands of San Benedicto and Todos los Santos, as well as maps of Cabo San Lucas, the Marías Islands and the Revillagigedo Islands. In 1779 he executed the map of the Alaskan coastline that faced the island of

p. 33. ANONYMOUS
MAP OF THE CURACY OF ORIZABA [18]

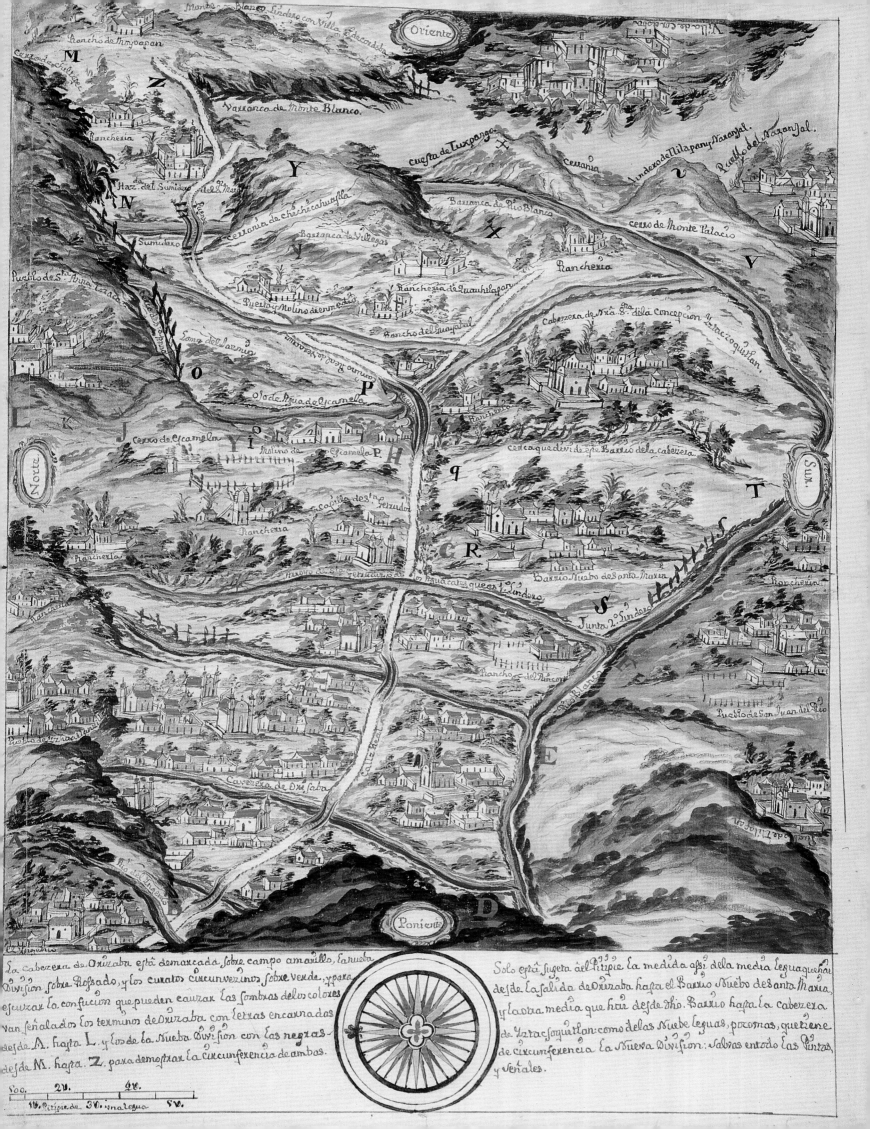

Oriente

Norte

Sur

Poniente

M Z
Y
N
O
P
L K J I
H
q
G R
T
S
A B C D E

Monte Blanco Lindero con Villa de Cordoba
Rancho de Moyapan
Varranca de Monte Blanco.
Rancheria
Haz. del Sumidero del S.r Mar.
Sumidero
Cerrania de Chichecahuasla
Barranca de Villegas
Pueblo de S.ta Anna Tzato
Loma del Sarmin.
Camino Real de Veracruz
Puerto y Molino de enmedio
Rancho del Mayatal
Ojo de Agua de Escamela
Cerro de Escamela
Molino de Escamela
Rancheria
Capilla de S.n Gertrudis
Rancheria
Rancheria
Pueblo de Ixhuatlancillo
Caverzera de Orizaba
Rio del Jnfierno
cuesta de Tuxpango
cerrania
Barranca de Rio Blanco
Rancheria
Rancheria de Quauhtlapan
Cabezera de Ntra. Sra. de la Concepcion Ixtaczoquitlan
cerca que divide este Barrio de la cabezera
Rancheria
Rio de Sn Gertrudis de los Aguacates que es el Lindero
Barrio Nuebo de Santa Maria
Junta 2.o Lindero
Rancho del Rincon
Rio Blanco
Pueblo de San Juan del Rio
Lindero de Nilapan y Naranjal
Puesto del Naranjal
cerro de Monte Palacio
V
V
U

La Cabezera de Orizaba esta demarcada sobre campo amarillo, La nueba
Division sobre Rossado, y los curatos circunvezinos sobre verde, y para
escusar la confucion que pueden causar las sombras de los colores
van señalados Los terminos de Orizaba con Letras encarnadas
desde M. hasta L. y los de la Nueba Division con Las negras
desde M. hasta Z. para demostrar La circunferencia de ambas.

Solo esta sugeta ael pitipie La medida assi de la media legua que hai
desde La salida de Orizaba hasta el Barrio Nuebo de Santa Maria,
y la otra media que hai desde d.ho. Barrio hasta La cabezera
de Ixtaczoquitlan: como de las Nuebe leguas, pocomas, que tiene
de circunferencia La Nueva Division: salvas en todo Las Pintas,
y señales.

500 2u. 4u.
16. P.tipie de 30. en una legua 8u.

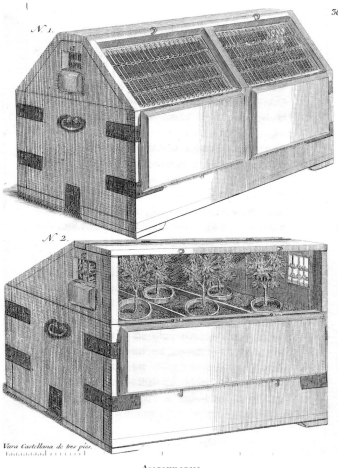

ANONYMOUS
HERBARIUMS FOR THE TRANSPORT OF PLANTS [19]

Santa Inés de la Magdalena. Between 1781 and 1782, further drawings of islands and coastal mountain ranges were elaborated by Juan Pantoja y Arriaga, José Mehei and José Antonio Vázquez.

Plans of ports also occupied the skilled cartographers who participated in the expeditions. Two of great importance are of Acapulco, one from 1778 and the other from 1792, products of the expeditions by Bodega y Cuadra. The latter of these served to fix Acapulco's position with respect to San Blas. During the latter voyage a plan was elaborated of Monterrey, on the California coast, fixing its position at 36°36' latitude and its longitude, with respect to San Blas, at 16°36'. The prolific commander Jacinto Caamaño, who traveled aboard the *Princesa*, executed six plans of the principal ports visited by his expedition in 1790. Two years later, the captains Eliza, Quimper and Alcalá Galiano elaborated the famous plan of the Strait of Juan de Fuca, assuring Spain of its claim to the discoveries in the region between 48° and 54° latitude, even before the reconnaissance by Vancouver. Among similar work aimed at securing the Spanish possessions

north of the port of San Francisco are the numerous plans of the strategic anchoring areas at Nootka, situated at 49°35' north latitude, first visited by Juan Pérez during his expedition of 1774, and the plans of the port of Bucareli, at 55°15' latitude, discovered by Bodega y Cuadra in 1775 and surveyed by the navigators of the *Princesa* and the *Favorita* on the expedition of 1779 and again, in 1792, by Jacinto Caamaño, who made revisions to the earlier plans. To this vast grouping of plans is added the no less numerous general maps of the extensive coastline of the northern Pacific. The expedition led by Juan Pérez allowed José Antonio Vázquez to delineate the coastline from Cabo Mendocino to Cabo Corrientes, a length stretching from 17° to 42° north latitude. In 1779, the coastal mapping had been completed as far as 59°30' latitude, the site of Mt. San Elías. As the expeditions ventured ever northward, reaching higher latitudes and navigating in polar ice, it was increasingly easier to elaborate maps of broader scope. The great map by Jacinto Caamaño, dated 1793, which reaches to 58° latitude, and that of López de Haro, covering as far as 64°, were doubtless the general maps from the last decade of the eighteenth century and the early nineteenth century of the greatest value from the point of view of the history of scientific cartography, not only in that they cover the area from Acapulco to Alaska (in the case of the Bodega y Cuadra maps, dated 1791 and 1793), but that they also established the positions of many points in the regions.

In conclusion, it should be noted that of all the voyages of exploration sponsored by the Spanish monarchy in the eighteenth century, the one headed by Alejandro Malaspina was undoubtedly the most relevant. In terms of duration and scientific achievement it can well be considered the most ambitious project from the period of the Spanish Enlightenment. During the five years between 1789 and 1794, he visited South America, Mexico, California, the northwest coast of North America as far as Alaska, the Philippines, Australia and many of the islands of the Pacific. His mission, political as well as scientific, historical and anthropological, was a faithful reflection of the Enlightened mentality of those who undertook it. Inscribed on the framework of the geopolitical conceptions of the Spanish Crown, the Malaspina expedition is also a portrait of the overseas Spanish empire capturing the moment in which Spain, after having negotiated a peace treaty with England, was attempting to establish a most effective political control over its colonies. It is within this framework that the great Spanish enterprise during the Age of Enlightenment must be placed.

ATANASIO ECHEVERRÍA
ASCENSIÓN AL VOLCÁN DE SAN ANDRÉS TUXTLA [20]

Nevertheless, it is probably within the history of the sciences where, today, the accomplishments are most recognized in terms of the contributions to geography, cartography, astronomy, physics, botany and zoology made by these global voyages of decades ago. The men of science who participated in the expeditions, outstanding among them the naturalist Antonio Pineda, attempted to stay abreast of the scientific knowledge of their day so that their labors would not be simply a collecting and recording of data but also of classification. Among them were men of various nationalities, such as Tadeo Hanke and Luis Nee, who found that, in the eighteenth century, being a foreigner did not imply any form of exclusion. Additionally, the expeditions included distinguished naturalist artists of the stature of Tomás de Suria, whose capacity for observing animals and plants, as well as human types, clothing, faces, weapons and diverse objects, is made obvious in each of the beautiful works he executed and that, fortunately, have been preserved.

In summarizing his voyage along the north coast of the Pacific in 1791, von Humboldt made the following evaluation of its contributions in his *Essai politique sur le royaume de la Nouvelle Espagne...* (Political Essay on the Kingdom of New Spain...):

This campaign of five months was not sufficient, without doubt, to survey and draw up the plan of an extensive coastline, with the painstaking care that we admired in the voyage of Vancouver that had lasted three years. The Malaspina expedition, nevertheless, is of special merit, that consists not only in the number of astronomical observations, but also, notably, in the clever method he has used in achieving correct results. The longitude and the latitude of four points along the coast have been fixed in an absolute manner, that of Cabo San Lucas, Monterrey, Nootka and the port of Mulgrane.

The labor of all these travelers and explorers is of great importance in understanding the nature of the impetus received by the life sciences, as well as the physical sciences, during the following century, and that its origin is to be found in the science of the Age of Enlightenment.

p. 36-37. FERNANDO BRAMBILA
VIEW OF THE TOWN AND PORT OF ACAPULCO [21]

ADVENTUROUS EUROPE
(1800-1899)

GUADALUPE JIMÉNEZ CODINACH

The year was 1808. The shadows of night had given way to the first rays of sun in the village of San Miguel el Grande, in the bishopric of Michoacán in New Spain. The village was filled with stories and rumors as it witnessed the escorting of an unusual prisoner: Count Octaviano D'Alvimar (also known as Gaetano Souch d'Alvimart or Dalmivar),[1] envoy of the emperor Napoleon I, an individual said to be carrying an order from Charles IV of Spain to "take command of this America."[2] Among the residents of San Miguel who approached and spoke with him were Captain Ignacio de Allende, Captain Pedro Lámbarri, don Francisco de las Fuentes and don Sebastián Aguirre. During his conversation with the prisoner, Allende was surprised to hear that Joseph Bonaparte still reigned in Madrid. He believed the Frenchman to be lying but later found out that it was true and realized that the population of New Spain had been kept in the dark as to what was happening in Madrid. Allende saw D'Alvimar twice. He related that, on the first visit, the Count complained of a broken jaw and the risk of its becoming infected. Allende recommended treatment with quinine. The following day Allende again visited the prisoner. D'Alvimar asked if he were a doctor and Allende replied that he was not. Nevertheless, he invited Allende into an adjoining room, removed the bandages and showed him the injury. While they were together, the prisoner asked Allende as to who the Viceroy in Mexico City was and if he thought that they might take him to the capital. During the interrogation conducted in Chihuahua, in 1811, Allende stated that he had not again seen D'Alvimar after this last visit.[3]

Father Miguel Hidalgo also met D'Alvimar. They spoke in the town of Dolores "at dusk, for about an hour and a half,

together with various other Creole and European neighbors ... during which time he talked about Emperor Bonaparte, General Moreau and general news...." Hidalgo never again saw the mysterious Frenchman.[4]

The viceregal government jailed D'Alvimar for espionage and deported him to Spain. However, he reappeared in 1822 with the intention of approaching Agustín de Iturbide, from whom he wanted to request a commission as lieutenant general in the Mexican army. Iturbide refused and D'Alvimar took part in a revolt against Iturbide's Empire that was launched in the village of San Miguel el Grande. The Frenchman, according to accounts by Justino Fernández, was apprehended and condemned again to "perpetual exile from this America."[5] D'Alvimar appealed and begged in vain. On September 20, 1822, he wrote to Iturbide explaining that, in order that he not feel thrown out of the Empire, he would stay in Mexico a few more days: "I am going to distract myself by completing two paintings that I have begun. Oh, wretched me! God is my witness that I expected nothing apart from my post as captain general in offering Your Majesty a beautiful miniature of your respected father [don Joaquín de Iturbide]...."[6] The Empire collapsed. Iturbide left the country in the summer of 1823. Months later, on November 7th, the republican government issued an order that D'Alvimar be escorted to the port of Veracruz for deportation.[7]

One painting exists by the count/spy/painter. It is a view of the Plaza Mayor (Main Plaza) in Mexico City, a work considered by the art historian Justino Fernández to be the first executed by a foreigner of this site that so interested other artists, both foreign and native. The work is in tempera. The plaza is observed from the southeast corner, with the National Palace at the right and

the Cathedral in the background, under a beautiful sky. D'Alvimar portrayed the plaza on a festive day, August 13, 1822, on which Iturbide had gone to the Colegiata de Guadalupe to establish the Order of Guadalupe. The scene depicts the return of the royal carriage to the Palace.[8]

D'Alvimar was not faithful to the reality of his subject, eliminating the Parián building and its stalls, as well as the equestrian statue of Charles IV, which had been covered by a large tarp and was later, in 1824, removed to the patio of the university. The artist did, however, achieve a beautiful composition of the plaza, capturing a historical moment in the brief Empire of Iturbide.

Although not all of the traveling artists, diplomats, technicians, scientists and European visitors that arrived in independent Mexico after 1821 had a past as troubled as that of D'Alvimar, their origins and lives did reflect the turbulence that existed in nineteenth-century Europe. Mexico was the theme of more than six hundred accounts by authors from England and the United States,[9] doubtless due to Mexico's having been born as a nation in 1821, a period in which travel literature was extraordinarily popular.

In 1811, the year in which *Essai politique sur le royaume de la Nouvelle Espagne...* (Political Essay on the Kingdom of New Spain...), by Alexander von Humboldt, was published in London, many Europeans—with the exception of the Spaniards—saw New Spain as a distant, exotic and unknown land. The Spanish ambassador to England reported to his government the difficulty he had encountered in obtaining a copy of the work in that the edition had sold out quickly.[10] This work by von Humboldt was the most widely read by the English public on the topic of New Spain, as well as the most often noted in the press and in official circles. The same had occurred in France, where the *Essai* had first become known in 1808. In his work, Baron von Humboldt described a New Spain that was unknown to nineteenth-century Europe. It contained scientific, cultural, economic and political information, as well as statistical data on natural resources, population and commercial activity. Although some of the numbers were erroneous, the *Essai* resulted in the

p. 38. Hubert Sattler
THE PORT OF VERACRUZ (DETAIL) [22]

Daniel Thomas Egerton
THE PICO DE ORIZABA [23]

JOHANN MORITZ RUGENDAS
THE VOLCANO AT COLIMA [24]

opening both of the eyes and the pocketbooks of speculators and businessmen in Great Britain and France.[11]

One hundred and seventy-five years ago, in September of 1821, Mexico became an independent nation. It was evident that Mexico, although from this point on responsible for its own destiny, continued to remain dependent—above all, economically—on foreign powers. The country's first feeble steps in its relationships with the power centers of the early nineteenth century were characterized by the ambiguity and insecurity with which they were taken. The posture adopted by the new nation in facing these governments was one of great ingenuity. Immediately after the consummation of independence, foreigners who had participated in the numerous pre-emancipatory conspiracies, those who had financed expeditions to New Spain, the arms dealers and the many creditors of both the rebels and the royalists, presented themselves before the new government to claim payment, privileges and compensation. The family of Viceroy José de Iturrigaray, the aforementioned French general, D'Alvimar, and such personalities from the United States as Peter Ellis Bean, James Wilkinson, Joshua Child, John Mason and Dennis Smith, among others, arrived in Mexico City to reap the fruits of the emancipation. All were seeking some personal privilege or benefit.

Admiral Thomas Cochrane, of Great Britain, appeared personally in Acapulco, on January 22, 1822, to offer his services to the Mexican Empire. Iturbide instructed his coastal officials to treat

Cochrane and his men kindly, but to remain alert to any false moves by these recent arrivals.[12] Also arriving in Acapulco were Colonel Felipe O'Reilly and General Arthur Wavell, both English, who presented themselves to the Mexican officials as officers of the government of Chile. Later, General Wavell presented himself before the British government as having been "dispatched" by Mexico to Great Britain, and delivered a report on the state of the Mexican nation.[13] In the report, Wavell strongly emphasized the opportunities that mining in Mexico presented for British investors advising them that, according to a Mexican law (and an earlier Spanish law), all mines that had ceased to be worked for ten years would revert to the government which would, in turn, grant them to Mexican citizens. As nineteen or twenty mines had been abandoned due to flooding, and as a result of the rebellion, Wavell argued that it was imperative that English machinery and capital be employed to increase the production of silver.[14]

For their part, those in the United States viewed with suspicion the British interest in the newly independent Mexico. Those who had been involved in financing and arms deals with the rebel groups now showed an interest in securing mining contracts. As a consequence, the two groups of investors became rivals: the British, in deals made with Lucas Alamán, Tomás Murphy, José Mariano Michelena and the Fagoaga brothers—all players in the independence movement prior to 1821—and such Americans as James Wilkinson, Dennis A. Smith and John Mason, supported by the former rebels Guadalupe Victoria and Vicente Guerrero. Dennis A. Smith, for example, was one of the principal Baltimore financiers of the Xavier Mina expedition.

Mexico's independence offered a broad playing field for the foreign investors, as well as for the artists who came to these lands due to the political, economic and social problems that shook the Old World throughout the nineteenth century. Mexico, the country with the mysterious name, attracted not only speculators and investors, but cultured men and women of other countries as well. Scientists, writers, painters, sculptors, lithographers and, later, photographers traveled throughout these lands both arid and fertile, hot and cold: writers such as Henry George Ward and his talented artist wife (1823-1827), William Bullock (1823), Madame Fanny Calderón de la Barca (1839-1842), and artists such as Claudio Linati (1825-1827), who landed in Veracruz in 1825, introducing lithography to Mexico, and Frédéric Waldeck (1825-1837), traveler, painter and engraver, native of Prague, disciple of David, veteran of Napoleon's cam-

paigns in Egypt in 1799, corsair of the Indian Ocean, who came to Mexico to work as an engineer in the mines at Tlalpujahua. Waldeck arrived at the port of Tampico in 1825. After working for a year in the mines, he settled in Mexico City where he gave classes in drawing and painting. In 1831, he proposed a project to the Mexican government regarding the study of Mayan ruins. He spent from 1834 until 1836 in Palenque and Uxmal. Because he sent reports and archaeological objects to Europe without the knowledge of the Mexican government, his drawings were seized and his protected status revoked.[15] Greatly impressed by Mexico, Waldeck wrote: "It is now time that the attention of Europe be directed toward a world perhaps equally as rich in scientific treasures and attractive mementos. America is yet little known...."[16] This same idea is reflected in the words of Henry George Ward who, in his work *Mexico in 1827*, affirmed:

Nothing could have been more imperfect until now than our knowledge about this vast country. Even many of the principal towns and rivers remain incorrectly located and, consequently, not even the elements for a good map exist. Von Humboldt did much to correct the prevalent errors in his time, but his personal observations were confined to a relatively reduced circle.... Within a short time, however, considerable additions to our store of information shall be made since among the foreigners that are currently exploring the Mexican territory there are some men of science that utilize their leisure time in making observations and plotting their routes throughout the various parts of the country that they feel obliged to visit because of their occupations.[17]

Ward's reference was to people such as the director of the Compañía de Real del Monte, and to one of the officials of the United Mexican Association, who had made observations and elaborated a map.

The lives and works of the various European artists who portrayed the landscapes and life of nineteenth-century Mexico is dealt with in other sections of this catalog. In this essay we will briefly reflect on the Europe from which they had come. What political, economic, social and ideological atmospheres enveloped them and drove them to these distant shores in search of their personal adventures, artistic or otherwise? The fact that Claudio Linati was a revolutionary and a member of the society of the *Carbonari* in Parma; that Daniel Thomas Egerton belonged to an aristocratic English family exemplary of the transition taking place in British society during the Georgian period and the beginnings of the Victorian era; that Johann Moritz Rugendas was the descendant of an illustrious family of engravers from Augsburg and a member of Baron von Langsdorff's expedition to Brazil; that Carl Nebel was a young designer, born in Prussia, in 1805, and that his work *Voyage Pittoresque et Archeologique dans la partie le plus intéressante du Mexique pendant les annés 1829 et 1834* (Picturesque and Archaeological Voyage Through the Most Interesting Part of Mexico During the Years 1829-1834), from 1836, included a prologue by none other than Alexander von Humboldt; that John Phillips, the English artist, published in London, in 1848, an album of lithographs and drawings that led to his visiting the country; that all of them, to one degree or another, had mixed their artistic talents with adventures that led to deportation by the Mexican government, such as the case of Rugendas; to being murdered under strange circumstances, as happened to Egerton in the Tacubaya neighborhood of Mexico City; to becoming indignant and critical of the Mexican authorities, as did Waldeck; to being denied both recognition and a military post, as was D'Alvimar; indicate that these artistic travelers came not always with aesthetic motives. Some were motivated by survival, others by commercial interests, and yet others sought to flee the problems that existed in their native countries.

Europe in the nineteenth century was a continent in profound turbulence. A period of revolution versus the restoration of absolutism, of popular liberation versus repression, of capitalist liberalism versus socialism, of constitutionalism versus the old regimes, of romanticism versus realism.

Within the century, it is possible to distinguish four stages that were born under the aegis of a dual revolution: the French Revolution and the Industrial Revolution in England.

a) In the first stage, from 1800 to 1815, is placed the confrontation between multi-ethnic and multinational armies. The mobility of the European had accelerated. Napoleon's armies pulled together great contingents formed by French, Poles, Hungarians, Swedes, Danes, Italians, and others from as far as the steppes of Russia. The French of the First Empire (1804-1815) considered themselves the heirs of the revolutionaries of 1789, convinced that they were bringing liberty, equality and fraternity to oppressed peoples. It did not matter that "liberation" was being imposed at the point of the bayonet. To

José Arpa
POPOCATÉPETL [25]

counter the "liberators," the allied powers rallied from England and Austria to the plains of Castile and the peninsula of Italy. The battle at Waterloo, which occurred in 1815, shifted the balance in favor of the allies who soon decided the fate of France, and of its former emperor, in an occupied Paris. The veterans of the *Grand Armeé*, as Napoleon's elite forces were known, dispersed throughout Europe, many of them crossing the Atlantic to seek fortune and glory. Among their plans was a failed attempt to liberate New Spain from the Spanish Crown.[18]

b) The second stage, from 1815 to 1848, was marked, in turn, by three revolutionary waves that occurred in 1820, 1830 and 1848. The first of these was preceded by vigorous turmoil within the universities of Germany that attempted to oblige the various German princes and ministers to grant constitutional rights to the people. The universities became centers of revolutionary movements due to the fact that the students, having returned to their cities after the Napoleonic wars, had organized secret societies, or *Burschenschaften*, for the promotion of nationalistic ideals. By 1816, a central organ existed which had organized representatives from sixteen German universities.[19] The government's response was repression. In September of 1819, the secret societies were dissolved by decree, inspectors were named for each university, and the press was censored. The organized opposition in Europe was concentrated in the secret societies, of which the oldest in Italy was that of the *Carbonari* in Naples, founded in 1810. Before the fall of Napoleon I, this group had been clerical and anti-French, however after 1815, it became liberal and nationalistic. Its program had been reduced to the fight against the Austrians, who occupied part of Italy, and against tyranny. The *Carbonari* sparked a revolution in Naples, in 1820, and another in Piedmont, in 1821. In the latter insurrection, the city of Turin was taken by the rebels, but the Austrian army put down the uprising just as it had in Naples.[20]

The secret societies also appeared in Spain. Young soldiers directed a liberal revolution headed by Colonel Rafael de Riego. In January of 1820, a Spanish army contingent was being prepared to be sent to Spanish America to fight against the rebels. The soldiers abhorred the idea of setting sail and became sympathetic to the subversiveness of some of the officers who advocated the restoration of the Constitution of 1812. By March, the rebellion extended to La Coruña, Oviedo, Zaragoza, Valencia and Barcelona. King Ferdinand VII found himself obliged to accept the Constitution but at the same time sought the support of the French legitimists. The liberal Spanish revolution was smothered, in 1823, by French troops under the command of the Duke of Angoulême.[21]

The second revolutionary wave spread over France in July of 1830. From Paris, the revolution moved on to Brussels where it took on a marked nationalistic character. The Belgians sought to shake off the yoke of Wilhelm I, King of the Low Countries. A mutual antipathy had long existed between the Dutch and the Belgians, based on religious, ethnic and cultural differences. The Dutch were Protestant and viewed their Catholic neighbors as inferiors. Wilhelm I had obstinately refused to grant concessions to the Catholics which explains why, on the monarch's trip to Brussels to visit an industrial exposition, pamphlets were distributed announcing: "August 23rd - Fireworks. August 24th - Celebration of the King's Birthday. August 25th - Revolution."[22] Finally, the Belgians triumphed. In November of 1830, a Belgian national congress was elected and a constitution elaborated, the most liberal in the Europe of the period.[23]

Between 1846 and 1848, Europe passed through a profound economic crisis. In France, discontent was mounting. Alexis de Tocqueville warned the members of the French Chamber of Deputies: "We are sleeping on top of a volcano."[24] The opposition had adopted the English custom of the political banquet for the holding of their meetings. The government, alarmed by the tone of the speeches by orators such as the poet Alphonse Lamartine and the radical lawyer Ledru-Rollin, prohibited a banquet scheduled for February 22, 1848, in Paris. Neither sluggish nor idle, the workers, students and intellectuals took to the streets, demanding reforms. The minister François Guizot ordered the National Guard to repress them. Many of the guard, however, joined the masses with shouts of "Down with Guizot!" The Parisians were indignant when one regiment killed twenty-three demonstrators and injured thirty. They threw up barricades and raided armories. The King saw fit to abdicate in favor of his grandson, the Count of Paris, a boy of ten years. The new monarch was, however, pushed to the side and a provisional government organized in which participated Lamartine, Ledru-Rollin and Louis Blanc.[25] From February until May, enthusiasm reigned in Paris. Liberty trees were planted and the red flags of the revolution waved. In June of the same year, however, fighting renewed in the streets of the French capital until the "forces of order" had achieved control. Many of the rebels were executed and four thousand were sent to penal colonies. Louis Blanc fled to England and the Revolution of February was ended.[26]

c) The third stage begins with the birth of the Second Empire in France and ends with the Commune of Paris of 1871. The regime of Napoleon III was dictatorial with a certain veneer of nationalist liberalism. He reinstated universal suffrage but at the same time organized an effective secret police, exercised control over the press, manipulated elections, persecuted and jailed his principal critics, and maintained control of the legislature. The new emperor nourished businesses, publicly-owned companies and the stock market, and reduced the regulation of private enterprise. He introduced a period of greater free trade in Europe with the reduction of duties on imports from Great Britain, Belgium, Switzerland, Austria, Portugal, Sweden, Spain and other countries. The Second Empire stimulated the undertaking of a great variety of public works, with an eye to stimulating employment, commerce and industry. Paris was transformed under the direction of Baron Haussman, becoming the most beautiful city in the world. A new opera house was built and gas lighting was installed in the streets, all set within the grandiose and ornamented architectural framework typical of the era.[27]

Napoleon III had not forgotten the workers. He subsidized workers' organizations and proposed labor laws, one of which allowed the right to strike, although with some limitations. In a period in which the European powers were expanding into Africa, the South Seas and Asia, Napoleon III sent a naval expedition to occupy various islands in the Pacific, among them New Caledonia, in 1853. Five years later he pacified Algeria, establishing a permanent civil government under the direction of Marshal MacMahon, and sent an expedition to Cochin-China—now Vietnam—to avenge the death of several French missionaries. In 1863, he established a French protectorate in Cambodia.[28] One year earlier, in 1862, he had intervened in Mexico, supporting the Second Empire headed by Maximilian of Hapsburg, brother of the Austrian emperor Franz Josef. Napoleon III believed, as did many of his countrymen, that France needed to maintain a presence in the Western Hemisphere in the face of the political and commercial advances being made by England and the United States. Paris had to become the beacon for "Latin America," a term coined in this period. In 1867, Napoleon III recalled what remained of the French army in Mexico and Maximilian was executed by a firing squad.

In Europe, Napoleon III confronted Prussia. The French emperor had not wanted war with his neighbors; however, the astute Prussian prime minister, Otto von Bismarck, obliged him to take part in the conflict. When the Prussian military assured him that they were in favor of the war, von Bismarck altered a telegram—the famous telegram from Ems—sent by Kaiser Wilhelm I of Prussia to the French ambassador. The original text had merely indicated that the Kaiser would not be able to receive him as he was about to leave the summer resort of Ems. Von Bismarck altered the telegram in such a way that it insulted the French. After six weeks of war, his defeat at Sedan obliged Napoleon III to surrender, in the company of 81,000 of his soldiers.

In 1871, the citizens of Paris known as the Communards again took up arms. In desperation, the rebels took the Archbishop hostage and burned several public buildings, including the Palace of the Tuileries. The Communards were repressed by the French army and their leaders either killed or sent into exile.

d) The fourth and last stage of the nineteenth century covers the years from 1871 to 1899. The example set by the Prussian victory affected other countries. Several of the powers tried to organize armies in the manner of the Prussians—inspired, in turn, by the French Revolution—that is, based on conscription from broad sectors of the population. The European countries engaged in a sort of arms race that only presaged great disasters. Between 1871 and 1914, there were various outbreaks of war between the powers, although none reached the point of a formal declaration. Europe was to wait until the twentieth century to live out two world wars, the most bloody in universal history.

The nineteenth century had not resolved man's eternal dilemma: to construct or to destroy his own destiny. In the words of Camillo Cavour:

> The more I observe the course of events and the behavior of men, the more convinced I am that the *juste-milieu* (middle road) is the only correct policy under the circumstances, capable of saving society from the two rocks that threaten to crush it: anarchy and despotism.[29]

OCTAVIANO D'ALVIMAR
MAIN PLAZA OF MEXICO CITY [26]

ALEXANDER VON HUMBOLDT'S EXPEDITION THROUGH MEXICO

FRANK HOLL

When Alexander von Humboldt disembarked in Acapulco on March 22, 1803, he had already spent almost four years in South and Central America. In the territories that are known today as Venezuela, Cuba, Colombia, Ecuador and Peru, the Prussian scientist and traveler had undertaken studies in a great variety of disciplines. Besides his achievements in geography and the natural sciences, von Humboldt had won the admiration of his contemporaries by climbing nearly to the summit of Chimborazo. At the time, this volcano in the Andes was considered the highest mountain on earth. Another show of von Humboldt's prowess had been an expedition through the jungles of what is today Venezuela, where he canoed the Casiquiare River, among others, and found evidence that the Casiquiare linked the Orinoco River system with that of the Amazon.

With his fellow travelers Aimé Bonpland and Carlos Montúfar—the latter of whom had accompanied him since Quito—von Humboldt headed for Mexico City. Twenty-one mules were necessary in order to carry the scientific instruments and the botanical, zoological and geological specimens that had been collected. The caravan moved slowly over well-trodden paths. "All the way from Acapulco to Mexico the route is crammed with mules. You have a hard time getting through," von Humboldt noted in his diary.[1] The observation led him to ask: "Why haven't they introduced camels into this country?"

In addition to meticulous measurements and experiments, comparison—in this case with the means of transportation commonly used in Africa and Asia—was a basis of von Humboldt's scientific method.

During the journey toward the viceregal capital of the dominion of New Spain, von Humboldt carried out his usual topographical measurements. The data compiled was later included in his great atlas of New Spain, *Atlas géographique et physique du royaume de la Nouvelle Espagne...* (Geographical and Physical Atlas of the Kingdom of New Spain...), which was published, in Paris, in 1811. The volume contains a great number of detailed charts, as well as the first profile of a country outside Europe: New Spain from Acapulco to Veracruz. In the course of the nineteenth century, the general map included in this volume was long considered the best available of Mexico.

The diary of the journey, which was published in Berlin, in two volumes (1986 and 1990), reveals the systematic analysis which von Humboldt conducted on the landscapes through which he traveled. First he would determine the precise topographical location of each point and then turn his attention to the geological characteristics of the soil, the relief, the climatological circumstances and, finally, to the flora and fauna. Additionally, he would observe and describe the inhabitants of the region within the context of their economic and historical conditions. "Everything is interaction...," he remarked his Mexican diary.[2] It should be emphasized that von Humboldt always considered the landscape as an area of interaction within nature itself, as well as between nature and human beings.

In 1811, the aforementioned atlas and the two volumes of *Essai politique sur le royaume de la Nouvelle Espagne...* (Political Essay on the Kingdom of New Spain...)[3] were published in Paris. The latter contain the results of von Humboldt's research in and around Mexico, where he stayed for almost

PHILLIPE RONDE
MINERS AT THE SAN PEDRO MINE, CHIHUAHUA (DETAIL) [27]

one year. This work is considered a milestone in modern geography.

The study on Mexico forms part of a greater work that totals thirty-four volumes describing von Humboldt's scientific expeditions throughout Latin America. Parts were written in collaboration with Bonpland and others. The volumes were published between 1805 and 1839 and are still considered the most valuable and, probably, the most extensive work that a single scientist ever financed with his own funds. The project consumed what remained of the fortune that von Humboldt had inherited and which he had previously utilized to finance his travels. The work contains a total of 1400 engravings, many of them in color. Among these, 1240 are illustrations of plants, as well as plates of mammals, birds, fish and insects. It also includes a great number of charts and profiles of landscapes, as well as illustrations of antiquarian objects and landscapes.

These last two types of illustrations can be found in the large-format volume *Vues de Cordillères et Monumens des peuples indigenes de L'Amérique* (Views of the Mountain Ranges and Monuments of the Indigenous Peoples of America), which was published in Paris, in 1810, together with a second volume of explanatory texts. This work, which is also known as *Atlas pittoresque du voyage* (Picturesque Voyage Atlas), con-

ALEXANDER VON HUMBOLDT
PYRAMIDE DE CHOLULA (DETAIL) [29]

tains sixty-nine engravings, forty-two of which are dedicated to Mexico.

Departing from Acapulco, von Humboldt and his companions went to Mescala, passing through Chilpancingo. They crossed the Mescala River on a raft made from gourds. They arrived at Taxco on April 6th but found that the prosperity of the old mining city had long vanished. In von Humboldt's opinion, there was a striking contradiction between the beauty of the local church and the enormous amount of money that the former owner of the mines, José de la Borda, had spent on its construction: "The Supreme Being doesn't need this kind of building, so disproportionate to the smallness of the cabins surrounding it. He would have been much better served had the example of His charity been imitated. But the vanity of man prefers more visible and more durable monuments."[4]

From the hills surrounding Cuernavaca, von Humboldt and his fellow travelers contemplated the ruins of Xochicalco. The scientist later regretted not having studied them himself. After his return to Europe, von Humboldt's description and illustrations included in *Vues de Cordillères...* inspired a great number of travelers, such as the painter Carl Nebel and the Hungarian photographer Pál Rosti, to visit and graphically document this archaeological site.[5] Von Humboldt owes his illustration of a lateral relief of the temple at Xochicalco to an

ALEXANDER VON HUMBOLDT
ROCHERS BASALTIQUES ET CASCADE DE REGLA [30]

engraving by Mexican geographer and naturalist José Antonio de Alzate y Ramírez, which had been published in 1791. The patterns in the illustrations of the temple at Mitla[6]—another site that von Humboldt had not visited on his own—were the work of Luis Martín, with whom the Prussian scientist made a number of geological excursions in the areas surrounding Mexico City.

Von Humboldt did not refrain from including drawings by other artists and scientists in his volume of illustrations and always credited their respective sources. In his scientific texts he observed the same criterion and produced models of masterful compilation of his own and other people's knowledge. Originality, which for many artists seemed imperative, was not overwhelmingly important to von Humboldt. Rather, he strove for scientific documentation and reinterpretation—including the knowledge already at hand—within the largest possible context.

On April 12th, the travelers arrived in Mexico City, which was to become the base for von Humboldt's scientific work in New Spain. From there he headed off on a number of journeys and expeditions in all directions. Nevertheless, he spent most of the time in the capital of New Spain, which had cast a peculiar spell on him: "There is probably no city in all of Europe that, as a whole, is more beautiful than Mexico. It has the elegance, the regularity, the uniformity of the lovely buildings of Turin, Milan, the elegant neighborhoods of Paris and Berlin."[7] Yet von Humboldt could not shut his eyes to the misery which most of the population suffered: "Nowhere in Europe can you see more poverty in the streets. 30,000-40,000 men (Indians), nude, wrapped only in woolen blankets or dressed in rugs. A sad and disgusting thing to see. And countless lice! Unequally distributed fortunes."[8]

In Mexico, von Humboldt was particularly impressed by the reforms undertaken by New Spain's former viceroy, Juan Vicente de Revillagigedo. Under his government, a number of improvements in justice, agriculture, industry and the educational system had been achieved. A major part of the statistical material later published by von Humboldt in the volume dedicated to Mexico was drawn from the census that had been conducted during Revillagigedo's reign.

On the other hand, von Humboldt was disappointed to see the little appreciation and the inadequate conservation relative to the Aztec hieroglyphs which archaeologist and his-

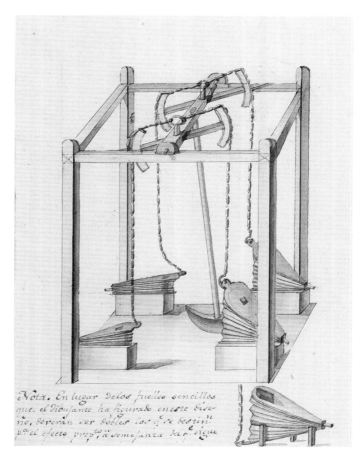

JOSÉ DE GOROSTIETA AND JUAN ANTONIO DE AYERDE
BELLOWS MACHINE USED TO EXTRACT METALS WITH FIRE [31]

torian Lorenzo Boturini Benaduci had compiled sixty years before. They had been piled in a humid room in the Viceroy's Palace where, von Humboldt noted: "A great number of them have already fallen to pieces, for every time they're opened they get more and more torn apart."[9] In the course of his investigations, von Humboldt found a series of indigenous hieroglyphic texts written after the Conquest, noting: "We can't but marvel at the creative power of the Mexicans when it comes to inventing new hieroglyphs for objects that were introduced by the conquerers and which they had never before seen. For example, a head from which emerges a string holding two keys is used to symbolize a person called Pedro."[10] Von Humboldt further noted: "It is horrible to follow the chronology of the Mexican hieroglyphs because you can be sure to note the arrival of the Spaniards as soon as you see representations of Indians strung up."[11] Von Humboldt acquired

C. ROCHUSSEN
COSTUMES OF THE INDIANS OF MICHOACÁN [32]

a series of Aztec hieroglyphs from the estate of Mexican scientist Antonio León y Gama and took them back to Europe. He was to include these and others that he studied later on (some of them in the Vatican's archives) in his volume *Vues de Cordillères....*

This same volume includes engravings of the three premier works from the Aztec culture: the *Piedra del Sol* (Stone of the Sun), the Stone of Tizoc and the statue of the goddess Coatlicue, all discovered in 1790 during restoration work on the *Zócalo* (Main Plaza) in Mexico City.[12] The *Piedra del Sol,* which the scientist interpreted to be a "calendar stone" (a contemporary interpretation of it is provided by Faak),[13] provided him with the opportunity to write his first text on the calendar systems

of the ancient cultures of the world and to compare the calendar system of ancient Mexico with those of Egypt, India, Japan, China and Tibet.[14] The statue of the goddess Coatlicue, which had been reburied, was again excavated at von Humboldt's request, but immediately after he had finished his studies it was again buried where it had been before. Later on, von Humboldt requested the statue for an exhibition at the Academy of Fine Arts, together with the plaster casts of ancient European statues, since, in his opinion, it was on the same artistic level. He also composed a detailed description of the designs, in relief, found on the Stone of Tizoc, which he compared to Trajan's Column in Rome.

While in Mexico, von Humboldt befriended the sculptor

and architect Manuel Tolsá. In November of 1803, both were present at the public inauguration of the equestrian statue of Charles IV that Tolsá had executed. As the statue was being hoisted onto its pedestal, the agave ropes being utilized broke. The statue toppled and almost crushed Tolsá and von Humboldt under its weight. While in the capital von Humboldt also enjoyed an intimate collaboration with the mineralogists Fausto d'Elhuyar, founder of the College of Mining, and Andrés Manuel del Río. Like von Humboldt, both had studied at the mining academy in Freiberg (Saxony). In November of 1803, von Humboldt was invited to attend the examinations at the College. Von Humboldt considered Tolsá's *Palacio de Minería* (Palace of Mining)—the architect's masterpiece, at the time still under construction—a "fortress." The ironic observation sprang from the fact that the German scientist would have preferred to see the new mining academy built in Guanajuato, where the theoretical and the practical sides of mining would have meshed as fruitfully as in Freiberg, and because Guanajuato would have presented better conditions for an intense collaboration between teachers and miners.

An important scientific goal of von Humboldt's during his stay in Mexico was the meticulous topographical measurement of the capital and its surroundings. From the roof of the newly-built mining academy, for example, he completed trigonometric studies of the volcanoes Popocatépetl and Iztaccíhuatl. A drawing of the mountains from this same point of view, created by Luis Martín, was later included as an engraving in von Humboldt's atlas of Mexico.

The atlas also contains a profile of the *Real Desagüe*, a drainage system built in the seventeenth century. Von Humboldt viewed it with much skepticism. On one hand, he could not but admit that it fulfilled its aim of efficient drainage for the city; on the other hand, he argued that the canal contributed to the dehydration of the fertile fields in the surrounding Valley of Mexico. His comments show evidence of his ecological point of view: "The Spaniards have treated the water as if it were their enemy," he wrote. "It seems as if they want New Spain to be as dry as the interior of the Spain of the Old World. They want to make the landscape look like their moral frame of mind, and they have succeeded quite well in doing so."[15] "Old Mexico was full of canals, like Venice. They want to dehydrate it all and place the city on solid ground. But in order to reach this goal, in case they should someday do so, they'll have to sterilize the

whole Valley and drain all the lakes"[16] The *Real Desagüe* was also an object of von Humboldt's acerbic criticism because its construction had cost the lives of thousands of Indians.

The excursions and journeys von Humboldt undertook from Mexico City were mostly motivated by his interest in geology and mining. Thus, he visited the mining regions of Pachuca, Regla and Guanajuato, as well as the Jorullo volcano. On May 13, 1803, he set out for Pachuca. He passed by Teotihuacan without visiting it although the archaeological site was only a few miles off his path. Later, in his volume on Mexico, he was to provide an extremely detailed description of the site based on measurements and studies done by the historians Sigüenza, Boturini and Oteiza. Generally speaking, during his stay in Mexico von Humboldt's interest in archaeology was rather secondary, with the exception of the studies he made of the pyramid at Cholula.

Von Humboldt was enchanted by the beauty of the Valley of Mexico: "A plain of more than 110 square miles, covered with pastures, lakes, expanses of *Fraxinus americana*, *Betula nigra*, small groups of cacti, *Yucca filamentosa*, and countless villages with pretty churches."[17]

On May 18, 1803, von Humboldt entered the shaft of the mine at Cabrera, not far from Pachuca: "The descent has something terrifying about it. Instead of stairs there are round trunks with notches. One doesn't know where to place his hands and knees. If your feet slip, you're lost."[18]

On May 21, 1803, von Humboldt paid a visit to the cascade and the basalt formations at the Hacienda de Regla: "The landscape is very picturesque. ... What a pity the waterfall isn't higher. The water drops from a height of only twenty feet. On both sides there are steep basalt columns. The little river that pours over the cascade at Regla has carved its bed through a deep valley surrounded by walls of basalt. Part of these walls can be seen rising above the surface of the water. Up above *Yucca filamentosa* and cacti grow. In the foreground there are trees with leaves of exceptional beauty. The surface of the water is covered with foam."[19] His studies revealed that the geological formation of basalt occurs in various regions of the planet under quite different climatic circumstances, which led him to conclude that they are all created under similar geological conditions. The illustration of the basalt formations at Regla in *Vues de Cordillères...*—sketched by von Humboldt himself, drawn by Gmelin and engraved by Louis

DANIEL THOMAS EGERTON
MINE SHAFT AT LA VALENCIANA [33]

Bouquet[20]—inspired a number of artists and geologists to visit the site, among them Baron de Courcy, Daniel Thomas Egerton and Johann Moritz Rugendas.

On May 24th, von Humboldt took measurements and made sketches of the "Organs" at Actopan and he observed that when contemplated from a distance, the rocks appear much bigger than from close up. The "Organs" are represented in a plate from *Vues de Cordillères...*,[21] which further documents von Humboldt's interest in illustrating geological and rock formations.

After this first of excursion, lasting nearly two weeks, von Humboldt and his traveling companions returned to Mexico City around dawn on May 26th.

Their second excursion—from the 1st of August to the end of September 1803—was also directed toward the study of mines. The route led them through Huehuetoca, where von Humboldt visited the *Real Desagüe*, traveling on to San Juan del Río and Querétaro until arriving in Guanajuato. Von Humboldt remarked that his stay there was "one of the most exhausting in all my life." Equipped with a barometer, he climbed all of the mountains in the region. His measurements of altitude resulted in what, for a long time, was to be

Baron de Courcy
the "la gallega" mine near zacatecas [34]

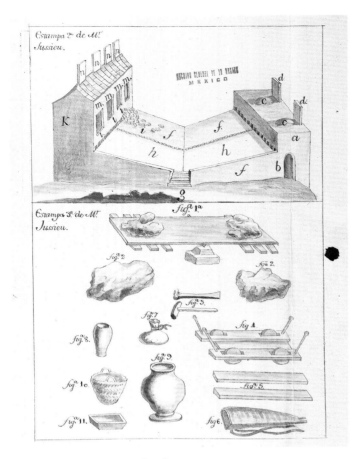

PH. SIMMONEAU

OVENS AND UTENSILS FOR THE SEPARATION OF QUICKSILVER [35]

sisted of carrying others around on their backs. As the prosperity of the Guanajuato region depended solely on the income from two mines, von Humboldt feared that the area might someday fall into insignificance as had Taxco.

After a visit to the mineral springs at Comanjillas, on September 11th, the travelers headed for the volcano at Jorullo, whose formation was described by von Humboldt as "one of most horrific phenomena that History has to offer."[24] On September 17th, 1759, the volcano[25] had emerged suddenly in the open plain of sugar hacienda known as San Pedro de Jorullo, causing "an uproar as if five thousand cannons were fired off at the same time."[26] Soon after, the volcano's summit had risen to a height of 1803 feet.

Von Humboldt climbed to the summit of the volcano and descended into the smoking crater. Later, he dedicated a number of illustrations to the Jorullo volcano: the *Atlas géographique...* contains not only a chart and a profile, but also a small landscape of it,[27] while *Vues de Cordillères...* also includes an engraving depicting the newborn volcano.[28]

In Valladolid (today the city of Morelia), the traveler's attention was attracted by little puppets that the indigenous people created with remarkably skilled craftsmanship.[29] They are fine examples of a fusion of elements of Spanish dress with those of the indigenous cultures. Together with the ornamental figures in the views of landscapes, they are the only human depictions included in the volumes that document von Humboldt's journey. By way of Acámbaro, Maravatío and Ixtlahuaca, the group arrived in Toluca on September 28th, 1803. There, von Humboldt and his companions climbed the Nevado de Toluca (14,944 feet), where he took measurements and studied the geological structure of the volcano. The group returned to Mexico City in the last days of September 1803.

On January 20th of the following year, von Humboldt, Bonpland and Montúfar departed from the capital of New Spain for the last time. On their way to Veracruz they passed through Puebla and visited the pyramid at Cholula,[30] the only Mexican pyramid that von Humboldt studied and measured himself. He referred to it as "the largest, oldest and most famous of all the monumental pyramids. ... Today it is considered to be a man-made mountain and, when seen from a distance, it might indeed be taken as a natural hill covered by vegetation."[31] "A small chapel surrounded by cypresses" now supplanted Quet-

the most correct and detailed chart of Guanajuato and its surroundings. Still, von Humboldt took an even greater interest in the mines. At La Valenciana he descended three times to the very bottom of the shaft; in Rayas he did so twice. He visited the mines of Mellado, Fraustros, Animas, San Bruno, Villalpando, Santa Rosa and Los Alamos. He criticized the lack of systematic procedures in the extraction of ore and the absence of useful charts and maps of the mines: "You have to walk through the whole house in order to get from one room to the next."[22] He referred to the main shaft of the mine at La Valenciana as the "greatest enterprise to have been undertaken by man, not in terms of depth, but because of its enormous breadth."[23] Von Humboldt also criticized the taxing and poorly paid labor of the *tenateros* (ore-carriers), who were exclusively indigenous or mestizos. He viewed with disgust the so-called "human horses" in the mine, whose work con-

zalcóatl, the deity to which the place was consecrated in the beginning, "and every day an Indian priest says mass from the top of this ancient monument."[32] The illustration of this site found in *Vues de Cordillères...* and the plates of the ruins at Cañar (Ecuador) are paradigms of von Humboldt's intention to represent pre-Columbian monuments within the context of their environment.

On the way to Veracruz, von Humboldt completed sketches of two other mountains, the Cofre de Perote[33] and the Pico de Orizaba.[34] In these, he paid particular attention to the precise representation of the region's flora and fauna. "The foreground of my drawing," he noted, concerning the view of the Pico de Orizaba, "is a forest made up of *Liquidambar styraciflua,* melastomas, and species of *Arbutus* and of *Piper*."[35]

On February 18th, 1804, the travelers arrived at Veracruz, whose harbor von Humboldt described as a "pierced bag."[36] Stormy winds from the North kept them from embarking for Cuba until March 7th.

The work *Essai politique...* and the illustrations in *Vues de Cordillères...*, in particular, had an enormous influence on the scientific and artistic exploration of New Spain. Although von Humboldt's Mexican itinerary rarely led him to unexplored sites, his great accomplishment was that he coherently structured the knowledge at hand, providing new comparisons, uncovering connections and interactions, and compiled it all in a new and comprehensive manner, through the use of both texts and illustrations.

Besides the scientific value of von Humboldt's texts and the high artistic quality of his illustrations, also notable is his remarkable talent for interchange and dialogue, which made his work so valuable to both the sciences and the arts. Thus, von Humboldt assured that both his works and his scientific point of view would be continually read and discussed anew. He maintained personal contact and correspondence with an impressive number of fellow scientists and traveling artists such as Johann Moritz Rugendas, Carl Nebel and Pál Rosti. In the year prior to von Humboldt's death, Rosti had the chance to show him his photographs of Venezuela, Cuba and Mexico. Old and afflicted with disease, von Humboldt was profoundly touched at their sight. The Mexican itinerary of Rugendas, who von Humboldt called the "most masterful painter of the characteristic forms of the tropical world," turned out to be almost identical to the route followed by von Humboldt three decades

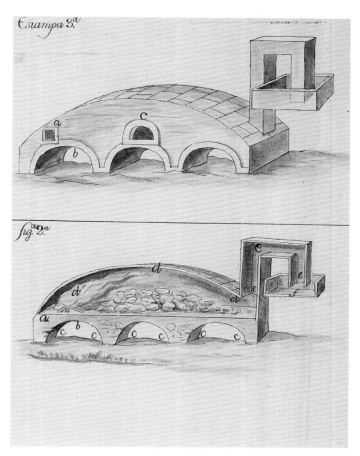

PH. SIMMONEAU
OVENS FOR THE SEPARATION OF QUICKSILVER [36]

earlier. Among other traveler-artists, Carl Nebel, a draftsman who specialized in architecture, was also influenced by von Humboldt. Nebel closely observed von Humboldt's counsel and also visited sites that the earlier traveler had not been able to see. Another important impetus within the plastic arts attributable to von Humboldt was the publication of his theoretical justification of the importance that landscape painting held for the natural sciences, in the second volume of *Kosmos,* in 1847.

Alexander von Humboldt transmitted to the arena of plastic arts his boundless passion for compiling, classifying and presenting the available knowledge about Latin America. Due to his influences, some artists attempted to capture the characteristic features of landscapes from the point of view of the natural sciences. Right up until his death, in 1859, von Humboldt keenly participated in keeping his work and his journey through Mexico alive in the minds of his contemporaries.

p. 62. EUGENIO LANDESIO
THE "LA PURÍSIMA" MINE AT REAL DEL MONTE (DETAIL) [37]

PROFILE OF THE TRAVELER-ARTIST IN THE NINETEENTH CENTURY

PABLO DIENER

On the American continent, the denomination traveler-artist is applied to the foreign painter, draftsman or photographer, generally European, who executed his creative work using the world through which he traveled as his theme. Within the nineteenth century we find a very broad range of personages who can be identified with this term. The nineteenth-century traveler-artist represents a singular category in the history of art. From the accidental traveler, be he a soldier, diplomat or businessman who dedicated his leisure time to the fine arts, to the academic painter who left the studio in order to practice his painting in the open air or in search of motifs to interpret on canvas, all are joined by their manner of observation and by their curiosity about the landscape, the people, their lives, their history and their monuments. Also to this category belongs he who traveled for pleasure or for adventure, or the man of wealth or of nobility who wanted to know the world, regularly making notes in his *carnet de voyage*. However, the archetype is, without doubt, the romantic artist, heir to the enlightened tradition of Absolutism and, at the same time, a pioneer who longed to learn of the world from a subjective perspective. His immediate predecessor is the scientific illustrator who accompanied the research expeditions to the most hidden reaches of the world. This figure, however, represented a role that he intended to surpass. The traveler-artist of romanticism restated his relationship with the sciences via an idealistic perspective and intuited that his contribution was not only that of a servile illustrator, but of someone capable of penetrating the profound comprehension of man and nature.

The attraction that the work of the travelers of all walks offers us today stems from the documental value that it continues to possess, as well as its artistic quality. The traveler-artists awoke in their American contemporaries an interest in the landscape as a pictorial motif. There are outstanding examples such as the Italian, Eugenio Landesio, who created a school of Mexican landscape painting, opening the way that his disciple José María Velasco was to follow to the culmination of *plein air* painting. Beyond those few cases in which a direct master-disciple relationship can be cited, the traveler-painters contributed, as a group, to the enrichment of the tastes of lovers of art. In Chile, for example, the shipping magnate William (Guillermo) Wheelright commissioned Rugendas to execute a portrait of his family, with the bay at Valparaíso as the backdrop. More than strictly a portrait painting, the artist offers a view of the port, the city and the ships, the subjects of the portrait becoming little more than small figures which decorate the foreground. Still, judging by the series of copies and variations that Rugendas painted of this work, the scene satisfied the wishes of Wheelright as to the representation that he had hoped for. Similarly of note are the numerous views of haciendas that Landesio painted in Mexico, works that, together with portraits, offered their owners the possibility of a type of identification.

The participation of the traveler-artists in archaeological discoveries and, in general, in the investigation of historical-cultural monuments was frequently pioneering, and in many cases their works contain information of interest to historical studies. The illustrations by Carl Nebel and Frederick Catherwood, the drawings and oils by Waldeck, and the photographs and watercolors by Adela Breton studied, reproduced and interpreted the pre-Columbian past of Mexico from a nineteenth-century perspective. The archaeological notes taken by Rugendas in the

Andean valley of Ollantaitambo are, due to their precision, a source for the reconstruction, for purposes of study, of buildings that have now mostly disappeared. The drawings made in the city of Lima by the French diplomat Leonce Angrand, between 1820 and 1840, contribute to the rediscovery of the baroque architectural riches of this former viceregal capital. The antiquarian tastes of the traveler-artists often manifested themselves in certain facets of collecting and commerce that overlapped with history and archaeology in quite different ways.

The third thematic area, or chapter, in which the traveler-artist played the part of innovator was that of ethnography and folklore. Herderian historicism evoked in the travelers a vision that, more than just fixed on the exotic, was attentive to the physical characteristics of the American peoples, as well as one that nourished a curiosity about their daily lives. From the time of the Napoleonic Wars, the writings by Herder had appeared as the principal theoretical support endorsing the deepening of knowledge of the historical past and the traditions of its cultures. Thus was initiated the romantic vision of "the people" and the idea that any loss of this cultural legacy, whether in terms of traditions, customs or poetry, constituted a loss to the essential substance of a country. This proposition found fertile ground in the emergence of the nation states and, on the American continent, the traveler-artists were instrumental in the creation of innumerable series dedicated to the study of typical inhabitants, which coincided with these longings on the part of some of the intellectual elite.

If the documental interest held by the works of these traveler-artists is undeniable, whether for the information they offer on their subjects or in terms of their reception during the nineteenth century, their artistic value is dissimilar. In viewing the art of the European travelers in Mexico during the nineteenth century, we should take a broad enough look that permits us knowledge of their works from the most diverse points of view. Just as Rugendas, Landesio, Egerton or Gros deserve attention as personalities from the history of art, the genre studies by Schönowsky, the sketches of landscapes and daily life by Bullock, and the antiquarian notes by Vischer are charming artistic documents, although some of them minor, that reflect the fluctuations in Mexico's reception in Europe.

THE ACADEMIC AS TRAVELER-ARTIST

By definition, the academic artist did not fit the stereotype of the traveler. His topics of interest were defined by means of a

Eugenio Landesio
VIEW OF THE HACIENDA DE SÁNCHEZ [38]

ADELA BRETON
CHICHÉN-ITZÁ. CARYATIDS [39]

ADELA BRETON
CHICHÉN-ITZÁ. CARYATID IX [40]

rigorous scale of values. His preferences centered on the painting of historical or religious themes, on the allegory or the portrait, while the motifs that attracted the travelers seemed barely to rise above the horizon of what, in the academic's eyes, was worthy of the fine arts. After much inconstancy, it wasn't until well into the nineteenth century that instruction in the painting of landscapes had been admitted, in a generalized form, into the curricula of the academies. As to genre painting as a pictorial motif, the words of Louis XIV, upon viewing some popular Dutch scenes, continued to echo within the halls of the academies: "Get those vulgar sights away from me!" Lastly, antiquarian themes were only worthy of attention if they appeared within the context of a historical reconstruction, thereby elevated to the level of historical painting, but not simply as documental illustration. Likewise, the academic aesthetic was nourished by the canons of classical beauty, while life studies—essential to the traveler—were considered merely a step in the creative process. However, in reviewing the work and the teaching practices of some of the foreign

academics in Mexico, one discovers features that can be associated with the work that the travelers left in their wake. An unmistakable example of this type of interrelationship can be found in the personalities of the Catalan, Pelegrín Clavé and the Italian, Eugenio Landesio.

Clavé practiced sketching in oils in Mexico and some examples of this work are still to be found, such as *Paisaje en Durango* (Landscape in Durango) and *Las cuevas de Cacahuamilpa* (The Caves of Cacahuamilpa). Certainly, these are small studies of a personal character, oils on pasteboard, done with rapid brushstrokes and paying more attention to color than to the silhouette. They are stupendous examples of work done using this technique, a practice that was recommended by the academics but which achieved autonomy only with the emergence of Turner and Corot. With their vistas of Alpine passes and the countryside around Rome, these European painters instilled, over a period of decades, a new way of viewing and painting nature. Running parallel to this, during the first half of the century, Alexander von

Humboldt had provided theoretical nourishment to the practice of sketching in oils. This technique represented one of the greatest rediscoveries made by the traveler-artists both within and outside of Europe. Pelegrín Clavé, in painting these types of works during his sojourn in Mexico (1846-1868) became, for a time, a traveler-artist, whether measured against the classicist tradition or in terms of receptivity toward the new currents in art. In fact, his preoccupation with the problems posed by the painting of landscapes figured in his invitation, in his capacity as director of the Academia Nacional de San Carlos, made to Landesio to conduct classes on this subject.

Eugenio Landesio transferred the idyll of the perfect Arcadias painted in Italy to that "most transparent region," the Valley of Mexico. His stay in Mexico (1855-1877) was determined by his commitment to the teaching of landscape and perspective painting. He had crossed the Atlantic not to participate in the rediscovery of the New World but, rather, with the purpose of imparting lessons on European culture and art. In his artistic production, however, his approach to the Mexican landscape is as novel as those of the travelers Egerton, Rugendas and Gros. The pictorial language of his Italian landscapes reappears in the vistas of Mexico, but now subjected to profound modifications, in topographical definition as well as in the solidifying and materiality of the coloring. As a teacher, he posed his own theoretical problems relative to landscape painting in Mexico and, in the manner of a traveler, studied ways to resolve the matters specific to his new surroundings. This sense of finding oneself between two worlds was characteristic of the traveler-artist and, from an academic perspective, Landesio fulfilled this principle completely. In this manner, in addition to writing general instructions to be utilized by young artists, as in *Cimientos del artista, dibujante y pintor. Compendio de perspectiva lineal y aérea, sombras, espejos y refracción con las nociones necesarias de geometría* (Fundamentals of the Artist, Draftsman and Painter. Compendium of Lineal and Aerial Perspective, Shadow, Mirrors and Refraction with the Necessary Notions of Geometry), from 1866, and *La pintura general o de paisaje y la perspectiva en la Academia Nacional de San Carlos* (General Painting or of Landscapes and Perspective at the National Academy of San Carlos), from 1867, he also dedicated himself to the writing of *La excursión a la caverna de Cacahuamilpa y ascención al cráter del Popocatépetl* (Excursion to the Cavern of Cacahuamilpa and Ascent to the Crater of Popocatépetl), in 1868. Among other topics in this work, he declared his

Adela Breton
CHICHÉN-ITZÁ. JAMBS WITH RELIEF [41]

concern, as an artist, with the deformations in the perception of color experienced at a great altitude, noting "that with the lack of atmosphere existing around one, and the great refraction, the effect is that, instead of blue, the sky appears black." Neither Clavé nor Landesio fit completely with the archetype of the traveler-artist yet, although from the Academy, their production coincides on essential points with that of the foreigners.

Another artist from the classicist tradition, spiritually connected to the Academy, is the Frenchman, Edouard Pingret. Within the scope of the Versailles aesthetic, Pingret was a traveler-artist. Already in Europe he had acted in the capacity of illustrator on a royal voyage, in 1844, on which he accompanied King Louis Philippe to England. In 1846 he traveled to Tripoli, Morocco and Algeria, at which time he began incursions into the sophisticated painting of Orientalism. Pressured by the crisis in France in 1848, he ended up traveling to Cuba and, soon after, to Mexico, where he resided from 1851 until 1855. From his position of prestige, he introduce genre painting as a pictorial theme at the Academy's exhibition of 1854. His work is more aristocratic, more idealized yet, in terms of subject, analogous to that of Linati, Blanchard or his contemporary in

pp. 68-69. Desiré Charnay
MITLA. HALL OF THE COLUMNS [42]

Mexico, Hegi. The genre work by Pingret, for the most part, parallels that of his fellow countryman and classicist, Raymond Quinsac Monvoisin, who worked in South America, principally in Argentina. Monvoisin's representation of the gauchos is as ideal, as perfectly attenuated, and as classically proportioned as the cultured images of the muleteer, the *charro* or the water vendor captured by Pingret. Each contributed to the acceptance of the genre and created a market for this type of painting among the nations' bourgeoisie. Both, as traveler-artists, took advantage of the possibilities presented them by this type of painting, as well as in portraiture and the casual antiquarian trade, in order to make a living.

THE ACCIDENTAL TRAVELER

With the consummation of Mexico's independence, an increasing number of travelers arrived in Mexico for professional rea-

sons. Impresarios and businessmen, military officers and those individuals who formed their retinues, and diplomats constituted a heterogeneous group of visitors. In spite of the differences of personality that characterized them, whether based on their positions or nationalities, as foreigners in Mexico—or in any other country in the Americas—they shared a position of privilege. They were generally well-to-do, often belonging to a cultural elite even within their countries of origin. The fact that they traveled as a result of their situations at least had broadened their horizons and sensitized them to observing the world with a certain curiosity. On a social level, during their stay in Mexico they established a broad network of relationships and had access to all kinds of information. Their work generally obliged them to write reports, perhaps explaining why often they transcended the production of simple accounts related to their work by also putting down on paper their impressions of these voyages. In tandem with such dilettante exercises in the literary genre, they turned to the practice of drawing and painting and, within one area or the other, many of them merit attention for their obvious sensitivity and intuition, and for the artistic heights they reached. If, as travelers, they could be identified, with greater or lesser precision, according to their personal brilliance or the company, institution or country they represented, as artists it is difficult to situate them since, generally speaking, they belonged to the vast family of the amateur.

The themes to which these artists dedicated their free time cover as broad a range as their backgrounds, nor was there necessarily any relationship between their professions and what they chose to paint. The Swiss, Lukas Vischer, for example, traveled to the United States in 1823 and, five years later, moved on to Mexico. He undertook the voyage with the purpose of managing the expansion activities of a prosperous family business, a textile factory specializing in silk ribbon, that was based in Basel. His album of drawings dedicated to Mexico features mainly studies of local characters, with some notation of plants and antiquarian pieces. His primordial interest in the human figure is evident from the caricatures he created as a youth, for amusement, in his native city. What was new, in his work executed in the United States as well as in Mexico, was the attention directed toward folkloric motifs. In Vischer's case, as well as in those of the other travelers, we know or can reasonably assume that he associated with artists, scientists and politicians. It wasn't difficult, therefore, for them to stay abreast of cultural and social news, as well as the

PÁL ROSTI
REAL DEL MONTE [44]

goings-on within public administration circles. As such, we can assume that Vischer had seen the album *Costumes Civils, Militaires et Religieux du Mexique* (Civil, Military and Religious Dress from Mexico), which Claudio Linati had published in Belgium in 1828, the same year in which Vischer arrived in Mexico. The studies by the Swiss are precious miniatures, of more careful stroke and more classical, and by far better than those of Linati. This does not diminish the influence that Linati had had on Vischer, and on society in general, thanks to his revolutionary genius as an editor and lithographer. In this sense, the cultivation of the "popular" that Linati propagated represented a pioneering work that also must be considered as setting the stage for Vischer. The link between Vischer and the "professional" traveler-artists is

documented in the case of his encounter with Rugendas, who painted his portrait, on horseback and attired *a la Mexicana*. His observations of daily life were as precise as his art, such as when he related the details of his trip from Veracruz to Mexico City, in a letter to his sister from April of 1828. He speaks of having made the trip in a sort of elaborate litter, harnessed at either end to a mule which was "sufficiently roomy to be able to stretch out. In New Orleans I had bought a mattress, a pillow and two blankets which had served as my bed on the boat, and I was able to utilize them again in the litter. I lay within it as if in a cradle since the litter rocked back and forth. It was carried by two mules and accompanied by two horsemen and a second pair of mules, which took turns carrying the litter, and as such we formed a sort of small caravan."[1]

In Mexico City, an antiquarian interest was also awakened within him. He visited Xochicalco, as had so many other travelers, and began to collect pre-Columbian pieces, occasionally even making notes on archaeological objects and monuments. Finally, outstanding within his collection were a group of traditional figures in wax which, as a memento, he took back to Basel with him and which today form part of the collection of Basel's Museum of Ethnography.

On the other hand, in the case of the English banker George Henry White, the only theme that we find among the watercolors he produced during his stay in Mexico (1862-63) are landscapes. This interest may well be interpreted as a heritage of his British upbringing. The assurance with which he directly applied his watercolors, without any prior pencil outlines, his skillful use of color and, particularly, the care shown in his studies of clouds, suggest that the author had a deep knowledge of the tradition of landscape painting of his homeland. The route followed by White, as well as by Vischer and the majority of the rest of the travelers, was conventional, the selection of motifs nearly always encompassing the preexisting iconographic tradition, whether landscapes, typical local scenes or historical-cultural themes.

The group of European military men with artistic leanings are associated primarily with the 1860's, a result of the wars provoked by the Second Empire. They found within their professional passion the expression of their dilettante exercises in the arts. Uniforms, troop formations that arose from military strategies,

JEAN BAPTISTE LOUIS, BARON GROS
POPOCATÉPETL AND PICO DEL FRAYLE [46]

and the painting of battle scenes were their favorite topics. Generally, due to this monothematic practice, they tended not to exhibit any curiosity in genre painting or landscapes. There did, however, exist exceptions in such outstanding figures as Juan Galindo, an English officer of Spanish and Irish descent who ended up dedicating his life, in Mexico and in Guatemala, to antiquarian studies, leaving a series of notes that were later published, in part, in the *Bulletin de la Société de Géographie* of Paris, in 1832. An important area to which the military contributed, whether as travelers or not, was that of cartography. Some, such as Major Adalbert Schönowsky of the Austrian army, personally executed this type of work while others delegated such duties to subordinates. The German, Eduard Harkort, for example, offered his services to General Santa Anna as both strategist and cartographer and between December of 1833 and February of 1834, on an expedition from Mexico City to

Manzanillo, opened new perspectives on the comprehension of landscapes for Rugendas, based on his knowledge of geography and cartography.

Among the accidental travelers, Jean Baptiste Louis, Baron Gros, an official of the French legation in Mexico from 1832 onward, overcame, by far, his status as amateur in the arts. His paintings reveal a professional technical knowledge in the use of oils, and the specific motifs and focus that he chose demonstrate the criteria of an artist steeped in tradition. Jean Baptiste Louis, who was a relative of the Napoleonic painter Jean Antoine, Baron Gros, a title bestowed upon him by the emperor, inherited the title, becoming the second Baron Gros. The little work he left us is dedicated to the landscape. They are naturalistic studies, carefully finished vistas composed in the luminist tradition of Dutch landscape painting, yet without the operatic sense of the classicist landscape. His painting was born,

primarily, of a careful observation of nature. The naturalistic scientific enthusiasm stands out as one of the principal motivations that led him to painting and, in the end, to becoming involved with the other travelers. Indicative of his interests, he scaled the Popocatépetl volcano, in April of 1834, in the company of the Prussian consul general von Geroldt and the English painter Egerton. In the account that Gros made,[2] of note is that, in conjunction with the spirit of adventure, he was motivated by scientific curiosity. He mentions, for example, that they collected plants for the herbarium of the German botanist Schiede, and speaks of having brought him "a new plant, a charming bush, analogous to our pink laurel, but whose flowers seem like beautiful clusters of lilies-of-the-valley, of a tone between white and rose." On the trip they had brought "a barometer, a mining compass, for want of theodolite; we also brought some thermometers, a small instrument for measuring the boiling tem-

perature of water as affected by the altitude, a good telescope and a hygrometer. All these instruments had been compared with those of General don Juan de Orbegoso and of the professor of physics, don Joaquín Velásquez de León, in order that when we returned to Mexico City we could accurately compare the results to those experiments that had been carried out simultaneously in the city and at the summit of Popocatépetl." Pico de Fraile (Friar's Peak) is one of the points where measurements were taken and Gros mentions in his writings that at 9:00 in the morning "the sky was darker than at dusk. Lamentably, we had no instruments with which to measure its intensity." During breaks in the trek, Gros notes that: "I dedicated myself to examining the summit of the volcano with the telescope and made

Lukas Vischer
typical character in "carnet de voyage en mexico" [49]

Lukas Vischer
typical character in "carnet de voyage en mexico" [50]

precise notes of the rocks, the fissures and the courses that had been marked by the lava flows on the south side of the mountain." Analogous to this is the predominant naturalistic interest that motivated the vista in oils he called *Pico de Fraile*, in reality a study of the rock formations of the mountain, whose focus denotes the attention paid to the form, texture, and coloring of the stone, more than being a picturesque view. All his paintings seem associated with a zeal for knowledge and documentation. Likewise, in 1832, when he painted the Pyramid of the Sun, at Teotihuacan, the only work known on an antiquarian theme by this author, he added an inscription that provides information about the meaning and importance that this monument held within the realm of archaeology. And at the same time as he offered us a detailed study of the pyramid, he was meticulous as to the observation of plants and the pictorial values of the ground and the clouds, composing the space with an interplay of light and shadow.

Like Gros, Elizabeth Ward, wife of the British diplomat, dedicated herself to a painstakingly careful depiction of the landscapes

of Mexico, in her case to be used to illustrate her husband's book. A taste for the genre of travel literature was especially common among the accidental travelers in diplomatic circles.

THE GRAND TOUR OF AMERICA

The first features of the journey, in the modern sense, appeared with the humanist spirit of the Renaissance. The religious pilgrimages, mostly to Rome, little by little gave way to the journeys of study to the fountains of Western art and culture such as those undertaken by Memling and Dürer and numerous other Central European scholars who headed to Italy. Toward the end of the sixteenth century, this journey became institutionalized as part of the education required for service in the royal courts and in the administrations of states, as well as for the "academic pilgrim," that is, the scientific journey that took him from one point in Europe to another in order to satisfy his hunger for the universal knowledge to be found in the great libraries, the archives,

JOHANN MORITZ RUGENDAS
PORTRAIT OF LUKAS VISCHER [51]

or through contact with other scholars. The growing importance acquired by this form of access to information was indicated by the academic status that was granted to the teaching of "the art of adequately organizing the journey," a subject on which, toward the middle of the eighteenth century, the historian Johann David Köhler lectured at the University of Göttingen. In the first pages of his treatise, *Instructions to Young Researchers for Advantageous Travel* (Magdeburg, 1788), Köhler warns the scholar that "not only must books be read, but one must strive to see with one's own eyes and perceive with one's own senses. ... The final aim of the journey by the scholar is that of collecting experiences and, thereby, enriching his knowledge." The modalities, motivations and destinations of the cultural journey were to become increasingly diversified during the Enlightenment and due to the spirit of romanticism. The great scientific expeditions throughout the length and breadth of the globe, the studies that Winck-

elmann dedicated to Greece, the philosophy of Rousseau and the romantic fashions imposed by the English poet and revolutionary, Lord Byron, decisively influenced the definition of the individual who undertook the Grand Tour in the nineteenth century. New routes became accessible, admiration for the classical world found competition from a fascination for the "natural man," and the initial, purely academic character of the cultural voyage became sprinkled with an individualistic subjectivism. The American continent was to form part of the Grand Tour of the nineteenth century. One example is the Englishman, Sir Richard F. Burton, polyglot scholar, orientalist and occasional painter who dedicated his life to travel, part of the time in the service of the British government, generally with the aim of escaping Victorian society. He traveled to Afghanistan, visited Mecca and Somalia and, in a diplomatic capacity, spent time in Santos, Brazil, and while stationed there undertook a journey to the state of Minas

BARON DE COURCY
CALLE [STREET] DEL PRESBITERIO IN JALAPA [52]

Gerais. Later he was transferred to posts in Damascus and Trieste. He was the prototype of the legacy of Lord Byron, of one who fled English society and scandalized it at every turn. Even as a young official with the East India Company he took on the role of an outsider by choosing to live among the general population rather than in the company's quarters, provoking his contemporaries to write him off, declaring that "he went native." He abhorred what he felt was the spiritual narrowness of the British and attempted—and achieved—an intimate relationship with the countries that he visited.

A traveler arrived in Mexico in 1832 who, in a manner different from that of Burton, also formed part of the group of cultured travelers of European tradition, the Frenchman, François Mathurin Adalbert, Baron de Courcy. His travels, as far as we know, were limited to the Americas. He arrived in Canada and journeyed through North America until reaching the Gulf of Mexico. He entered Mexico via the port of Tampico and resided in the country for nearly one year. De Courcy is a personality of little mention in the annals of history. Rather, it is from accounts of his travels that we can learn something of his existence and the features of his personality. In Mexico he met Gros and was a traveling companion of Rugendas. His drawings and watercolors are indicative of a well-trained artist, although we have no knowledge of under whom he may have studied. By leafing through his *carnet de voyage*, we can intuit that he was a man who traveled and painted for personal pleasure, seeking out picturesque landscapes, yet also attracted by the sites and monuments that were visited by most of the other researchers and artists of the period, such as the mines of Guanajuato, the prismatic basalt formations at Regla, and the ruins at Xochicalco.

One of the last travelers whose life was evocative of the tradition of the Grand Tour was the German doctor Paul Fischer. Although his voyage to Mexico in 1890 might be better catego-

PAUL FISCHER
XOCHIMILCO [53]

rized as that of a contemporary emigrant, Fischer settled in the country only after having traversed Europe and the Americas, and gone as far as Hong Kong. At just over twenty years of age, he completed his studies in Munich and left on a tour of the world, painting along the way such subjects as Bahia and Rio de Janeiro, in Brazil, as well as various seascapes from the Eastern Pacific, until establishing himself on terra firma in Durango. His world tour seems to have been the last stage in his personal formation, even though it wasn't a voyage of study. The link with the humanistic idea of the voyage is reaffirmed by reading his travel journal. His style of drawing, that of the German academic school, and the vastness of the themes that he covers suggest a broad education of a universal sense that, by force of tradition, had to be culminated with a grand journey through unknown lands.

THE MÉTIER OF THE PROFESSIONAL TRAVELER-ARTIST

The most charismatic and, doubtless, the best example of the professional traveler-artist from the nineteenth century was the Bavarian, Johann Mortiz Rugendas. From his participation on a scientific expedition to Brazil, his relationship, as a disciple, with

Alexander von Humboldt, and his trip to Italy, to the undertaking, of his own volition and at his own risk, of his great voyage to the Americas, the stages of his biography document, step by step, the genesis, the conflicts and the interests of the nineteenth-century traveler-artist.

There exists an obvious evolutionary relationship between the romantic traveler-artist and the illustrator who had earlier accompanied the research expeditions during the Age of Enlightenment. Actually, his professional career began at the age of nineteen when he joined, in the capacity of draftsman, the expedition to the interior of Brazil organized by the German naturalist Georg Heinrich von Langsdorff, funded by the government of Russia. However, Rugendas never really assumed the responsibilities imposed under his contract which required the "diligent exercise of his art in all circumstances and, chiefly, the illustration of those objects that the head of the expedition pointed out to him as being important."[3] His relationship with von Langsdorff was strained, to the point that he left the expedition during a trip to the state of Minas Gerais. Beyond the personal discord and the circumstantial issues that surround this episode, the rupture is evidence of the incompatibility between the responsibilities

JOHANN MORITZ RUGENDAS
VIEW OF THE SLOPES OF POPOCATÉPETL AND IZTACCÍHUATL WITH THE VALLEY OF MEXICO IN THE BACKGROUND [54]

that the head of the expedition imposed on the draftsman and the ideas that the artist held as to his work. The positivist legacy of the Age of Enlightenment represented by von Langsdorff drove him to accumulate information, to be an instrument of the sciences or, simply, to serve the politics of colonial expansion by recording the riches to be exploited. On the other hand, imbued with the spirit of romanticism, Rugendas aspired to carrying out his work with autonomy. He wanted to become involved in the process of political independence which Brazil was undergoing at the time and, in the artistic arena, to define his own parameters, conceding preeminence to his artistic sensibility with the aim of penetrating to the essence of the subject of his interest. The weight of the growing romantic valuation of subjectivism rested upon him and, lastly, the desire to situate himself at the center of attention. He was part of the world through which he journeyed.

One of the most patent examples of this attitude, characteristic of the European artists of the period, is *Voyage to Italy*, by J. W. von Goethe (1816/17, 1829). In Verona, the German poet wrote, on September 17, 1786: "I make this marvelous voyage not to allow myself to be fascinated, but to come to know myself through these objects." He sought the essence of everything and challenged himself to "observe without thinking." For him, knowledge did not consist of the simple accumulation of information; rather, it lay in the interpenetration of the existence of objects, with the goal of "comprehending the most profound sense of that which man has been capable of creating." The desire to comprehend existence, whether of artistic objects or of nature, was the central purpose of his travels and of his work, and poetic introspection appears as his fundamental tool.

Friedrich Schiller also denied the validity of the collection of information unless it were conceived within a global vision. Accordingly, he wrote to C. G. Körner, in 1797, that "nature is something that, in itself, will always remain beyond our grasp and, in all its aspects, as venerable as it is unfathomable." Thus, in referring to the early scientific research by Alexander von Humboldt, he implacably criticized the man: "I don't understand how he can go on with such arrogance, utilizing as parameters his formulas which, in general, are no more than empty words and represent nothing more than limited concepts." He concluded with: "Nature has to be seen and conceived in the smallest of its manifestations, as well as in it most far-reaching laws."

The traveler-artist fluctuated between the extremes of idealistic poeticism and the scientific zeal of documentation. It was Alexander von Humboldt himself that resolved the conflict, based on his personal experience as a traveler, as well as on the existence of a profound coincidence with Goethe and, in spite of their personal differences, with Schiller. In the correspondence that he maintained with numerous traveler-artists, beginning in the 1820's, largely through the encyclopedic publication *Cosmos* (1847), von Humboldt defined the field of art as being auxiliary to the sciences. In the first pages of his analysis, in Volume II, he writes: "In order to illustrate Nature in all its monumentality, one must not pay attention only to its exterior aspect; Nature must also be represented just as it is reflected in the spirit of man..." He later states: "Each geographic zone, apart from its intrinsic charms, also has a singular character and each awakens different sensations within us. ... The blue of the sky, the configuration of the clouds, the perfume from afar, the succulence of the herb, the brilliance of the foliage, the silhouette of the mountains, are elements that

CAMERA LUCIDA [55]   CAMERA OBSCURA [56]

determine the global impression of a region. The work of the landscape painter is to capture and interpret this with intuition."

His thinking and his work on the Americas were always a point of reference, not only for his most direct German disciples such as Rugendas and Carl Nebel, in Mexico; Albert Berg, in Colombia; or Ferdinand Bellermann, in Venezuela; but also for the Hungarian photographer Pál Rosti, and the English watercolorist and photographer Adela Breton. Even as critical of the antiquarian studies of von Humboldt as was Waldeck, he used the same concepts as this wise Prussian in analyzing the work of the traveler-artist and coincided with his appreciation of the relationship between art and science. For example, in a critical commentary on the work of Rugendas pertaining to Brazil, he wrote in his diary, dated Sunday, November 11, 1831: "In the afternoon I went to visit Mr. Rugendas and saw his work. That on the subject of Brazil, which was lithographed in Paris, is picturesque from every point of view and plants are illustrated that this artist drew with great inspiration; but he concludes nothing from life and he relies too much on his memory. He draws the human figure skillfully, and I also saw one of his landscapes of a virgin jungle, that he himself lithographed, which is very beautiful in its detail, but weak in the interpretation of the whole."[4] Even while Waldeck finds fault in that which von Humboldt had praised in the plates from *Voyage Pittoresque dans le Brésil* (Picturesque Voyage in Brazil), it is worth noting that as to the *effet général,* they coincide in that this aspect, which von Humboldt calls the "global interpretation of the landscape," is the area of intrinsic

artistic creation in the work of the traveler-painter. According to Waldeck, even for the adequate illustration of a plant there must be *beaucoup d'esprit,* inspiration, and not simply dexterity. The same concept appears in a letter from von Humboldt to Rugendas, with his praising of "the intellectual elaboration of your drawings of the tropical world."[5]

Von Humboldt's thinking accompanied the traveler-artist throughout the nineteenth century and his commentaries and suggestions, with reference to the diverse techniques of representation, encompass even photography and the construction of panoramas. In concluding the chapter in *Cosmos* dedicated to the "Influence of Art on the Revitalization of the Study of Nature," he enthusiastically describes the possibilities offered by the panorama, the painting of 360°, as a visual spectacular "because the spectator imagines himself surrounded by a different nature, as though bewitched within a magic circle and withdrawn from every distortion that originates from the real world."

The traveler-artists took on the challenge of taking back to Europe their impressions of the landscapes, the life and the historical monuments of the countries in which they traveled. To fulfill their purposes they turned to the mediums available at the time. Waldeck, for example, included among his equipment a camera obscura, an optical instrument with a long tradition among landscape painters, which incorporated a lens that projected an image onto a mirror which, in turn, was reflected in such a way that the artist could execute a drawing by following the silhouette. Catherwood traveled with a camera lucida, a variation

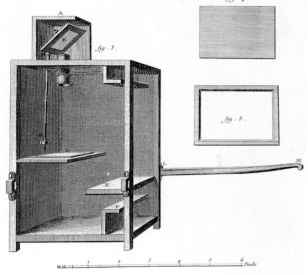

CHARACTERISTICS OF CAMERAS OBSCURA,
AS NOTED BY DIDEROT Y D'ALEMBERT [57]

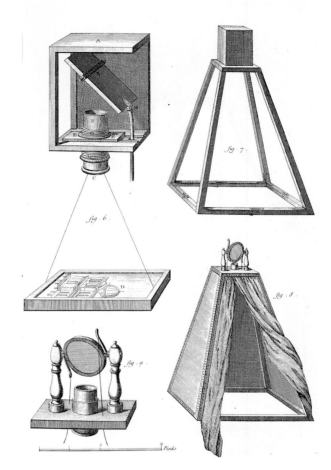

CHARACTERISTICS OF CAMERAS OBSCURA,
AS NOTED BY DIDEROT Y D'ALEMBERT [58]

of the former, patented in 1807. With the passing of the century, the use of photography was to become more and more frequent, whether as a mere auxiliary mnemonic instrument for painting or as an autonomous artistic expression. The travelers, too, realized that their images required a degree of staging if they were to transmit the emotion and the impact that they themselves had experienced. With apparent modesty, Rugendas summarized, in this sense, the artistic project of his life in a letter to von Humboldt: "I wanted to show the world what beautiful pictorial treasures were to be offered by the tropics, since there are very few institutions for which it is possible to agree to the difficult route that leads there. I felt the vocation to be a pioneer of art in an area that others would later develop to its furthest limits."[6] Waldeck, for his part, as an artistic testament, composed in Paris a great oil painting whose topic is a ritual scene in a pre-Columbian ceremonial center. The representation translates to the language of the painting of history the fantasies that had matured over the years in

his antiquarian work. The most spectacular modality for showing the marvels of the New World to the Europeans was the panorama. Through the initiative of William Bullock and his son, a vista of this type was presented to the London public in 1825, the first dedicated to the City and the Valley of Mexico.

This work, as with nearly all of those created by the traveler-artists, possessed documental value and had the ambition of being able to relive an adventure. All contributed to establishing the bases of an iconography of the country and its people. They are not, however, only documents of journeys. They cover an area that ranges from faithful naturalism to the most ingenious fantasies, since in the nineteenth century, as in one form or another in preceding centuries, the illustration of travels in the Americas combined credible representation with illusion and dreams.

pp. 86-87. EDOUARD PINGRET
KITCHEN IN PUEBLA [59]

EGERTON'S MEXICO
(1831-1842)

MARIO MOYA PALENCIA

A surprising number of Englishmen—painters, engravers, writers, miners, businessmen—visited Mexico in the nineteenth century. One such, Charles Joseph Latrobe, went so far as to qualify its capital as "the City of Palaces," so denominated in his book, *The Rambler in Mexico*, published in New York, in 1836, in which he wrote of the works of its founders and conquerors:

Look at their works:
the moles, aqueducts, churches, roads,
and the luxurious City of Palaces
which has risen from the clay-built ruins
of Tenochtitlan...

When Latrobe came to Mexico, a year or two prior to publishing his book, Daniel Thomas Egerton was residing in the Tacubaya district of Mexico City, at 4 Coliseo Street. Egerton, the British painter and engraver, born in the upscale London suburb of Hampstead on April 18, 1797, had arrived in Mexico in 1831 at the suggestion of his older brother William Henry, who at the time had dedicated himself to real estate dealings in Texas, then an integral part of the Mexican Federal Republic.

Daniel Thomas Egerton, the son of a slightly eccentric Anglican clergyman, had studied pictorial art in the London academy of Dr. Thomas Monro, a consummate watercolorist who served as one of the psychiatrists to King George III. He distinguished himself by copying the works of Joseph M. W. Turner, Thomas Girtin and John Robert Cozens, at the apogee of the period of enlightenment that suffered the intellectual shock produced by the French Revolution. Egerton couldn't make the

"Grand Tour" to what today we would consider the tourist centers of Italy and Greece, countries that the English admired as being the origins of Western culture and art, so he sought contentment in developing his skills in the plastic arts in London. It was there that he published, in 1824, a book of humor and acerbic criticism entitled *Fashionable Bores -or- Coolers in High Life*, containing three plates, signed by him, and text that he penned under the pseudonym Peter-Quiz. His biting caricature of the cheeky "dandies" of the period was quite successful and served to popularize such fashionable London haunts as St. James, Covent Garden, Chalk Farm (the dueling ground), Jacquier's Cafeteria and the Clarendon Hotel, among others. Beginning this same year, he exhibited his work at the Society of British Artists, where he held the post of treasurer. The themes were primarily English landscapes. During this period, he was awarded an important prize for his artistic sensibility. Also about this time he married Georgiana Dickens, with whom he had two daughters.

A descendant of nobility, the Egertons of Ellesmere and Bridgewater, he decided, in 1831, to separate from his wife, leaving her with an alimony agreement. Then, like so many of his compatriots, prisoners of the desire for adventure and burning with a curiosity about exotic lands, he moved to Mexico. Apart from his brother's influence, he had been captivated by the expressive force of the exhibition of "Mexican Idols" staged in Piccadilly by the archaeologist Bullock.

From his arrival at the port of Veracruz, Daniel Thomas Egerton was mesmerized by the landscapes and the light found in this land, which he reproduced in innumerable watercolors, ink drawings, lithographs and oil paintings. He traveled tire-

DANIEL THOMAS EGERTON
SAN AGUSTÍN DE LAS CUEVAS [60]

lessly throughout the country, returning to London in 1837 to produce an excellent book of twelve Mexican lithographs titled *Views in Mexico*, published in 1840 by James Holmes, which became the most famous and widely diffused of his works, including a Spanish version that has enjoyed great success in Mexico. It includes incisive literary descriptions of Veracruz, Puebla de los Ángeles, Mexico City, Zacatecas, Real del Monte, San Agustín de las Cuevas (Tlalpan) and other sites. Egerton also created watercolors, drawings and oils of the volcano Popocatépetl, Guanajuato, the areas surrounding Mexico City, Chalco, Morelia and the Nevado de Toluca, in which he captured not only the beauty of the landscapes but also the humanity and customs of the country, the forms of dress of the indigenous peoples and ranchers, and the characteristic Holy Week celebrations.

Egerton returned to Mexico City toward the end of 1841, in the company of a young lady of less than twenty years, named Agnes Edwards, with whom he lived first at an inn located at 10 Vergara Street (today Bolívar), where they were observed by Mrs. Calderón de la Barca, the Scottish wife of the first Minister of Spain in Mexico, who referred to them as "the mysterious English couple." Later they resided at the Casa de los Abades (House of the Abbots) in Tacubaya near which, in a place called Pila Vieja, adjoining the hermitage of San Juan, they were both treacherously murdered on the afternoon of April 27, 1842. The great majority of the works of Daniel

Thomas Egerton, most of them dedicated to Mexican themes, are to be found in Mexican collections, with the exception of one of the two originals of *El Valle de México* (The Valley of Mexico), a splendid oil painted in 1837, which belongs to the government of the United Kingdom and is displayed within their embassy in Mexico City. The collection of Banco Nacional de México (Banamex) contains some of his better oils, including *Ascensión al Popocatépetl*, *El Popocatépetl: vista del cráter*, *Vista del Popo desde Atlauta*, and *Vista del Popo desde Atlauta y el Bosque de la Cuesta hacia 1833*, all on the subject of the volcano Popocatépetl which lies just southeast of Mexico City, as well as the works *Ranchero* and

Rancheros cruzando un arroyo (Ranchers Crossing a Stream). Among the observations made by Egerton was that Mexico should assume, as soon as possible, the bold attitude of an empire or face fragmentation, province by province, until its very name disappeared. It appeared to him that no other country in the Western Hemisphere held a position more suitable to constituting a great power. The Mexico that Egerton painted and described was a country that had, and has, everything needed for the conquest of the future, and which Egerton loved and respected as revealed by the passion he injected into the descriptions of its majestic beauty and the human qualities of its inhabitants.

JOHANN SALOMON HEGI
(1814-1896)

PABLO DIENER

Swiss-born painter Johann Salomon Hegi lived in Mexico from 1849 to 1860. During these eleven years he made countless sketches of the country, especially its people and its everyday life. His work includes more than a thousand drawings and watercolors on Mexican themes. Hegi's artistic activity blossomed simultaneously with his affinity for literature; in fact, a good number of his works as an artist were accompanied by his own texts, be they of explanatory or simply anecdotal nature. The delight which Hegi took in literature is an important element of his artistic personality. This passion was nurtured, among other ways, by over five decades of friendship between the artist and Gottfried Keller, the most distinguished author writing in the German language that Switzerland produced during the nineteenth century. At the same time, Keller was intrigued by Hegi as a paradigmatic personality who was to inspire him in the creation of a number of literary characters. Particularly in his novel *Green Henry*—with its precise analysis of the life of an artist during the middle of the nineteenth century—Keller found inspiration in the life of artists such as Hegi and used their experience as a point of departure for creating his own fictional characters. A typical instance of this interplay between the painter and the writer can be found in these excerpts from a letter that Hegi wrote, from Mexico, to Keller (in Heidelberg) on March 10, 1850:

"... I have now spent about two months here in Mexico, but only a week ago was I really accommodated in a room of my own, so that within these four walls my existence is no more that of a traveling artist, and I'm adapting myself to the way of the people here. Until a short time ago, I'd been very eager to know what might come, and wrote but a few lines home while seated at the camp fire. I'd love to give you a detailed account of my journey to Mexico, of how I like it, whether my hopes are bathed in sunshine or clouds, but I'd never end, and that would be quite boring. After I left you [in Heidelberg], I traveled quickly. In Frankfurt I only stayed for one day, and I sacrificed a visit to Saint Paul's Church to the Städel Institute [picture gallery and collection of graphic arts]. As I was bound for a continent with little art, I preferred to take as many artistic impressions as possible with me. ... I stayed only a short time in Mainz and Cologne because I was really too busy trying to reach Antwerp. Here I tried to find out where my fellow travelers were, but to my surprise and great anger they had not yet shown up. Acquaintances told me that there was no possibility to cross within the next three months. After two weeks I finally received a letter from my fellows, who told me they would soon arrive. I'd spent more than four weeks in Antwerp before I embarked on a steamboat to Rotterdam, where we continued to The Hague. There we found a ship to New Orleans, but which put to sea only two weeks later. ... On May 10, [1849] we slowly sailed out of the harbor of The Hague ... and I leaned over the deck rail, and my heart said goodbye to everybody and everything I had left behind. The city and the coast were already full of the perfumes of the evening sunset. I was in a happy frame of mind, because I let my thoughts go to the bliss I was going to feel upon my return to this coast. The things that were expecting me seemed easy; it wouldn't occur to me that there might be no return. ... In the Gulf of Mexico I had the chance to enjoy the sight of a thrillingly multicolored sunset, and when we passed by Cape San Antonio, in the west of Cuba, we were lucky to observe an extraordinary scene in the eastern part of the horizon:

Johann Salomon Hegi
MARKETPLACE [62]

Johann Salomon Hegi
SELF-PORTRAIT [63]

Johann Salomon Hegi
MULETEERS [64]

Johann Salomon Hegi
GOOD FRIDAY [65]

93

JOHANN SALOMON HEGI
PICADOR [66]

a thunderstorm approached us from three sides; on two sides, dark but smooth clouds flashing with lightning, while from the third side, in the east, strong winds blew. A sailor made me understand that something good was waiting for us. ... Here it's impossible to make any money with art, for the landscape painter even less so than for the portrait painter or the painter of human figures. The public prefers colorful daubs to well-done paintings; in case they should by chance enjoy one of the latter, they're not likely to pay any more than they pay for some smearing by a Mexican painter. He who only comes to study should prepare himself to deal with a thousand sufferings and high costs, for here tropical nature isn't found just around the corner. From Veracruz to Mexico I couldn't find anything extraordinary. Special sites have really to be looked for, and that's where the nature of the trouble of working begins, because much stealing is done in this land. You can't leave the city alone without being followed by one of these villains. Of course, when acting decidedly you needn't fear anything from a gang of two or three of them. But while immersed in your work, you don't always have the time to pay attention; before long, your head might get caught in a lasso or be struck by a stone. It's always better to have a fellow accompany you, but it's not easy to find them. ... I don't enjoy myself here. They hardly conserve the national costumes and usages; the Indios are the only people that have something to offer. I hope to find something in other parts of the country. I'll return as soon as I can, that is, when I have enough studies and sketches to present, and when I've gotten enough money together to travel."

GEORGE HENRY WHITE

JOHN ORBELL

George Henry White's background belies his accomplishment as an artist. He was born in 1817, the son of a farmer in eastern England and grew up in modest circumstances in the countryside about 50 miles east of London. For reasons unknown he moved to central London with his younger sister and brother in the early 1830's and in 1834, at the age of seventeen, he joined Baring Brothers & Co., by then one of the leading merchant banks in London.

At the time, Barings competed with Rothschilds for the leadership of the international capital market in London, and White was employed as a clerk dealing with routine matters related to securities. He performed well and by 1850 had been promoted to one of Barings' most senior clerk positions. By the middle of the decade he had assumed the role of troubleshooter, a position that involved being sent abroad when an important issue needed to be solved. He made his mark at the firm in 1856 while on a trip to Buenos Aires where he negotiated, on behalf of Barings, the rescheduling of the Argentine government's international debt. The arrangement proved beneficial for all parties involved and he returned to London a hero.

Parallel to his business life, he set out to provide himself with the education that he had missed as a child. He studied the classics and poetry and specialised in lexicology. He also learnt to paint with watercolours, but the identity of his tutor is unknown.

In early 1862 Barings dispatched him to Mexico, accompanying the Anglo-Franco-Spanish naval and military expedition whose arrival at the port of Veracruz marked the opening of an especially unhappy period in Mexican history. White, however, had no role to play in either the expedition or the result-

ing French invasion. His task was to negotiate with the Mexican government for the resumption of interest payments to its London bondholders. Although his mission was ultimately unsuccessful, he was to remain in Mexico until December of 1863, a time during which he became a careful observer of both Mexico and Mexicans.

Many of his observations were recorded in the letters he wrote fortnightly to the partners of Barings in London. They provide long and detailed accounts of the politics, economy and society of Mexico, and today survive in the archives of ING Barings in London. They give details of the advance of the French army and of the resistance by the Mexican forces, as well as accounts of the devastation caused to the Mexican economy and the deprivations suffered by the people.

"This French invasion has produced incalculable mischief," he wrote in May of 1862, "and it is impossible to foresee the results which may ultimately follow from it.... The country is now plunged into a disastrous war and, with no available revenues, is compelled to raise money by all sorts of expedients and of course on the most onerous terms." A year later he witnessed the evacuation of Mexico City ahead of the French advance: "The 31st May was a scene of indescribable confusion; it was the intention of the government to have retired with some show of dignity ... but the retreat was converted into a flight. The members of the government went off sometime during the afternoon, and the remainder of the troops the same evening. They have taken away treasure estimated at $1,300,000 and all the state archives leaving the national palace quite empty."

He also describes his own life and the sometimes dangerous

George Henry White
san juan de ulúa, veracruz [67]

George Henry White
the pico de orizaba as seen from the sea [68]

GEORGE HENRY WHITE
XOCHIMILCO [69]

situations in which he found himself. In April of 1863 he was set upon by bandits outside Mexico City and lost his watch and money, receiving wounds to his head which laid him up for a month. He also found problems with food: "Everything eatable is drenched with a composition of garlic and tomatoes," he wrote to Barings, "and it is impossible to get any plain decent food."

Alongside his written record, he recorded in watercolour the Mexican landscape, returning to London with a portfolio of about eighty watercolour works. At Barings they were a source of wonderment because although the bank had done business in Mexico since at least 1800 and had been the government's financial agents in London during the 1820's and 1830's, nobody at Barings had any firsthand knowledge of this country which had been so important to their business.

His landscapes depict the countryside through which he travelled. He arrived at the port of Veracruz in March of 1862 and painted the harbour showing the French invasion fleet, the customs house and the French tricolour flying above it. He moved on to Orizaba, Puebla and Mexico City and subsequently travelled regularly between those places. He spent much of his time in Tacubaya, where most of his watercolours were painted. The great mountains of Iztaccíhuatl and Popocatépetl, as well as Lake Texcoco, appear in many of them. Others are views of Mexico City, including one of the Gardens at Xochimilco. In a few instances he made studies of trees and plants and more occasionally, of specific buildings such as the Church and cloisters at Acatzingo.

His works reflect the beauty and tranquillity of the Mexican landscape and contrast with the turbulence of Mexico at the time.

GEORGE HENRY WHITE
POPOCATÉPETL AND IZTACCÍHUATL AS SEEN FROM TACUBAYA [70]

Many of the landscapes he painted are now covered over by the urban development of Mexico City while others remain unknown to today's residents and travellers due to the shroud of air pollution. Several have an atmospheric quality that reveal White to have been experimenting with the techniques of such English artists as William Turner. Most, however, are clearly landscapes executed by an artist who had learnt to paint in the English countryside. They possess a distinct pastoral quality; Whites trees and grazing cows are English, transported to the Mexican landscape.

On his return to London, White resumed his work with Barings and went on to undertake other missions abroad, although none as prolonged or as exciting as the journey to Mexico. The lifestyle of a troubleshooter took its toll on his health, however, and he retired from Barings at a relatively young age, in 1872. For the sake of his health, he moved to England's West Country and there worked on the establishment of both Torquay's Natural History Society and the town's Government School of Art. He died there in 1889.

Today 103 of White's watercolours of Mexico, France and England hang in the London headquarters of ING Barings, while his letters and other Mexican papers are available for study in the bank's historical archives. It appears that the watercolours in the ING Barings collection are the only surviving examples of the work of this capable amateur artist.

FRANÇOIS MATHURIN ADALBERT, BARON DE COURCY

KATHERINE MANTHORNE / PABLO DIENER

Baron de Courcy, a traveler-artist from the lower echelons of the French aristocracy, is doubtless a personage worthy of study. Very little is known about the man, hardly any biographical data is to be found, yet he left a body of at least 114 works of art executed in pencil and watercolor. The geographical area covered by his work stretches from Canada and the United States, with a total of 63 landscapes related to these two countries, to Mexico and the Caribbean, resulting in another 51 works that demonstrate not only his fascination with geography but the emergence of a gradual discovery of the pictorial richness to be found among the populace and their daily lives. As a whole, the known works by de Courcy are to be found in two large-format albums that cover a period of just over two years, about 1830-32. Beyond this work there are but a few documental references as to who the traveler was. The most conclusive evidence is to be located in Mexican archives which contain his application for a Letter of Security, or safe conduct pass for traveling, which is dated July 5, 1832, a document that, interestingly, carries the signature of another painter, Baron Gros, who signed in his capacity as the French chargé d'affaires. A surprising association with another artist who came to know something of this mysterious personality was that with the German traveler Johann Moritz Rugendas. Among Rugendas' work are three portraits of de Courcy, all dated August of 1832. Further delving into Rugendas' notebooks reveals that the Frenchman and the German were traveling companions on a 15-day excursion from Mexico City to the hacienda of Santa María Regla.

But what other friendships did he establish? Who else advised him as to the places he should visit? And, in the end, what were the motives behind the undertaking of this voyage?

From a careful review of de Courcy's albums we can intuit that we are dealing with well-schooled and well-practiced artist and not simply an affable amateur who wanted to capture memories of his voyage. His work is aimed in multiple directions and we can summarize the value of his art on three essential points.

First, his views of the landscapes of Canada and the United States are among the earliest executed in North America of a naturalistic character. While other artists had certainly turned their attention to the continent's scenery long before de Courcy (1801-02), the predominant tone of their work was rooted either in a classicist schema or in the tastes of romanticism. De Courcy, by contrast, allowed his observations of nature to dictate the detail as well as the overall composition of each landscape. His views of the Hudson River and of Niagara Falls, for example, were executed virtually at the same time as those of Thomas Cole, founder of the Hudson River School of landscape painting. This poses the question of what knowledge de Courcy had of the local painters in the United States, and they of him and his travels through the area.

A second outstanding feature of the work of this artist is the broad geographical range that he covered. He began his travels in Quebec and ended up in the Caribbean, along the way capturing scenes of such rivers as the St. Lawrence, the Passaic and the Hudson. He entered Mexico via the port at Tampico and traveled to the interior as far as Aguascalientes, then moving on to Mexico City and, finally, exiting the country by way of the port of Veracruz, making his way from there to the Caribbean. This tour of the length of the North American continent permits a unique example for the comparative analysis of North Amer-

BARON DE COURCY
THE PYRAMID OF THE SUN. TEOTIHUACAN [71]

ican landscape painting which has been generally limited to the comparison of an artist from the United States to one from Mexico and to another from Canada, the process always suffering from the differences in their background and training.

The third aspect, beyond that of geographical or historical-cultural issues, that lures us into following the trail of this traveler-artist is the quality of his work. As a whole, the portfolio reveals a notable receptive sensitivity and a strong pictorial sense. Each of his pieces beg comparison with those of the more notable traveler-artists that toured the Americas such as Karl Bodmer, who traveled through the American West; or George Catlin and the work he elaborated on the theme of indigenous Americans; and, as we have seen, with Rugendas, with whom he shared a brief stage of his artistic adventure.[1]

BARON DE COURCY
CHURCH AT TEOTIHUACAN [72]

JOHANN MORITZ RUGENDAS
PORTRAIT OF BARON DE COURCY [73]

Baron de Courcy
WATCHTOWER OVERLOOKING CORN FIELDS [74]

HUBERT SATTLER

NIKOLAUS SCHAFFER

The name of the Sattler family is closely associated with the "Great Panoramic View of the City of Salzburg, Austria". This image is one of the few examples that has been conserved among those created during the heyday of the genre. During an extended exhibition tour that lasted from 1829 to 1839, the panorama was shown with enormous success in various European countries and brought Salzburg—which at that point had drifted into near oblivion due to political circumstances—back into public discussion. The triumph of the exhibition was certainly an important factor in the decision by Hubert Sattler (1817-1904) to choose the same profession as that of his father Johann Michael Sattler (1786-1847), the painter of the Panorama. At twelve, young Hubert had already studied at Vienna's Academy of Fine Arts. Later, in the course of the adventurous yet difficult tour with the Panorama of Salzburg, he became quite familiar with the profession of a traveling painter. Nevertheless, it should be noted that Hubert Sattler's work places particular emphasis on the so-called "cosmoramic views" which, at first, had been only an added feature of the exhibitions, offering the public an opportunity to get to know many of the historic sights of Salzburg, as well as presenting views of the town's outskirts, famous for their particular natural beauty. In order to satisfy an increasing public interest, Sattler continually expanded the geographic horizons of his representations, adding mostly oriental, exotic and archeological motifs. As time went by, the great Panorama (16 x 88 feet), with its view merely of the sights of the city of Salzburg, was totally supplanted by an almost encyclopedic gathering of the world's wonders. Sattler still, however, used the peephole-like format chosen by his father, the illusionistic perfectionism of these pictures further augmented by optical devices and the effects of illumination. This is the reason why today's presentation of these works as easel-paintings gives a distorted impression of their original effect. For example, they could only be looked at in completely darkened rooms and through tiny peepholes, anticipating the atmosphere and the technique of the cinema which was soon to develop.

Although Sattler did make efforts to lend authenticity to his works, through intensive studies of nature, his wish to fascinate his public was doubtlessly stronger than the intention to represent what had been seen in sober reproductions. This was the point where hyperrealism ended and the marvelous and the fantastic took over. But it was just that, in evoking the mysterious magic of the distant and the unknown, which brought success to Sattler's creations at a time when traveling options were few and the mass media was not yet omnipresent.

Upon his retirement, in 1870, Sattler donated the cosmoramas to Salzburg, his native city, under the condition that they be exhibited together with his father's Panorama in a rotunda constructed especially for that purpose. Sattler, however, continued to travel tirelessly and painted cosmoramas until his death in 1904, his legacy including more than 140 of these works. His journeys led him to Damascus, Cairo, Jerusalem, Constantinople, Rome, Lisbon, Edinburgh, Paris, Moscow, Toledo, Seville, Havana and Boston. After the exhibition building was destroyed in 1937, a genre whose fascination had greatly suffered from the rise of tourism and photography began to drift into obscurity. For a long time, panoramas were merely considered as an obsolete or old-fashioned version of pictorial reports. Only in more recent years, with an increasing general interest

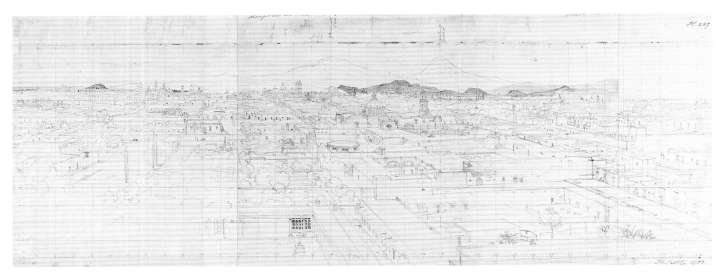

in genre painting, has the special role of panorama painting in the history of civilization, as well as its artistic value, once again been duly appreciated.

The precision of Sattler's works make them invaluable documents of their time. New York and Mexico City, with an almost village-like architecture, or Egypt's or Yucatán's archeological sites, only partially excavated, already attract our attention as such. When we compare the past with the present, we often can't help but feel a sort of nostalgic yearning for the variety and vividness of color, most of which is now lost. Even traveling itself has turned into mere routine and almost nothing is left today that seems mysteriously strange or distant. Maybe the recently rediscovered attraction of Sattler's works is due to the fact that they can bring back some of the magic that has vanished through exaggerated exposure. They still convey astonishment in light of the wonders of the world and fill even today's spectators with an eagerness to get to know distant countries.

The illusionism of Sattler's images was augmented by the well-calculated use of elements which show that he had also mastered the art of psychological manipulation. An equally distributed focal depth relative to each detail—even the most distant ones—makes the motifs, which are represented from a slightly higher point of view, seem "purified" from all atmospheric influences, as if they were under a glass cover. The depth of the com-

position and the carefully combined effects of color and light create a fascinating magnetism which corresponds with the almost photographic smoothness of the painting. Sattler made efforts to create stereometric effects by using a rather forced relief of light and shadow. The horizon—generally low and with skies agitated by stirring clouds—conveys a feeling of surpassing limits, of losing oneself in the distance. Such a concept goes far beyond a merely didactic representation of the sights from distant countries.

After having covered almost all of Europe and the Near East, Sattler left for the United States in 1850, where he successfully presented exhibitions of his cosmoramas in New York, Boston and Philadelphia, taking time out to travel through the U.S.A., Mexico (especially the Yucatán) and the West Indies. The sketched material produced in the course of these journeys was used periodically in his later cosmoramas. The *Total View of Mexico at Sunset* was done in 1854, one year after his return to Europe, whereas the *Valley of Mexico* was painted in 1868. Sattler had already anticipated his personal knowledge of the country in 1836 with *The Tulum Temple at Yucatán*, for which he apparently utilized a lithography by Catherwood. It seems that this was the only occasion where Sattler—who always used exact topographical drawings as models and, later on, also his own photographs—parted from the scrupulous principles that characterized his work.

Hubert Sattler
VIEW OF MEXICO CITY WITH POPOCATÉPETL AND IZTACCÍHUATL [76]

JULIUS HOFFMANN, ARCHITECT TO MAXIMILIAN

FERDINAND ANDERS

October 6, 1866, and January 21, 1867, were two important dates within the increasingly agonizing reign of the Austrian-born Emperor of Mexico, Maximilian. They are also symptomatic of the circumstances of the time and illustrate the way the Emperor and former Archduke thought and felt. The irrevocability of his decisions was a principal trait of Maximilian, and he proudly referred to it as a forte of his character. In politics, however, this attitude had fatal consequences. Maximilian's perseverance also becomes evident in an almost exaggerated way in his architectural projects, which are considered to be the true legacy of this sovereign of the House of Hapsburg. Each of these architectural creations bears a relationship to the other and they form a whole of which Maximilian never lost sight. Even while imprisoned in Querétaro, his thoughts clung to the continuing of these projects.

The dates mentioned above lie within a hapless period of increasing political instability and mark the two days on which Julius Hoffmann presented the plans for the rebuilding he had been asked to carry out for the sovereign. At age 18, Hoffmann (born in Trieste, February 20, 1840) had already collaborated with his father, Julius Hoffmann the Elder, on the works at the Miramare Palace which Maximilian had ordered built on the shores of the Adriatic Sea near Trieste. In 1864, he traveled to Mexico in order to serve Maximilian as court architect. His plans are true masterpieces of architectural drawing. The sense of unity maintained between the architectural concept of the building and the carefully chosen decoration of the interiors would today be termed as a "total" work of art. In addition, the surrounding gardens were to provide a fitting frame. The gifted architect fulfilled the Emperor's wishes with masterful solutions.

Thieme-Becker's *Encyclopaedia of Plastic Arts*[1] notes that in 1867, Hoffmann intended to go to Dalmatia to "survey the reconstruction of the monastery of Lacroma on orders from Maximilian." Yet this plan was never to be carried out due to the turbulent events at the end of Mexico's Second Empire. That same year Hoffmann signed a contract with Louis II of Bavaria. During the last years of his life he was responsible for the decoration of the interior of the castle of Neuschwanstein. He died in Munich on August 5, 1896. Some of the projects originally conceived for Maximilian seem to have found application in the architectural creations for the Bavarian king, particularly in the plans for the castles of Herrenchiemsee and Neuschwanstein. A selection of drawings from Hoffmann's portfolio is now included in the Orozco y Berra collection in Mexico, while others belong to the Graphische Sammlung Albertina in Vienna. Among these drawings we find the sketches for the projects mentioned earlier and for the reconstruction of the monastery at Lacroma, which was conceived as a retreat for an emperor who could have abdicated at the age of thirty-five.

As the younger brother of Austrian Emperor Franz Josef I, the Archduke had always felt "closest to the Crown," yet it seems that destiny didn't mean for him to enjoy the honors and the esteem bestowed upon his brother, who was two years older. Authority seemed beyond the grasp of the younger brother. For some time he served as governor general of the Lombardo-Venetian kingdom. He strove hard to do well although this particular office had been designed as a mere figurehead post. As Commander in Chief of the Austrian Navy, he embodied what he called the "maritime principle" in a empire that considered itself an inland country. He wrote a number of articles in which he laid down his ideas on this subject. Under his command, the

Austrian Navy turned into an efficient body which proved its abilities in the historic naval battles of Helgoland (1864) and Lissa (1866). On September 9th, 1866, after she had returned to Europe, the Empress commented on her husband's achievements: "Everybody admires the two accomplishments of the absent prince: the battle of Lissa and the palace at Miramare."

At the age of 17, Maximilian had already built a small Swiss-style mansion called Maxing in the area surrounding the Viennese palace of Schönbrunn. For the future he planned the construction of the castle-like Neu-Maxing on the same grounds, where the Commander in Chief of the Navy was to reside. In keeping with Maximilian's strong dynastic spirit, one of the stairways was to lead up to a gallery containing his forefathers' portraits. The formal dismissal of the Archduke after the failure of the war in 1859, that resulted in the loss of Lombardy, turned the eager young admiral completely away from making important decisions. The subsequent chilling of his relations with the Viennese court drove Maximilian to concentrate on his property: Miramare and the island of Lacroma, near Ragusa (today Locrum and Dubrovnik). Carlota had acquired the island with funds from her dowry and had given it to her husband as a present. The old, reconstructed abbey was to become the favorite residence of the Commander in Chief of the Austrian Navy, who would move from one residence to the other every two weeks. "Miramare is our town house, and Lacroma is our home in the countryside," the Archduchess proudly remarked. Later, his Mexican correspondence demonstrated that the young Emperor yearned for both Miramare and his beloved island. For this reason he attempted to create something similar to what he had known in Europe in the New World. Thus, he sent for a number of artists, Hoffmann among them, in order to materialize his architectural ideas. Moreover, Maximilian also wished for science and the arts to flourish in his newly adopted homeland. The enrichment of these fields had already been an important aim of his in Europe, but it was his passion for construction that would turn out to be the most characteristic trait of the young Emperor of Mexico.

A comparison of Hoffmann's projects (from the Albertina Collection, Vienna) with what is left of the plans for Maximilian's earlier projects in Trieste (particularly those contained in the archives at Miramare), and with the vast portfolios of drawings in the Austrian National Library, allows us to make a kind of a "tree diagram" of the Archduke's architectural ideas (see the appendix to this article). Not only can we locate a great variety

of plans for Neu-Maxing, but there is also evidence affirming that the initial plans for Miramare stem from a small villa set in the rocks at Grignano (overlooking the bay near Trieste), where young Maximilian had once found shelter from a storm. Although the project grew larger and larger, the Archduke finally had to opt for a simpler but economically more realistic version. The Austrian architect Karl Junker later received orders to elaborate the plans for the project. Maximilian's words, "All I ask of life is a beautiful palace with a big park by the sea," provide a concise description of the palace and the park at Miramare. Yet the project's dimensions grew incessantly. When Maximilian and Carlota moved in, the construction was not yet finished and the work was to continue beyond the couple's departure for Mexico.

As the new Emperor and his wife found conditions at the Palacio Nacional in Mexico City unsuitable, remodeling was quickly begun in order to give the palace an appearance appropriate to the official requirements and to the new ceremonial ambiance of the court. It was during this undertaking that the Salón de Ceremonias (also called the Salón de Embajadores) was redecorated. In keeping with his appreciation of history, and for reasons of continuity, the Emperor commissioned a series of oil paintings of the heroes and the main predecessors of the Independence Movement in Mexico. The construction of the building's main staircase involved extremely high costs. It was carried out in accordance with the young Emperor's ideas for Neu-Maxing in Vienna, but the project was never to be completed due both to economic factors and the direction that political events were taking. Manuel Payno's review of the costs of the French Intervention (1861-1867) do not bear out the embezzlement that had been suspected. What can be drawn out was the criticism of a number of his contemporaries in the light of the "construction mania" and the senseless waste of public funds. Without the help of a supervising architect, Maximilian himself had ordered substantial rebuilding, then later canceled it: "From June 1864 onward, major construction work was again taken up. Maximilian ordered the demolition of various parts of the Palacio de México, moved offices to other buildings, closed down the General Treasury, built a chapel and a theater, had rooms for Carlota, Princess Iturbide and his intimate servants restored and decorated; maybe the so-called plan wasn't made up of anything other than demolishing what had been there before and substituting it with new constructions. Although he had a number of architects, it was really he who directed

the rebuilding. The archives don't contain a single document worked out by any one man with a homogeneous and complete plan for it all; building was done to the extent it was believed to be necessary or according to Maximilian's spontaneous ideas."[2]

Treasurer Jakob von Kuhacsevich, who handled the accounts having to do with construction work, wrote to Miramare: "It is frightening how they construct at the Palace of Mexico and in Chapultepec. The Emperor's well-known passion! If it were me, I'd have waited until the end of the honeymoon, because it's not yet sure at all what direction this mar-

riage is going to take [i.e., between Maximilian and Mexico]."[3]

Had his empire lasted longer, Maximilian would certainly have completed an even greater number of constructions. The National Palace and the *Zócalo* would have been rebuilt according to the characteristics of historicism. An extended series of projects of the same style was already planned, but they were never carried out due to the lack of time and funds. In Chapultepec, Maximilian found an equivalent of his own creation at Miramare, the old Viceroys' Castle, which rose up from the rocks like a throne and seemed more likely to satisfy his criteria for a residence. The breathtaking view from above had already

been enjoyed by Alexander von Humboldt, and it also left a profound impact on Maximilian. The tower of the *azotea* (roof terrace) completely bewitched its new resident. Shortly thereafter, the name of the residence was changed to Miravalle, analogous to Miramare. The reconstruction carried out by the Emperor's architect Rodríguez Arangoiti turned the former *Alcázar* into a building in the style of a villa in Pompeii. In 1866, the walls were decorated with the famed bacchantes by the painter Santiago Rebull.

Manuel Payno commented on the construction activities: "In Chapultepec, the old Palace, the platforms, the stairways up the hill and the park were all rebuilt and restored. Although it is undeniable that many improvements were achieved, the results fall far from justifying the high costs, especially in the gardens. The bills for civil expenses state that a number of times four, six, eight, even eleven thousand pesos were spent on the gardens. Had these funds been used to economical and discrete effect, these amounts would indeed have ultimately transformed this park, beautiful by nature."[4]

The severe criticism by another author, Simon Leo Reinisch, fully confirms Payno's statements. Reinisch had worked for the

Archduke as an Egyptologist and joined his court in Mexico to work as a curator for the yet-to-be-created National Museum. His diary contains the following confidential entry from February 22, 1867: "The other day, when asked by the Emperor about the financial situation of the country, the secretary in charge replied: 'Majesty, you spent all this money pouring it down the drain.' Colonel von Schaffer, an intimate friend and an always benevolent counselor to the Emperor, confirmed to me that the secretary's words were the plain truth. The Emperor's love of luxury and his boundless passion for building were completely senseless. The decoration of the Palace, of the castle in Chapultepec and of the summer residence in Cuernavaca consumed millions. Add to this the lack of order and planning in the economy of the acquisitions. Today, so-and-so is told to order or to buy something, tomorrow the same thing is said to another person and, the day after tomorrow, to another one, etc. As a consequence, the cashier has to deal every day with a number of persons who ask for and are supposed to receive money by order of His Majesty. And as there are many who address the poor

guy, it is difficult, if not to say impossible, to verify it all. What splendid times for cheats! Now that the vaults are empty, the Emperor says that everybody stole money from him. The least accused are the real thieves, for they know how to handle his capricious ways. He's not quite what you'd call a keen observer of human nature. Someone who today takes an oath as his secretary and whom the Emperor praises for his genius, immense talent and as a personification of honesty, a week later might be dismissed as a 'fool' or 'rascal'. That's how the Emperor has made himself a number of bitter enemies. Not a few were those who had served him devotedly, but who were dismissed from their office for trifles or without any reason, just for simple vanities. However, the Emperor had a strange affection for and confidence in the great and well-known impostors, although

he had been warned of the danger involved. From November through December of 1866, he let it all go and went to catch flies and bugs with Father Bilimek (curator at the Museum of Natural History), or drew plans for the gardens at Miramare and Lacroma. As a reward for filling plenty of boxes with flies, Father Bilimek was awarded the Gold Medal of Civil Merit. The plans for the gardens drawn by Our Majesty should be copied and hung in frames in the palace, so that in case he leaves the country, the Mexican people will become aware of the great variety of occupations he engaged in while on the throne."[5]

The projects for the castle reached an extent that would have equaled a total rebuilding. The plans were drawn by the Austrian architect Gangolf Kayser. Today, most of the corresponding plans belong to the collection of Manuel Orozco y

Berra. By error, they also include some studies by Hoffmann, such as the plans for a stairway that was misinterpreted as belonging to Chapultepec, but which really is part of the pier and the harbor at Miramare. These architectural plans were not drawn before the autumn of 1866 as can be concluded from the fact that the buildings bear inscriptions in Latin which were done by Dr. Samuel Basch, the Emperor's physician at the time.

The plans for the two architectural projects mentioned at the beginning—a plan for the interior decoration of the *Alcázar* in Chapultepec and an overall project for the residence called Olindo, in Acapatzingo, near Cuernavaca—are conserved in the Graphische Sammlung Albertina in Vienna and consist of a set of loose, dated sheets. The sheet dedicated to Chapultepec is only an overall plan, drawn up shortly before the sad news of the Empress' illness. The sheets regarding Olindo include one front view, a cross-section, details of the decoration of the walls of the Emperor's room and of the central dining room, a cross-section of the living room and of the valet's room, as well as drawings of furniture and lamps.

Although the Empress' return from Europe grew more and more unlikely, the cross-section of Olindo has symmetrical notes that read "Rooms of H.M. the Emperor" and "Rooms of H.M. the Empress," but a detailed planning of Carlota's rooms was postponed. As the drawings conserved in the Albertina include a plan for the reconstruction of the Castelletto, located in the park at Miramare, we can obviously deduce that, prior to the works in Lacroma, Hoffmann was supposed to have carried out the construction of a residence for Carlota. The minor building would have allowed for better nursing of the ailing Empress than the spacious palace itself.

Around 1900, when an extensive number of studies concerning the era of the Intervention and the Second Empire appeared, the memoirs of Maximilian's private secretary, José Luis Blasio (1842-1923), became an important source of information about the Archduke-Emperor's private life. The Porrúa Dictionary (5th. ed., 1964, p. 366) refers to the book as "fundamental to the knowledge of the inner aspects of the Second Empire," and in his monograph about the imperial couple, the author Conte Corti quotes Blasio's work as the "well-known book of memories."[6] It seems, however, that this intimate diary—whose author's memory had slightly faded after so many years, but which at the same time was augmented with court gossip and by what Blasio calls "the truth about the imperial love affairs"[7]—entered the

realm of secondary literature without having undergone any thorough criticism.

The Emperor soon returned to his habit of moving from one residence to another every two weeks, this time between the Borda Garden and Chapultepec. As to the emperor's stays in Cuernavaca, Blasio notes: "The reception was extremely heartfelt as always. In the afternoon a big meal was served, and in the evening there was an imposing fireworks display. As Maximilian wished to come more frequently, he thought that there was possibly a way to arrange a residence for himself in Cuernavaca, and old Pérez Palacios, who knew the city very well, said that none was more fitting for the purpose than one called Jardín de Borda, but that it was abandoned and in such a poor state that it needed substantial rebuilding. The sovereign went to visit it the next day. He was thrilled with the beauty of the place, whose vast gardens, spacious rooms and ponds made it worthy of being an emperor's mansion. The administrator prepared the documents for the rent, steps were taken toward the necessary rebuilding, and within a few days the rooms were papered and the gardens cleaned."[8]

Regarding the acquisition of Olindo, Blasio writes: "On his rides on horseback through the surroundings, the Emperor discovered and bought a vast tract of land in a place named Acapazingo, where he built a Pompeian-style mansion for the Empress which he named El Olvido [i.e., 'Oblivion']."[9] The author suspects that the hacienda was soon to turn into a "love nest." The comments written on the walls of the Borda Garden and the name "Casa de la India bonita" (House of the Pretty Indian Girl) are convincing proof of what gossip can do.

The name "Casa de la India bonita"—a gift from Maximilian to his wife, with which he returned the favor that she had done him with the gift of Lacroma—even appears in the publications of the Instituto Nacional de Historia (INAH) and is further evidence of the obstinacy of the gossip. Contemporary documents and reliable sources, however, often reveal altogether different historical truths. It seems an irony of history that Maximilian and Carlota's personalities were misinterpreted on the basis of their own creations, be it with slanderous intentions or simply due to a lack of understanding.

The Archduke-Emperor was indeed a contradictory character. In a number of situations he proved that he was capable of acting. Personalities of even greater determination would have admitted failure in light of the complex and desperate political

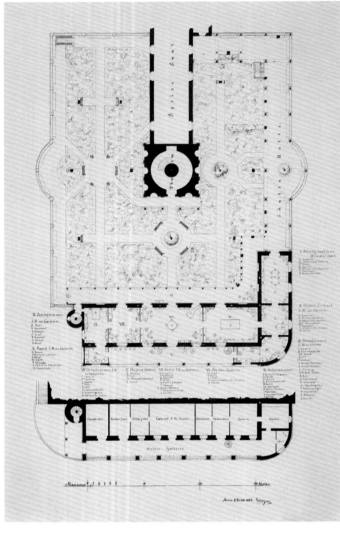

JULIUS HOFFMANN
CHAPULTEPEC. REMODELING PROJECT [81]

situation that the Emperor was forced to face. His romantic side, however, was only taken into consideration much later. Other characters with similar traits were Louis II of Bavaria (called the "Fairy Tale King") and Empress Elizabeth of Austria. Not only did all three sovereigns have similar personalities as far as their withdrawal from reality is concerned, but they were also united by family ties.

The pursuit of tranquillity and complete isolation emerges as a result of the desire to create, of dedicating oneself to metaphysical meditation. It is a characteristic trait of the patrons of the works of historicism. Maximilian is certainly one of the most prominent creators of that style within the realm of architecture. Although his life was quite short, a large number of sources which help to create an image of this fascinating character are still accessible. His absolute necessity for being alone in order to create has been interpreted as whimsical, just as his need to retreat was seen as a way of creating opportunities for love affairs. The fact that the imperial couple didn't have any offspring was another source of malign comments and has not kept people from attributing illegitimate children to both Maximilian and Carlota.

It has often been asserted that Maximilian was merely an amateur in many scientific disciplines. For his architectural projects, however, he certainly carried out precise preparatory studies. As the patron of these constructions, there is evidence to affirm that, beyond his role as a Maecenas, he enriched the projects with own ideas. As a creator of architecture, Maximilian materialized his own vision, detached from the real world and the life that surrounded him. Moods and impressions which could be captured by optical means were submitted to the intellectual aim of realizing a synthesis of architecture, painting, sculpture, and gardening. Maximilian knew how to penetrate this world of delusion and leave real life behind. Yet the hard facts of life made disaster seem inevitable. And although Maximilian lacked knowledge concerning human nature, he was able to choose artists of great talent, as is clearly evident in the case of Julius Hoffmann.

In discussing the architectural projects of the Archduke-Emperor and, especially, the huge debts created by his "construction mania," it seems fitting to make a survey of the amounts invested with the help of historic documents. The lack of some data can be explained by the fact that many payments were made from private funds which,[1] of course, would not appear in the official accounts.

Concerning the appanage payments made to Maximilian, one should bear in mind that, according to a decree by the Mexican

Council of Government from the year 1863, the Emperor could spend a yearly amount of 170,000 pesos on his own needs. This is the same amount that Emperor Agustín I had had at his disposition from 1822-23. Facing a critical financial situation in 1866, the Emperor refrained from spending two thirds of this amount.

The inherited fortune belonging to Princess Carlota had a value of more than three million francs. After difficult negotiations that included the Archduke Ferdinand Maximilian and one of his representatives, 250,000 francs were added as a dowry from the Belgian King, as well as one million francs paid by Leopold I, the father of the bride, who was famed for his stinginess. The Emperor, on the other hand, contributed an equivalent amount, which lead to an annuity of 50,000 francs (or 20,000 florins). In other words, the capital which Carlota brought with her when she married Maximilian was more than 1.7 million florins. In addition to the annual interest of almost 82,000 florins, there were about 25,000 as a result of payments from Austria (see HHStA [Haus-, Hof- und Staatsarchiv], Vienna, Administrative Registratur Fl/182, no. 43: Vermählung Carlota [Marriage Carlota]).

These details are important in understanding the negotiations that took place in 1864 to fix the appanage destined for Maximilian and Carlota upon their departure to Mexico. They also point out the degree of coverage that existed in light of the Archduke's financial obligations, particularly those resulting from his architectural projects.[10]

In a confidential letter to the Austrian Secretary of Treasury written in 1864, it was laid down that from an amount of 150,000 florins of appanage, the recently elected Emperor of Mexico would receive 100,000 florins every year. The remaining 50,000 florins would be used in order to pay outstanding debts. In order to achieve a quicker payment of their debts, Carlota refrained from her right to spend the 20,000 florins for her personal needs. However, this amount didn't have any bearing on payments to private persons; rather, it went to the Austrian state.

During the negotiations over the Emperor's estate, it was discovered that for Miramare and Lacroma there were outstanding debts of 611,389.48 florins (see HHStA [Haus-, Hof- und Staatsarchiv], Vienna, Administrative Registratur Fl/100, 1867 I 126: Treaty between Austria and Belgium on Emperor Maximilian of Mexico's Estate). This shows that, all in all, the late Archduke's debts were not as enormous as have often been stated in literature.

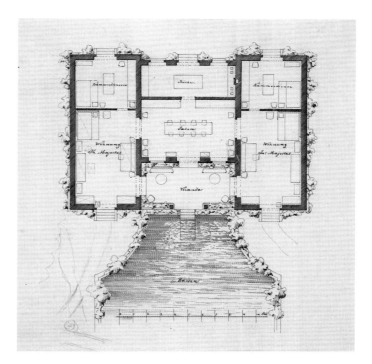

JULIUS HOFFMANN
PALACE AT CUERNAVACA. GROUND FLOOR [82]

p. 116. WILLIAM BULLOCK
WATER CARRIER (DETAIL) [83]

Water Carrier

WILLIAM BULLOCK: SHOWMAN

JONATHAN KING

William Bullock was an artist and showman who turned his talents to a myriad of projects, including the promotion of the first exhibitions about Mexico, in London, in 1824. He was born into a large family in Sheffield, probably in the 1770's, and in his youth worked as a designer developing, meanwhile, a lively interest in the commercial exploitation of museums. Beginning in the 1790's as an itinerant curator with 300 objects, Bullock turned his collection, within about ten years, into a static museum, based in Liverpool from 1800-09. [Bullock 1807] After a successful move to London, about 1810, he set about creating an all-purpose exhibition palace and emporium, the Egyptian Hall, which opened in 1812. [Bullock 1810 and 1812] In this suite of exotic galleries he displayed his renamed London Museum of Natural History, and also retained galleries for a wide variety of shows and events. It was Bullock's genius to be able to combine side show-type entertainment—which, in earlier generations, might have taken place in booths at fairs—with smarter displays of scientific intelligence. Each exhibition was, for the first time anywhere, to combine disparate elements: models, collections of natural history, antiquities and ethnography, painted panoramas, natives, catalogues and the full panoply of press attention. The most startling of his ventures was the acquisition of Napoleon's coach from the Battle of Waterloo and its presentation, with the coachman, Jan Horn, in 1816. Apart from making vast sums of money from the show, Bullock confirmed the British interest in Napoleonic France and reinvested his profits in further exhibitions on similar themes. This occurred at the same time as William Bullock's brother George (1778/83-1811), a cabinet maker, was providing furniture for Napoleon in St. Helena [Wainwright

1988]. After the novelty of these shows—the natural history museum, Napoleon's coach and the associated French collections—had worn off, they were simply disposed of at auction in 1819. [Bullock 1819]

After the sale, the Egyptian Hall was redesigned internally and brought up to date, in terms of style, and redirected as a series of galleries for varied events including exhibitions of paintings and auctions. Bullock then embarked on a series of travel-related projects. The first of these involved the Italian circus performer Giovanni Belzoni (1778-1823), who had turned himself into an Egyptologist and opened a model of the tomb of Seti I, appropriately, in the Egyptian Hall, in 1821. [Mayes 1959] Next came an exhibition about the Saami, or Lapps, and Lapland. [Bullock 1822] This Scandinavian venture closely paralleled the later Mexican scheme. After a visit to the north, Bullock developed ideas which he ran in parallel, emphasising the more propitious elements as it suited him. The Saami show was probably, initially, to do with the importation and breeding of reindeer—a means of farming British uplands; next it became a theatrical show, with a play by Thomas Dibdin. When most of the reindeer died, the project reverted to an exhibition in the Egyptian Hall. Here, as earlier, Bullock combined a static show of artefacts—sleds and dwellings and costumes—with an ethnic exhibition—the Saami family demonstrating their lifestyle—with a scientific gloss involving the propagation of the surviving reindeer. Finally, Bullock ran a large painted panorama round the back of the exhibition, thus giving patrons several different experiences for the price of one. [Altick 1978: 233-252, 273-5]

Bullock spent approximately six months in Mexico, from March to August, 1823. In a sense, the travel narrative, published

William Bullock
xochimilco [84]

Water Carrier

WILLIAM BULLOCK
WATER CARRIER AND MAN WITH COAT OF LEAVES [85]

soon after his return, is a conventional affair, describing his journey, companions, the country and inhabitants. [1824 a] But it is enlivened all the while by a passionate interest in natural history: the fish in the Gulf of Mexico, for instance, and their variety in the markets, followed later by discussion of birds, particularly hummingbirds, and mammals. Underlying all of this is a secondary interest, in commerce and trade and, particularly, in improvement and in betterment—what would later be called progress—using British capital and industry. Bullock notes, for instance, the excellence of the unfinished road from Veracruz to Mexico City and points out how it could be improved with a little tarmac. The silver mines, ruined during the gaining of Independence, could, he was sure, be brought back into production with European capital and steam engines. Bullock displayed his travelling equipment to good effect: a folding chair; a camera lucida, for drawing; and illustrated fashion magazines, the latter having the immediate intended effect of providing new clothing styles for the local population. He was always scheming on several different levels. When he talked about the dearth of

knives for eating, one knows that what he was really saying is that there was a ready market for Sheffield cutlery. When he talked about good Flemish paintings in churches, he was thinking as a dealer in the market for old masters. The account of his travels is, therefore, written less as a diary, although from time to time dates are introduced, and more as a luxuriant prospectus of commercial possibilities. Bullock comments on the excellence of the land, the superb quality of wheat, of tobacco, and of horses and the construction of coaches. In comparison he complained about the bad tailoring, poor barbering and the dreadful furniture—the latter necessitating the importation of American suites. As befits the good showman that he was, Bullock recorded accurately the entertainments of Mexico: he described circus acts including the ancient practice of pole juggling with the feet, a bullfight, cockfights, and gambling. Bullock also hired a Mexican servant to bring back to London. The engagement must have been carried out with an eye to the forthcoming show, *Modern Mexico*, just as he had earlier engaged the Saami family. Finally, Bullock, being Catholic

WILLIAM BULLOCK
PULQUE CARRIER [86]

and strongly nationalistic, is able both to comment on the Spanish view of British buccaneers as pirates and to review, for instance, the ecclesiastical architecture of Puebla as a sympathetic worshipper.

Bullock did not travel widely in Mexico but visited cities such as Cholula, Puebla and Jalapa on the road from Veracruz, Teotihuacan, and Texcoco, in the Valley of Mexico. He also made two brief visits to Temascaltepec, a silver mining town west of Mexico City and, on the second occasion, seems to have acquired the mine in association with an American. While he does not seem to have spoken very much Spanish, Bullock carried out what must have been relatively complex, but poorly recorded, negotiations. He obtained permission to excavate around two major antiquities, Coatlicue and the Stone of Tizoc, in order to make casts, and to erect scaffolding over a third, the Calendar Stone. Then he negotiated the loan of perhaps eight Mexican manuscripts. [Graham 1993] Finally, he obtained permission to enable him to purchase the silver mine in Temascaltepec, on his second visit there, in June 1823.

From this visit to Mexico, Bullock created three or four exhibitions in the period 1824-1826. Within a year of his return, *Ancient Mexico* and *Modern Mexico* were opened in the Egyptian Hall to excellent reviews and wide acclaim. They constitute a display of Bullock as the virtuoso showman, including models and casts, antiquities, natural history and economic geography, a panorama, an Indian and, of course, publications using the new technique of lithography for the illustrations which, as Bullock noted, had not yet reached Mexico. Then, quite quickly, at the end of 1824, Bullock closed *Ancient Mexico* and relocated some of the casts and antiquities in a combined show, *Ancient and Modern Mexico*. In 1825, this exhibition, too, was closed and the separate publication was employed as an auction catalogue to dispose of the remnants of the show. [Note 1] Even then Bullock was not finished with Mexico. A new separate *Panorama of Mexico* opened in Leicester Square [Burford 1826], eventually travelling to New York a couple of years later for display in the Rotunda.

Bullock returned to Mexico to run his mine, apparently without much success. He returned to Europe, via the United

WILLIAM BULLOCK
VIEW OF THE CITY AND VALLEY OF MEXICO [87]

States, during the spring and early summer of 1827, travelling through the riverine heart of the country to Cincinnati, then the preeminent city of the American West. There he visited an estate on the Kentucky side of the Ohio River, slightly downstream from the city. This establishment, with a 1000 acres and a fine Federal-style mansion, Elmwood (ca. 1820), Bullock purchased, determining later to create an ideal community and rural town of 300 dwellings. [Note 2] This was to be named Hygeia, after the Greek goddess of health. On arrival in London he published an account but the London press did not welcome the idea, one journalist and close supporter of Bullock, William Jerdan, preferring the earlier interests in Mexico and natural history. Nevertheless, despite the lack of enthusiasm for Hygeia, Bullock retired there for ten years before resuming travels in South America and Europe, dying in London in his 70's, in 1849. [Alexander 1985].

Bullock's importance was as a businessman who combined scholarly vigour with entrepreneurial talent, always aware of the need for new ideas with the vigorous development necessary for the creation of successful enterprises. In each exhibition he would take an idea, stretch it, and then dispense with it, moving on to a new project. He seems always to have been prepared to change course, moving from London to Mexico as a manager of a mining concern, then seeking to achieve something of a cross between a Southern gentlemen and a real estate developer by moving outside Cincinnati. This venture was abandoned, in turn, and he returned to London, still travelling, still restlessly seeking interesting opportunities in old age. In his career, Bullock sits between Sir Ashton Lever (1729-1788), an eighteenth-century gentleman collector who created a museum in a disused royal palace in Leicester Square, and P. T. Barnum (1810-1891). But whereas Lever lost rather than made money, and Barnum valued money above all, Bullock combined showmanship and financial acumen with a scholarly integrity that the other two lacked.

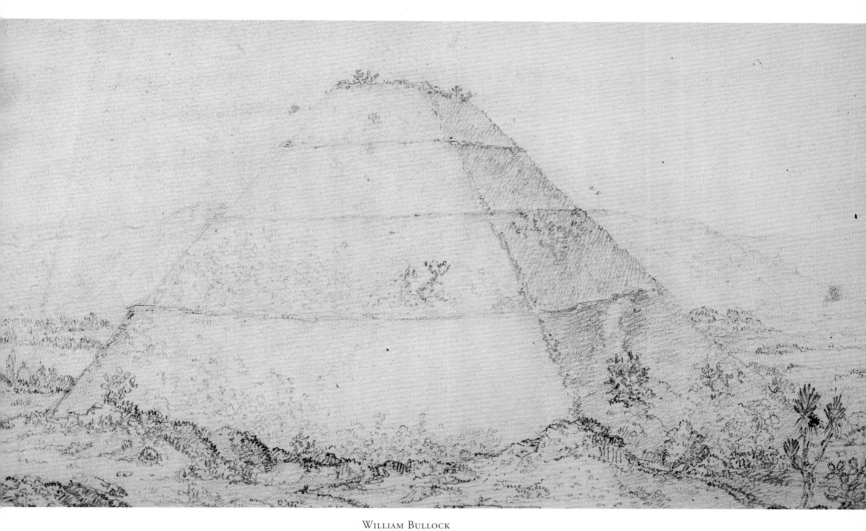

WILLIAM BULLOCK
TEOTIHUACAN. THE PYRAMID OF THE SUN [88]

p. 126. FELIX ELOIN
PANORAMIC VIEW OF MEXICO CITY
SEEN FROM THE ROOF OF LA ENSEÑANZA [89]

Yxtaccihualt
La Santisima
Soledad de Cruz

Popocatepetl   Jesus Maria   Sta Teresa   Jesus   S Miguel
S. Lucas   Prison

St Fernando   Concepcion   S. Domingo
San Lorenzo
Prison
de la Enseñanza
1 noviembre 1867

Carmen   S Sebastien   S Pedro y   el Peñon   Loreto   Prison de la Enseñanza
                                        S Pablo   12 Octubre 1867

THE PANORAMA OF LEICESTER SQUARE

SCOTT WILCOX

The panorama, as it was presented to its original audiences in the late eighteenth century, was an experiment in verisimilitude, an attempt to expand the mimic capabilities of art[1]. The experience of being completely surrounded by a painting of a full 360-degree view was, in itself, so novel and exotic that its subject matter did not need be. Indeed, familiar subjects were the order of the day, so that the spectator could better gauge the success of the illusion. When Robert Barker, the inventor of the form, first displayed an oversized circular painting to an Edinburgh audience in 1788, the subject was the Scottish capital itself. When Barker moved his operation to London the following year, the initial presentation of the Edinburgh painting was succeeded by one of London. It was only after 1800, when Barker's rotunda for the display of his panoramas in Leicester Square had became a fixture of the London scene and imitators and rivals had sprung up in London as well as in other cities, both in Britain and abroad, that exhibitors began to recognize that the panorama's startling verisimilitude could be put to the service of bringing before a local audience the far-flung reaches of the globe. The sustained popularity of the panorama phenomenon through much of the nineteenth century rested not just on its illusionism but on its complex nature as a nexus of art, entertainment, and education. The exhibition of a *View of the City of Mexico and Surrounding Country*, by Barker's successors at the Leicester Square Panorama, from 1825 to 1827, took its place in a seventy-year-long series of panoramas at that venerable institution, ranging in subject from Macao, in China, to the Polar Regions.[2]

Robert Barker, an entrepreneur, portrait painter and teacher of drawing and perspective, developed his notion of a 360-degree

painting in Edinburgh sometime around 1786. He devised a moveable frame on a pivot to enable an artist—in the earliest instances his son Henry Aston Barker—to isolate and draw successive segments of a view from a single vantage point. These drawings would be linked together to form a full 360-degree composition which would be enlarged and transferred to canvas. H.A. Barker produced the first set of such drawings on Calton Hill in Edinburgh, and the resulting painting, twenty-five feet in diameter, was opened to the public in a meeting hall in the city on January 31, 1788. Robert Barker had already taken out a patent on his idea, which at the time he called *La nature a coup d'oeil*. The patent's specifications dealt almost exclusively with the mode of display, leaving no doubt as to the importance of presentation to the goal of making spectators "feel as if really on the very spot." Of the painting itself, Barker only remarked that "the painter or drawer must fix his station, and delineate correctly and connectedly every object which presents itself to his view as he turns round, concluding his drawings by a connection with where he began," and that "he must observe the lights and shadows, how they fall, and perfect his piece to the best of his abilities." There was no mention of the moveable framing device, nothing of the problems of presenting the perspective of a 360-degree view, and no acknowledgment of the difficulties of representing straight lines on a curved canvas. Instead, Barker detailed the circular building or framing needed, the top lighting, the central viewing platform "which shall prevent an observer going too near the drawing or painting, so it may, from all parts it can be viewed, have its proper effect," and the awning, or roof, and wall, or paling, that should mask the top and bottom edges of the canvas. Barker sought to eliminate anything that might detract from the illusion or call attention to the painting as a painting. He was also at pains not to obstruct the full sweep of the panoramic view, stipulating that the entrance to the viewing platform must be from below "so that no door or other interruption may disturb the circle on which the view is to be represented."[3]

That first painting of Edinburgh, although it seems to have been quite successful in both its Edinburgh and London showings, certainly did not embody the ideal envisioned by Barker in his patent. It was not until his creation, in 1793, of a permanent establishment for the exhibition of his 360-degree paintings, which he now called panoramas, that he was able to achieve the proper combination of scale and lighting to do justice to his original conception. Barker's Leicester Square Panorama was housed in a rotunda built specially for the purpose, to the designs of the Scottish architect Robert Mitchell. The main exhibition area was a drum, ninety feet in diameter and fifty-seven feet in height, which could accommodate a painting of about ten thousand square feet. A central pillar supported a viewing platform with a diameter of thirty feet so that the spectator was at a distance of thirty feet from the actual canvas. Visitors reached the platform by a dimly lit corridor so that when they emerged into the exhibition space it appeared to have the brightness of the daylight they had left outside. A second, smaller exhibition space, mounted above the larger compartment, was opened in 1795. This second space was fifty feet in diameter and held a painting of about 2,700 square feet. It was in this "Upper Circle" that the panorama of Mexico City was exhibited.

Robert Barker ran the establishment until his death in 1806, when his son Henry Aston, who seems to have been responsible for artistic matters from the beginning, took over all aspects of the operation. Under his direction, a group of assistants painted the vast canvases in a large circular studio in Southwark. In 1816, H.A. Barker made one of those assistants, John Burford, his partner. On H.A. Barker's retirement in 1824, John Burford and his son Robert became the proprietors. John died in 1827, but under Robert's direction the Leicester Square Panorama remained open into the 1860's.

Initially the Barkers promoted the panorama as both a novelty and a serious contribution to art. It was an "IMPROVE-MENT ON PAINTING, Which relieves that sublime Art from a Restraint it has ever laboured under."[4] While the novelty was a key selling point, they insisted on the seriousness of their artistic experiment. The panorama was not some vulgar sideshow but the result of "minute investigations of the principles of art" and "intended chiefly for the criticism of artists, and admirers of painting in general."[5] If the aim of art was to hold a mirror up to nature, as the proprietors of the panorama were, of course, anxious to assert, the panorama could indeed seem an epoch-making invention, with significant implications for the painting and display of all sorts of pictures.

The expiration of Barker's patent, in 1801, occasioned an outpouring of competing panoramas and related forms of scenic entertainment. As the landscape painter John Constable noted: "Panorama painting seems all the rage."[6] Until that point the Leicester Square rotunda had exhibited views of British cities and recent British naval victories. In response to the increased competition, the Barkers produced their first view of a foreign city, Constantinople, and announced their intention "to spare no expense or trouble to bring forward scenes of useful information, as well as gratifying amusement; and the public may expect to have the most interesting Views and the most noticed cities of Europe, in due time, laid before them."[7] Within a few years, the scope of the Barkers' geographical reach had extended beyond Europe, and the presentation of exotic and news-worthy locales became a key feature of the panorama's newly educational thrust. Constantinople was followed in the first quarter of the nineteenth century by views of Paris, Gibraltar, Dublin, Cairo, Malta, Messina, Lisbon, St. Petersburg, Spitsbergen, Lausanne and Lake Geneva, Bern, and the ruins of Pompeii. The view of Mexico City in the mid-1820's was the first of a number of panoramas of subjects in the Americas, which included Rio de Janeiro, Quebec, Niagara Falls, and New York City.

The educational value of the panorama's version of virtual reality was dependent on the closeness of that virtual reality to the real scenes it purported to represent. Establishing the accuracy of the panoramic representation and the authority on which that representation was based were primary concerns, already apparent with that very first panorama of Edinburgh. When the Barkers presented that view to a London audience, they claimed that they had first exhibited it in Edinburgh specifically "to gain it an indisputable character for correctness."[8] They also produced a statement from the Lord Provost of Edinburgh that their picture was "a most correct and just represen-

Section of the Rotunda, Leicester Square, in which is exhibited the PANORAMA.
Coupe de la Rotonde, dans laquelle, est l'exhibition du PANORAMA, Leicester Square.

Published May 12, 1801.

Robt. Mitchell, Architect.

ROBERT MITCHELL
CROSS SECTION OF THE ROTUNDA AT LEICESTER SQUARE [90]

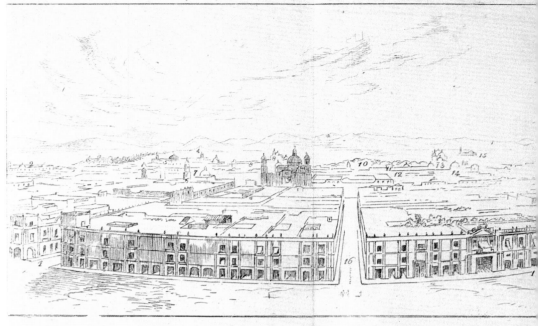

1. Calle Plateres.
2. De los Viscaynas.
3. Calzada canería de Chapultepec.
4. Chapultepec.
5. La Cigarros
6. Espiritu Santo.

7. Colegio de los Niñas Hospital for poor Girls.
8. S. Francisco.
9. Le Profaso.
10. La Alameda.
11. Mineria.
12. Belemitas Convent for Friars.

13. S. Ypolito.
14. Sta Clara.
15. S. Fernando.
16. Calle Lerrea
17. Casa de Stad
18. Concepcion

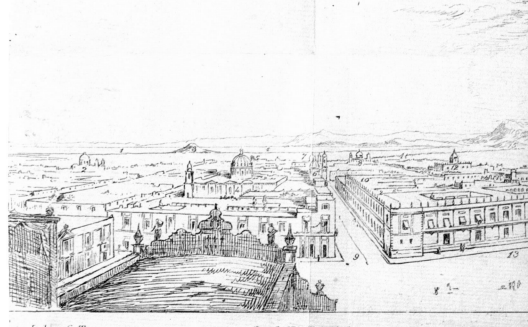

1. Lake of Tezcuco.
2. Nuestra Seigñora de Loreto.
3. Peñon de los Baños.
4. Sta Teresa de Antigua.
5. St Lazaro.
6. Sta Ynes, Convent for Nuns.

7. La S. Sma Trinidad.
8. Soledad de Santa Cruz.
9. Calle del Arzobispardo.
10. Casa de Moneda.
11. Calzaday.
12. Jesus Maria.

13. Palacio.
14. La Mercea.
15. Peñon Vieque.
16. Izlaccihuatl.
17. Popocatepetl.
18. Botanic Garde
37 Religious Proc

J. y R. Burford
PAMPHLET FOR THE PANORAMA OF THE CITY
OF MÉXICO EXHIBITED BY BULLOCK [91]

19. San Lorenzo.
20. Calle de Tacuba.
21. Imprinta general Printing Office
22. Cruz taba verterus,
    First Chapel built by Cortez.
23. S. Domingo.

24. R. Aduana, Custom House
25. Casa de l'Ynquisicion
26. S. Catalina de Sena.
27. Plaza de Galois.
28. Claverio, Treasury of the Cathedral.
29. Cathedral.

30. La Encarnation.
31. Mountain of Chiquiti.
32. Calzaday miena de Guadalupe.
33. Pyramids de S. Juan.
34. S. Pedro y S. Pablo in which the Congress meet
35. S. Yldefonzo.

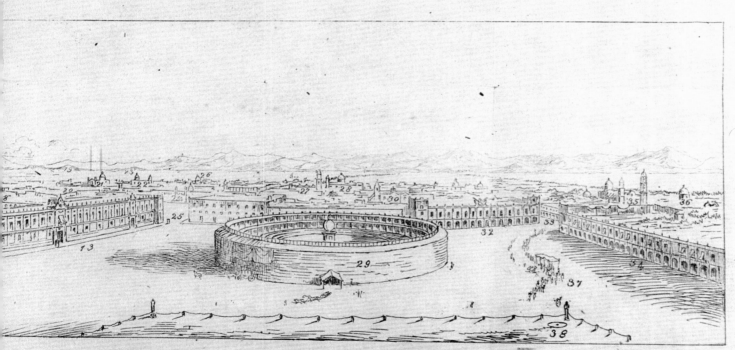

19. Licra de Molcagete.
20. Universidad.
21. S. Pablo.
22. Col. de S. Pablo.
23. Estapalapa.
24. Porta Cœli.
38. Sacrificial Stone.

25. Del Bolador Market.
26. S. Jose de Gracia.
27. Hosp. de Jesus de los naturales.
28. S. Miguel.
29. Casa de Tores.
30. S. Bernardo.

31. Leira de Ajusco.
32. Deputation, House of the Mayor.
33. Calle Monterilla.
34. Les Portales.
35. S. Augustin.
36. Regina Cœli.

DANTE ESCALANTE
RECONSTRUCTION OF THE PANORAMA OF THE CITY OF MEXICO BY WILLIAM BULLOCK [92-96]

tation of the city and its environs to the fullest extent of the horizon in every direction."[9] Such testimonials to the fidelity of their views became a standard element of panorama advertising, as did the information that a panorama was painted from sketches made on the spot either by one of the proprietors, Henry Aston Barker or Robert Burford, or by another artist-traveller, such as Frederick Catherwood or William Bullock.

Panoramic illusion took its place among the expanding means of gaining knowledge about an increasingly shrinking world. As a writer in the *Repository of Arts* put it in 1826: "What between steam-boats and panoramic exhibitions, we are every day not only informed of, but actually brought into contact with remote objects."[10] An article in *Blackwood's Magazine,* in 1824, calling panoramas "among the happiest contrivances for saving time and expense in this age of contrivances," more fully developed the theme of the panorama as a substitute for travel: "The fullest

impression that could be purchased, by our being parched, passported, plundered, starved, and stenched, for 1,200 miles east and by south, could not be fuller than the work of Messers Parker's [sic] and Burford's brushes. The scene is absolutely alive, vivid, and true; we feel all but the breeze, and hear all but the dashing of the wave."[11]

The panorama provided a vivid visual counterpart to the news that could be obtained through the print media, and topicality was an important factor in the choice of panorama subjects, as were imperialistic and commercial concerns. The panorama of Mexico City, which John and Robert Burford painted from sketches William Bullock had made in Mexico in 1823, brought the appearance of the Mexican capital to an audience that had been reading of the turbulent events in Mexico surrounding its independence from Spain in 1821 and the establishment of a Mexican republic. The text of the explanatory booklet that could be purchased at the Leicester Square

[93-95]

[96]

rotunda made explicit the commercial opportunities that gave the subject of this panorama an interest beyond mere intellectual curiosity:

> Possessing all the material for a most extensive exchange, Mexico offers the greatest advantages to commercial speculation: the employment of its present very numerous and unemployed population, by a combination of British talent, capital, and machinery, together with an active and unrestricted intercourse, will raise them from the lethargy and shackles in which they have been so long bound by the narrow and barbarous policy of Spain, to that rank amongst nations, which, from their character, the fertility of their soil, and the almost inexhaustible riches of their mines, they are so well calculated to maintain.[12]

The *View of the City of Mexico...* returned to the "Upper Circle" at Leicester Square from July to December 1853, and it was on display again when the Leicester Square Panorama closed its doors for the last time on December 12, 1863.[13]

As the nineteenth century progressed, the panorama's role in bringing home the world accurately and vividly was usurped by photography and, eventually, the newsreel. The last quarter of the century saw a resurgence in panorama activity, but the great panoramas of that period concentrated almost entirely on recreations of historical battles and biblical scenes. The Barkers' and Burfords' efforts to present their audiences with "scenes of useful information" from around the world had become outmoded; panoramic illusion was now in the service of bringing the past to life. Even that function of the panorama would soon be ceded to the new medium of the cinema.

p. 136. August Lohr
iztaccíhuatl [97]

LANDSCAPE PAINTING AMONG THE TRAVELER-ARTISTS

PABLO DIENER

In Hispanic and Portuguese America, it was the traveler-artists who discovered the landscape as an artistic motif. The oils by the Dutchman, Franz Post, of the Brazilian vistas that he captured around 1650, appear as a remote prelude to the enthusiasm for landscapes among the nineteenth-century travelers. Post interpreted the landscapes of the Americas in a Dutch pictorial language: vistas of very low horizons and compositions of classical taste, with a focus marked by abundant vegetation and broad perspectives of prairies, enlivened with scenes of daily life and by an interplay between light and shadow. Strictly speaking, Post had no immediate heirs among the traveler-painters. For instance, his descriptive spirit is quite alien to the rather melodramatic painting by William Hodges, the English traveler who accompanied James Cook on the expedition to the South Seas in the following century. Apart from their differences, the works by Post, as well as those by Hodges, were to serve as points of reference for the traveler-painters of the nineteenth century. However, the principal incentives and artistic precedents for the painting of landscapes by the romantic travelers weren't historicistic. Rather, more immediately, they were responding to the cultural and artistic restlessness of the period. The best reasoning behind these types of works is intimately linked to the revered position held by Nature within the philosophical, scientific and artistic climate of the eighteenth century and onward.

The changes in the conception of Nature were particularly relevant during the Enlightenment. Nature was to represent, with growing emphasis, perfection and the model—in the classical sense, the possibility of a Golden Age. In the art of the eighteenth century and that of the first part of the nineteenth century, Nature appeared as Arcadia, as an allegory of superhuman power, as sublime beauty or, at times, as the ideal materialization of an emotional state. In this context, the representation of Nature had to combine life study with the current artistic tradition. For the painters of classicism, life studies were the basic material for creating the *Idea* of the work of art. Masters such as Reynolds and Valenciennes insisted that these were the two aspects that the painter of landscapes must always take into account in their work. These artistic parameters are basically to be found in the landscapes created in the seventeenth century by Nicolas Poussin, Claude Lorrain and Jacob van Ruysdael. Beginning about 1800, the purely naturalistic observation began to gain more and more ground, in the pragmatic manner of the work of William Turner, John Constable and J.B.C. Corot. The observation of light and color, the naturalistic study of clouds and the sky, and the attention paid to the pictorial value of the subject matter, the land, the plants and of nature in general acquired a presence that surpassed the importance of tradition. With it was inaugurated a new form of artistic reception of Nature that Baudelaire summarized with the following words in his comments on the exhibition of the Salon of 1859: "...the current credo throughout the world is this: I believe in Nature and in nothing apart from Nature. I believe that art is and can be nothing apart from an exact reproduction of Nature."

The problems that confronted the artist in the transition from classicist tradition to a resolute naturalism demanded novel solutions and the turning to new techniques. Burning questions were put forth by all painters interested in the artistic representation of Nature, among them, certainly, the travelers.

The dynamic that Nature acquired as a theme in art had a counterpart in the field of the sciences, where the encyclopedic

JEAN BAPTISTE LOUIS, BARON GROS
THE VALLEY OF MEXICO AS SEEN FROM LAKE TEXCOCO [98]

Jean Baptiste Louis, Baron Gros
VIEW OF TEXCOCO (DETAIL) [99]

PÁL ROSTI
POPOCATÉPETL [100]

PÁL ROSTI
IZTACCÍHUATL [101]

spirit was the rule, with a keen desire for systematic universal knowledge. The scientific grasp of the world required illustrations—careful representations of animals, plants, crystals and the physiognomy of the landscape. The tradition of scientific illustration influenced the nineteenth-century traveler-painter as much as the purely artistic complexities. From his point of view, the boundaries that formed his field of endeavor straddled those of art and science. Alexander von Humboldt himself, writing on the painting of landscapes in the second volume of the encyclopedic publication *Cosmos* (1847), explicitly demarcated this area, evoking "the ancient link between the knowledge of Nature and artistic poetry and intuition." Von Humboldt proposed a "physiognomic representation of the landscape" equidistant from classicist composition and literal naturalism. In his opinion, "in landscape painting, as in all branches of art, one must differentiate between that which can be captured from modest sensory perception and immediate observation, and that infinite that emerges from profound sensibility and the force of intellectual abstraction." His proposal to the artist was that he faithfully paint the topography and that he be credible in the representation of Nature, inviting him to create a vista of the landscape in its optimum possibilities. Von Humboldt invoked the artists to work on the basis of such ideas: "Until the second world voyage by Cook, there had been a scarcity of inspired artists who followed the tradition of a physiognomic representation of Nature. The work realized by Hodges in the western islands of the South Seas, and our unforgettable compatriot, Ferdinand Bauer, in New Holland [Australia] and the

land of Van Diemens [Tasmania], has recently been surpassed with greater style and with a superior mastery in the American tropical world by Mortiz Rugendas, Count Clarac, Ferdinand Bellermann and Eduard Hildebrandt and, in many other parts of the world, by Heinrich von Kittlitz, traveling companion, around the world, of the Russian, Admiral Lütke." We see von Humboldt defining a group of traveler-artists that represented landscapes according to the principle of a creative naturalism, respecting and enriching the illustration of an ecosystem. In short, he conceived a school of landscape painting based on scientific and artistic postulates.

The landscape painting created by the traveler painters constitutes a small chapter in the history of art, yet one that is well defined and autonomous. Its greatest brilliance corresponds to the middle third of the nineteenth century and the works on themes from the American continent compose a body of work both numerous and of good quality. In the second half of the century, the figure of the traveler-artist as a painter of landscapes became diluted and, in fact, their work became increasingly removed from the artistic vanguards of the latter part of the century. By following the footsteps of the European travelers in Mexico, Brazil or Chile, we can recreate an ideal journey through this nineteenth-century artistic genre. Instruments, technical elements and forms of expression exist which were repeated among the travelers throughout the length and breadth of the continent. Furthermore, the traveler established a singular relationship with Nature and in Mexico, specifically, he was the artistic conquistador of a no man's land. Between the extremes

of pure topographical illustration of scientific intent and the picturesque vista which appealed to popular tastes, we find outstanding artistic works which can be placed within the tradition of landscape painting and are important links to its development.

Among the painters of landscapes and, in particular, among the travelers, the practice of sketching in color achieved great diffusion beginning in the first decades of the century, becoming one of the principle instruments in the execution of their work. Additionally, this modality of work provides us with a reflection of the changes in the relationship between man and Nature and, consequently, in the new reception of Nature that the artists postulated. From a historical perspective, the practice and valuation of the color sketch was a symptom that, relative to our topic of travelers, permits the placement of the painter within the framework of the interests and concerns of nineteenth-century art.

Already being imparted in the academies, for example in the manual *Éléments de perspective pratique à l'usage des artistes* (Elements of Practical Perspective in Use by Artists), by Pierre-Henri de Valenciennes, it was recommended to painters to realize detailed studies of trees and to be precise in the sketching of the silhouette of the orography, but it was also suggested to make color tests in order to recreate the atmosphere of the landscape. The oil sketches that Pelegrín Clavé executed in Mexico were faithful to this academic tradition. They are evidence of the occasional practice of this technique on the part of an academic artist and are exercises of a strictly personal character. However, in spite of the extraordinary character in the work of

Clavé, these works reveal that the academic master was sensitive to the problems facing the reception of landscape painting. This fact deserves even more note if one takes into account that it was he who, at the Academy, provided the initial impetus toward the creation of a school of landscape painting in Mexico. Just as Clavé introduced the practice of sketching in color in the purest academic tradition, other travelers were to infuse the color sketch with a connotation closer to the new artistic currents of the nineteenth century. The painters of the most enthusiasm and the richest production in terms of sketching in color in Mexico were Egerton, working in watercolors, and Rugendas, who worked in oils. In view of the lack of unequivocal documental proof, we can only intuit the importance that these two painters gave to this type of work, both in terms of the abundance, variety and quality, and on the impact on history that this body of work has had. Egerton executed a great quantity of rough landscape sketches. They are pencil drawings, finished in a narrow range of watercolors, generally incorporating brown, green and blue. More than simply colored notes taken of the landscape, or what appeared within it, they are studies of light, of the luminous atmosphere. Egerton attempted to recreate the chiaroscuro of a space. In this sense one can find analogies to the études by Chopin, similar in that they both play with an idea. Within Egerton's notebooks can be found, for example, three sketches of Teotihuacan—two sepias and a grisaille—that represent a study

DANIEL THOMAS EGERTON
SAN JUAN TEOTIHUACAN [105]

DANIEL THOMAS EGERTON
SAN JUAN TEOTIHUACAN, LATE AFTERNOON [106]

144

DANIEL THOMAS EGERTON
SAN JUAN TEOTIHUACAN AT SUNSET [107]

model of light and shadow. The first offers a vista of San Juan de Teotihuacan in the light of day. Over a rough pencil sketch Egerton painted, in sepia, the tone of light corresponding to each plant, construction and mountain. The second study is painted in afternoon light. The silhouettes of the church and the mountains are defined by the contrasts of chiaroscuro rather than by pencil strokes. The third is a *nocturne*, a study of the effects that the light had on both the landscape and the painter. The intention of these works, however, is distinguishable from that of Chopin's études in that those of Egerton possess, apparently, a strictly private character. They were never made public by the artist. This is precisely the topic of dispute among painters and critics: the valuation of a color sketch and the status that should be conceded it within the body of work of an artist. Turner provoked a scandal in Rome, in the winter of 1828-29, when he presented his great oils in which color, not line, dominated. He went beyond the limits of tradition by incorporating the sketched painting as forming part of his finished work.

Corot, by contrast, never valued his *études d'après nature* as finished works even though he knew that they were the essence of his creative work as early as the initial stage of his practice of sketching in oil, in Rome, between 1825 and 1828.

In a note dated 1856, in a notebook of drawings, he wrote that "it doesn't matter which place it may be or which object, we preserve the first impression." Around this time he had occasionally exhibited some of his paintings, cataloging them as études. For Constable, however, the oil sketch, on a one-to-one scale with respect to the final work, acquired an unequivocal value as an expression of the *Idea* of the painting. The painter composed a work in his most immediate language, abstracting and subordinating the descriptive detail. It is in the full-size sketch where Constable created the pictorial idea of a unitary space subjected to a coherent interplay of light and shadow, in the baroque tradition. This is also the artistic sense that we identify in the watercolors by Egerton, each of the works cavorting between naturalism and the tradition of European landscape painting of

Jean-Frédéric Waldeck
THE VALLEY OF MEXICO FROM THE BISHOP'S GARDEN IN TACUBAYA [108]

the seventeenth century. But just as Constable is closer to the well-defined painting of the Dutch, the work of Egerton evokes Claude Lorrain in the use of a type of ambient light that glistens in the particles of air more than on the subjects.

It was Rugendas who, among the travelers, conceded the most artistic value to the color sketch, though his stance didn't separate him from the classicist tradition. Rugendas painted medium- and large-format oils throughout his entire life, works carefully finished and composed in the manner of the Dutch baroque school. The education he had received in Munich was of a rigorous cultivation of the drawing, and his artistic values were learned in an academic atmosphere. Equally important, however, was the influence that Alexander von Humboldt had on him. Rugendas probably felt the initial artistic impulse to practice sketching in oil during the year he spent traveling in Italy (1828-29). The influence of Turner, and perhaps that of Corot, and the probable encounters in Rome with the Berliner, Carl Blechen—the German landscape artist who most decid-

edly practiced this technique—revealed to the young Rugendas a modality of painting which until then hadn't been practiced. Yet, with his arrival in Mexico, in 1831, it would become part of his daily work. The paintings that Rugendas sent to von Humboldt from Mexico were oil sketches, although not the first drafts—that Corot had spoken of as being so important. To date, nearly two hundred of the paintings sent by the artist to his mentor have been located, and many of them exist in earlier versions that the painter kept in his notebooks. The studies that Rugendas sent to von Humboldt have the same aim as the full-size sketches by Constable, the capturing of space and light, which for Rugendas was the physiognomic representation of Nature. Von Humboldt had defined this concept while speaking of the service that art could lend to science. During his voyages he had lived through the difficulties presented the artist by "field work" and through work on his own publications knew of the necessity and importance of good illustrations. He cultivated relationships with numerous young artists, and incited them to travel

JOHANN MORITZ RUGENDAS
GORGE OF THE RÍO GRANDE DE SANTIAGO [109]

to the Americas and take part in a renaissance of landscape painting, this time in the tropical world. Within von Humboldt's gigantic epistolary legacy is to be found a rich correspondence with young painters. He sent them instructions, induced them to draw with precision, as well as to make rough sketches in color, always with the idea that it might lead them to eventually compose a painting in the studio. But later, in the praise that the German scientist gave to the studies of the Mexican landscape that Rugendas had sent him, one can perceive that he recognized these works as artistic accomplishments that satisfied his own longings. With time, von Humboldt also took his passion for Nature to the same level as Corot. In a letter to the painter Albert Berg, dated May 1853, he suggested that he not alter his original drawings, that he conserve them "with the character of rough sketch that is original. Everything that is added later to the representation of subjects that have been captured in a state of felicitous animation, robs the sketch of a little of its vitality." Rugendas, in the end, also came to value his oil sketches, to the degree that he sent them to Germany for their study and

public exhibition. However, we also know that he wanted to develop, artistically, the work he had initiated in the Americas after his return to Europe. After donating his work to the Bavarian Crown, in 1848, he committed himself to the regular delivery of paintings executed in his studio. The weight of artistic tradition remained important throughout his entire career, the spirit of the Munich academy persevered within him. However, an affinity for the sciences, inspired by von Humboldt, induced him to execute *études d'après nature* and, like Corot, Rugendas realized that these pieces were not only good but essential to his work, as manifested in a letter to his sister from March of 1832.

Just as the traveler-artists practiced the art of sketching in color in order to draw nearer to Nature, they also turned to the use of optical instruments in their "field work" in order to achieve greater speed in compiling their notes and more fidelity in the vistas. One example of the use of these technical apparatus by the artists in Mexico during the first third of the nineteenth century is provided in a vista of the Valley of Mexico by Pedro Calvo. This is an outstanding work, although isolated,

ANTHONY CAREY STANNUS
VERACRUZ [110]

ANTHONY CAREY STANNUS
LA ALAMEDA AND FAÇADE OF THE HOSPITAL DE SAN JUAN DE DIOS [111]

DANIEL THOMAS EGERTON
THE BASALTIC FORMATIONS AND CASCADE AT REGLA [112]

ADELA BRETON
THE BASALTIC FORMATIONS AND CASCADE AT REGLA [113]

exemplifying the iconography of landscape painting from the brush of a Mexican artist from the early part of the century. In one corner of the painting Calvo includes a self-portrait of the artist at work using a camera obscura. The vista is broad, of a panoramic character, and is dated 1825, the same year in which William Bullock and his associates presented the panorama, *View of the City of Mexico and Surrounding Country*, in London.

Both works glorify the use of technical resources. The presence of the camera obscura can be interpreted in Calvo's case as proof of the authenticity of his *Vista de la Ciudad de México* (Vista of Mexico City), and the panorama, in turn, draws its life from optical illusion, an apparatus of fantasy that attempts to transport the spectator to another place. The art of the travelers frequently appeared in association with optical inventions. In some cases documentary evidence exists of such utilization, for example Waldeck's mention of the camera obscura among the vast inventory of objects he carried with him on trips. In other cases we can intuit that the artist had made use of, primarily, the camera lucida. This is evident in the case of urban vistas executed with precise detail, such as the profiles of Veracruz and the Valley of Mexico by the Englishman, Anthony C. Stannus, or in the panoramic

compositions of Mexico City that Pedro Gualdi painted in a series of works. It is plausible that, during the last stage of his sojourn, Rugendas also utilized this instrument. The silhouettes that he drew from the crater of the Colima volcano, among others of his rough sketches, are so lineal as to make one think that they were made from a camera lucida. Although Rugendas never mentions the instrument within his scant writings, his traveling companion on the trip to Colima, the engineer and cartographer Eduard Harkort, doubtless used one on a daily basis.

The landscape painting by the traveler-artists attempted to achieve the value of a document while at the same time earning the admiration of the public. The painter utilized, as the tools of his trade, technical resources both modern and not for precision in drawing. He also practiced sketching in color and, at times, he was aware of the necessity for the "staging" of his work. And in his relationship with the subject of his art, Nature, the traveler created a game of artistic conquest in the New World. His conquest of a no man's land in Mexico sometimes made him appear a bold explorer of the farthest reaches of the earth. When Rugendas scaled the Colima volcano, and Gros ascended to the top of Popocatépetl, they were not only study-

José Gutiérrez
THE HACIENDA DE REGLA [114]

Johann Moritz Rugendas
THE BASALTIC FORMATIONS AND CASCADE AT REGLA [115]

BARON DE COURCY
THE BASALTIC FORMATIONS AND CASCADE AT REGLA [116]

ing, measuring, drawing silhouettes and taking notes. They were also seeking the adventure of living within virgin nature. Harkort writes that he and Rugendas were the first in history to scale the Colima volcano. His account is sprinkled with ingenuousness, whether in the emphasis on their success or in the manner in which he referred to the mountain guides who, out of fear, accompanied them only for part of the climb. Gros and his companions planted flags on the summit of Popocatépetl, as if they had conquered the moon—their moon. Gros relates that "after six hours of pointless hiking through the eternal snows, abandoned by our guides, who didn't want to risk setting foot in 'the dominions of the evil spirit,'" the attempt ended in failure. A thousand obstacles retarded this conquest. But, thanks to the experiences gained by the failures, Gros writes that finally, "on April 29, 1834, we were able to plant the French flag on the highest peak of the Mexican Andes." The adventure

of the voyage, the pretension (well-founded in many cases) of having lived moments of an intimate relationship with Nature, made the artist feel, and be, a protagonist in his own play. His aspiration was to capture these unique experiences with the brush and transmit them to his contemporaries along with as much of the emotion that he himself had lived through. During his voyage to Ecuador, the painter Frederic Edwin Church, from the United States, described in his diary the fascination that he experienced upon seeing the Sangay volcano from a hill. The clouds, the gradual appearance of the peak of the volcano, the smoke from the crater, and the changes in color with the movement of the sun entranced him. In relating this experience, Church is carried away by enthusiasm and relives the dialog that he sustained with Nature in a sublime moment: "I commenced to sketch the effect as rapidly as possible, but constant changes took place and new beauties revealed themselves as the setting sun turned the black smoke into burnished copper and the white steam into gold. At intervals of two or three minutes an explosion would take place; the first intimation was a fresh mass of smoke with sharply defined outline rolling above the black rocks and immediately a dull rumbling sound which reverberated among the mountains. I was so delighted with the changing effects that I continued making rapid sketches of the different effects until night overtook me and a chilly dampness warned me to retrace my steps..."[1]

Of similar note is the dramatic dialog between the artist and Nature that is insinuated by the work that Rugendas painted of the Colima volcano, as well as that which Egerton and Gros dedicated to Popocatépetl. All seem to have been seeking an artistic synthesis of their experiences, imbued with a rhetoric that reaches exaltation and with an evident keenness of reportage. The specific curiosity about volcanoes is part of the common legacy that the traveler-painters owed to von Humboldt.

The eagerness for adventure and the tradition of science were to influence the selection of favorite motifs by the traveler-painter of landscapes. With the passing of the century, a repertoire of picturesque themes became consolidated. In Mexico, for example, the travelers made pilgrimages to the Hacienda de Regla to view and take notes on the prismatic basalt formations, or they traveled to the volcanoes—from the one near Orizaba and those of the central *altiplano*, to that of Colima. Vistas of the ports of Tampico and Veracruz, as well as that of Acapulco, are equally recurrent themes in the painting of landscapes, in part due to their inarguable attractiveness as notable examples of natural beauty under the influence of man's modifications. However, in part, the representations of these ports also carry an anecdotal connotation, that of the initiation or termination of the traveler's voyage. A "picturesque-ness" of the landscapes of the Americas was created in the nineteenth century. From Chile, there were frequent vistas of the mountains between the capital, Santiago, and the port at Valparaíso; in Lima the artists were in the habit of painting the city from the far side of the Rimac River; in Brazil, one of the first stops on many of the voyages from Europe, it was the city of Salvador, and then on to Rio de Janeiro—one or the other city always finding a place in the portfolio of the travelers who arrived at these latitudes. The repetition in the motifs of landscape painting indicate to us that interests were transmitted from one artist to another, as well as the solutions to the same pictorial themes that were exchanged among them throughout the century. For Eugenio Landesio, in Mexico, it was so evident that the view from the slopes of Popocatépetl and the interior of the caves at Cacahuamilpa posed problems of general artistic interest that he dedicated a short work to the academic-artistic analysis of these sites, thus actually enriching the picturesque value of both. In the literal sense of the term, the picturesque led the traveler to see the landscape not only in terms of itself, but in relation to other works of art. Paradigmatic is the case of Baron de Courcy, whose Mexican work seems to emulate that of his traveling companion, J.M. Rugendas. After touring the mining region around Pachuca together, de Courcy continued on alone from Mexico City to Veracruz. The vistas he painted on this stage of his trip found inspiration, nearly without exception, in the notes that he had seen within Rugendas' portfolios: a street in Jalapa, the Puente Nacional, and the port at Veracruz as seen from inland are picturesque motifs that de Courcy saw in the work of Rugendas and whose focus he carefully sought in the later continuation of his trip, in order to reinterpret them in his own artistic language. Another illustrative example of the elaboration and re-elaboration of the landscape of the New World meant to be interpreted in terms of European tastes can be found in a vista of Rio de Janeiro lithographed by the Englishman, Richard P. Bonington, based on a watercolor drawing by Rugendas. Bonington was, perhaps, the most brilliant romantic English watercolorist. He lived his artistic life in France and was a friend of Delacroix, with whom he shared a studio in Paris around 1825. Bonington's work bridged English romanticism, the legacy of Turner and Constable, and the baroque dramatism of Géricault and Delacroix. Bonington knew the same Paris as Rugendas. In the lithographic work that he undertook for the editor Engelmann, he came across the illustration that Rugendas had drawn and painted in Brazil. A young man of twenty-seven years, Bonington had never traveled to Brazil nor seen Rio de Janeiro's Guanabara Bay, only imaging its aspect from the study by Rugendas. The landscape by Rugendas is a pencil drawing of smooth, sharply pointed strokes, essentially descriptive. He had only colored the Pão de Açúcar (Sugar Loaf) and the other curious rock formations that contribute to the characteristic profile of Rio de Janeiro. It is one of

the most delicate leaves among all his landscape work. Boning-ton let loose a storm in the bay, with a red-tinted sky and a churning sea, ships tossed by winds and high waves. The masts of a ship cover details of the orography and the waves in the foreground push the city far into the background. It is difficult to imagine a more extreme contrast in the interpretations of the same landscape. Bonington composed an operatic painting over the landscape by Rugendas. In his future work, the traveler also turned more and more to granting a character not solely descriptive, but also emotive to his landscapes. In Mexico, Rugendas ended by developing a form of landscape painting that captured the subjectivity of Nature. The other landscape

painters from the century were to do the same, from George Henry White, the stupendous "Sunday painter," to the illustri-ous academic Eugenio Landesio. The painting of landscapes by travelers was to continue beyond the turn of the century in the watercolors of Adela Breton and in the oils by August Lohr, among others. Picturesque painting of double connotation was a secular constant among the travelers, perhaps even defining it in part. Thus, upon leafing through different notebooks, we often note the recurrence of motifs and in the development of the work—when it exists—what also becomes increasingly evident is the classicist archetype with which the traveler configured his mod-el in the capture and representation of Nature in the New World.

EDUARD HILDEBRANT
VIEW OF ACAPULCO [119]

JOHN TH. HAVERFIELD
SAN BLAS. HOUSES NEXT TO THE SEA [120]

JOHANN MORITZ RUGENDAS
SUNSET AT LAGUNA DE CUYUTLÁN [121]

p. 158. Johann Moritz Rugendas
MARKET IN MEXICO CITY (DETAIL) [122]

ETHNOGRAPHY AND GENRE IN THE IMAGES OF THE TRAVELERS

JUANA GUTIÉRREZ HACES

In the beginning all the world was America

J. Locke

On February 23, 1833, Johann Friedrich Conde de Waldeck (Frédéric Waldeck) executed a drawing in which he depicts an indigenous man dressed in a brief *taparrabo* (loincloth), his torso covered by a loose-fitting shirt. He is supporting himself with a long staff and on his back, slung over one shoulder, one can make out a bow. In the upper left corner is inscribed "Palenque," the date and, in diminutive lettering, a description of the man. Perhaps it was on this same day that he made another drawing, this of a young indigenous girl dressed only in a long skirt, apparently in a sustained pose with one hand raised, holding a bowl of fruit and the other hand outstretched, holding a string of freshly caught fish. Earrings, a necklace and a long chain with a cross help to cover the nakedness of her chest. At the top of the page is the inscription: "Philipa Sánchez, 12 ans."

In 1822, Waldeck had participated in the engraving of fifteen drawings executed during the Del Río-Armendáriz expedition to Palenque (1787), which for the first time had reached the general public in an English publication.[1] As a result of this work, Waldeck became interested in visiting this land and moved to Mexico in 1825, finally arriving in Palenque in 1833 where he executed a series of drawings of the archaeological ruins, as well as noting information about the inhabitants of the area such as he had done in the two drawings previously described.

There is a long history of artistic examination of the inhabitants of the American hemisphere, particularly with reference to the area that is now Mexico. What difference exists, then,

between Waldeck's drawings from 1833, so individualized that he would include the names and ages of his subjects and which were elaborated with faithful respect to their ethnic features, and those illustrations which, throughout nearly four centuries, had stimulated the imagination of the Europe as to what the inhabitants of these lands were like and what their customs were?

On one hand, it is evident that the greater part of the images of the people native to this land, which for centuries had nourished the expectations of the Europeans, were results not of the direct capture of the model in question but, rather, of the imaginations of the readers of chronicles by conquistadors and missionaries, images usually based on a single figure or a literary description. The few known images from the sixteenth century that were made directly from a model are those by artists who were present at some "performance" by indigenous Americans who had been brought to Europe, together with material treasures, to be presented to the king and, therefore, transplanted into a foreign environment.

Having a model in front of him obliged the artist to concentrate on his image and not on a written account. An example are the works executed by Christoph Weiditz, who attended a showing of indigenous Mexicans at the Court of Toledo, in 1528. The artist drew several of them individually and also illustrated their performances. The plates that capture individual aspects of the indigenous men are carefully crafted, focusing on characteristics that others, who attended similar events, were to record and which, later, a multitude of artists and writers would

repeat: the nudity, the use of feathers, the dark tone of the skin, the characteristic and peculiar facial features, their being in the company of exotic animals such as the macaw, their corporal decoration, their jewelry, etc. It seems, however, that the "scientific" image of these Mexicans, who played with a ball as well as with a wooden cylinder which they would rotate with their feet, was not sufficient, leading the majority of illustrators to abandon these models in favor of conventions created by literature and by the imagination, rather than images emanating from direct observation.

Draftsmen and engravers provided illustrations for publications on the Americas without ever having been on the continent or even having met one of its inhabitants in person. Thus, what they furnished were narrative images of activities, battles or rituals rather than portraits of individual men. If, on occasion, an isolated figure was portrayed, such as the case of the portrait of Moctezuma, literary stereotypes provided much of the descriptive material.

The result was that the figures were always based on images distorted by a given country and its people. Depending on who made the description, thus appeared the image of the indigenous American, generally a European image to which had been added garments, mannerisms and native color, since these new beings, who appeared to be cohabitating the world with them and who they had always thought of as being smaller, were recreated from the point of view of the known world. The fact that Columbus had taken a course to the West indicated that the Americans were westerners and, as such, the European had to accept the Indian as part of his cultural environment—as his mirror—and they were thus represented. With the discovery of the Americas, the two great islands of the world had been delineated and the indigenous American had been placed in the West.

On the other hand, the representations made of the indigenous Americans from the sixteenth century onward, whether natural or taken from literature, were realized as a form of imparting knowledge, the drawing becoming an instrument whereby that which was known was reproduced again and again while the unknown was pushed to the side, thus defining that which made the Americans equal to the Europeans and that which made them different.

Together with these drawings on physical knowledge, the literary descriptions delineated the personality of the American, establishing, over time, his humanity that of primal savagery both on a universal and, later, local level. Classified without any reference to a civilization, they were savages loose upon the earth who, when they could later be identified with towns and cities, with order and policing, became local savages, even "good savages."

For the indigenous Mexican, the savage personality was a recurrent theme throughout the centuries. In spite of the acknowledgment of their "civilized virtues" which, upon closer inspection, left the Europeans astonished, the theme of human sacrifice was always mentioned and represented and they never failed to address the cannibalism (in spite of the many apologists for this civilization) that bespoke their primitive condition. Typical of this genre are the drawings that decorate the 1555 map of the world by Grynaeus, and some of the drawings from *America,* by De Bry (1594), or in the allegory of *América,* from the beginning of the seventeenth century, by Crispijn de Passe, in which, in spite of the symbolic language, the allusion to cannibalism is excessively realistic.

From this point on, throughout the entire colonial period, the status of the indigenous American and his graphic representation were to suffer from a complete ambivalence which would appear to be linear were it not for the variations, depending on the author and the circumstances, in which he might experience a raising or lowering of category. Later, the indigenous Mexicans mutated from savages into barbarians, applying the cultural categories known by the Europeans. They were barbarians not only for being located on the fringes of the Empire, but because they were infidels. No longer being savages opened the possibility of their being Christianized. This rise in status came about thanks to, among other factors, the recognition that was given to the great city of Tenochtitlan and, consequently, to the Aztec civilization. In the case of the indigenous Mexicans, the standard against which they came to be measured was based on knowledge of the Aztec culture, effectively eliminating consideration of any of the other cultures in the area of New Spain.

In light of the promising riches to be gained from these cultures, the Spanish Crown opted for a simple extension of its feudal system and the indigenous Mexican, like all the other Americans, moved on to a new category: that of the vassal.

The representations of the indigenous Mexican made directly from models in the following centuries of colonialism remained a purely Spanish matter since foreigners were not looked on with approval in New Spain. Cases such as that of the Neapolitan, Giovanni Gemelli Carreri, who visited Mexico City during 1696-97 or the Englishman, Thomas Gage who, in his capacity as a Dominican, lived in the colony from 1625 to 1635, were practically the only exceptions. Thus, those in Europe continued to consume the Spanish chronicles, that is to say the internal literary sources, and no one was visually capturing the evolution of the inhabitants of these lands, not even local artists.

The artist working in New Spain, just as the foreign visitors before him, would habitually produce generic figures and, as had occurred with graphic expression elsewhere, it was difficult to distinguish features that spoke of any group apart from that which inhabited the center of the territory. Every portrayal of the inhabitants of these lands simply depicted "Indians" or vassals. In some cases, perhaps in a painting or a relief, one can find an indigenous subject who, by his dress, can be determined to belong to nobility, such as in the altarpiece in Xochimilco dat-

ANONYMOUS
WATER VENDOR IN MEXICO CITY [124]

ing from the sixteenth century. A more recent example is the portrait of doña Juana María Chimalpopoca that is found in the Museo Franz Mayer, in which one can begin to notice natural features that speak of true portraiture, but that until now had been the exception to the rule. In general, on the rare occasions in which colonial painting dealt with indigenous subjects, the personages were portrayed without the expression of physical features which might place them geographically, focusing only on the garments that indicated social standing. Even with the later emergence of the "caste paintings" in the eighteenth century, the models of social stratification continued to be illustrated. Of extraordinary interest is that some of series of caste

CLAUDIO LINATI
WATER VENDOR AND OTHER VENDORS [125]

paintings included, within their social scale of races and racial mixes, depictions of *mecos,* or savages. This indicates that the caste paintings can be considered, in spite of which has been previously noted, as a recognition on the part of the Europeans of the civility of these lands and their inhabitants, an admission that each civilization might have its inherent features, such as the savage, and that upon his incorporation into New Spain it was made implicit that he was a part of a compact group with its own characteristics, and that he might carry in his bosom something that marks the essence of his origins.[2]

In written descriptions we find an interesting phenomenon in the comparison of the indigenous peoples with the Greeks and Romans, something that was to occur repeatedly through-

out the centuries of Spanish rule although with differing explanations over the course of time. This comparison was never as clear in visual descriptions as it was in written accounts. These comparisons generally alternated between two ideas. On one hand, for example, Sahagún observed the gods of the indigenous civilizations with reference to those of the Romans. This comparison served only as a means of gaining knowledge, providing seeming identifications in the search to clarify the identity of each one of the gods. Others, such as Las Casas, approached the matter from the point of view of prestige, as was characteristic of classicism, drawing conclusions as to the virtues possessed by these gods in relation to their classical counterparts and finding them worthy of being defended and respected. The prestige granted in this manner seemed useful to the argument against the abuses suffered by the indigenous peoples at the hands of the Spanish, and the classical interrelationship formed part of a social philosophy in the humanist mold that, however, wasn't carried over into the plastic arts.

With the model of the indigenous Mexican fixed as that of a vassal and the only "direct" form of representation limited to local efforts during the colonial period, it was easy for the generic representation to mutate in other countries, becoming, in the seventeenth century, an allegory.[3] Both the Church and the State were extending their dominions and these representations found their way into the palaces and churches throughout the "humanized" parts of the world. The allegories regarding the New World, as well as other types of representations depicting the indigenous Americans in general and the indigenous Mexicans in particular, continued to preserve the primitive impression that had been established in the sixteenth century, an image that, in a certain sense, due to the ongoing racial as well as cultural intermixing, began to be increasingly divorced from reality. This distancing from the reality of the Mexican inhabitants was evident not only in the abstract and symbolic language of the various baroque allegories but also in the fact that nearly all of what was written during the period regarding the inhabitants was in reference to their historical past and the state in which they were discovered at the time of the conquest or, at the most, the state of a certain indigenous group described by way of justifying the work of the missionaries. Thus, the historical indigenous peoples were represented rather than the inhabitants of New Spain. This situation was to continue, with rare exceptions, until the eighteenth century. The native people who were described or illustrated no longer existed and, therefore, could not possibly be confronted, making an interesting justification for not having to change the model.

Due to the fact that the new allegorical image had nothing to do with reality, certain arbitrary changes could be made—if not to the essence of the image, at least to the details that would nevertheless transform the content that was being transmitted. In this manner, the nudity of the women became sensuality and in men it signified dignity and extreme heroism[4] since the fruit (the indigenous people) of the kingdom, under its imperial protector, could not be less than abundant and worthy of such paternity. One needs only look at the early engravings by Philippe Galle from 1581 or those by Maarten de Vos from 1594, passing

PHILLIPE RONDE
WATER VENDOR IN MEXICO CITY [126]

on to paintings by Rubens, Iñigo Jones, Paolo Farinati, Jan Van Kessel, Andrea del Pozzo, Luca Giordano, Charles Le Brun and on to the sculpture by Gianlorenzo Bernini until, in the eighteenth century, with Giovanni Battista Tiépolo's work in the Royal Palace in Madrid, or in that of Würzburg, to observe this process of carnival-like dignification, a process which was able to take place without any misgiving since none of the authors just cited had been to the Americas and had probably never seen an indigenous American.

In spite of the fact that absolutism sought through these allegories to create an image of power and glory, it is contrasted by the internal discussion in seventeenth-century Spain in which, according to official chronicles, there existed an open posture of hostility toward the natives, justifying the idea that the inferiority of the Indian required his subjugation. This argument had to be reinforced in the face of the criticism by foreigners as to the conquest and Spain's policies toward the indige-

pp. 164-165. JEAN-FRÉDÉRIC WALDECK
FIESTA DE LOS CINCO DÍAS [127]

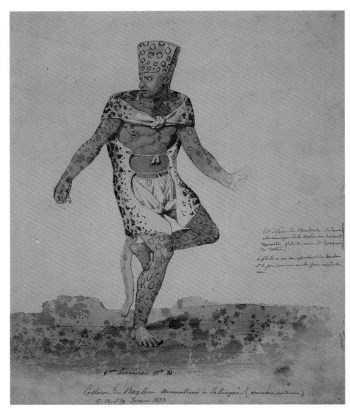

Jean-Frédéric Waldeck
DANCER DRESSED IN TIGER SKIN [129]

Claudio Linati
ATIGRADO DE CARNESTOLENDAS AT PALENQUE [128]

Jean-Frédéric Waldeck
MECAPALERO [130]

nous people.[5] This situation provoked an unforeseen change in the description of the native populace: some historians such as Antonio Solis exaggerated the ferocity and valor of the indigenous in order to extol the heroism of Cortés and the bravery of the Spanish soldiers in defending themselves, thus granting the Aztec natives the virtues necessary to convert them into worthy adversaries relative to the Spanish. The natives were depicted in this new light in the engravings by Jacob Schÿnvoet that were contained in the publication *Historia...,* by Solis, in its English edition of 1724, as well as those by José Ximeno for the edition published in Madrid, in 1784. It is interesting that the visual language, whether in mural allegories or in the engravings for books, glorifies while the text vilifies.

At the same time as the indigenous people were converted into allegory, during the seventeenth and part of the eighteenth centuries, their culture was again compared by writers to the classical world, but this time in terms of the pride in possessing an antiquity, some authors boldly suggesting that both ancient cultures, the classical as well as the pre-Hispanic, had drunk from the same fountain. This marked the beginning of what would later develop into the Creole's pride in possessing an antiquity of his own.

After their ascendancy to the highest rungs of respect within the palaces and churches, where images of the indigenous were on a par with their counterparts from other continents, due to their representation as fierce and valiant warriors or the establishment of their relationship to the ancient Greeks and Romans, the fall from favor was to be brutal when the "Dispute over the New World" was initiated. This eighteenth-century controversy, carried on by a series of "enlightened" personalities and headed by Buffon, Raynal, De Pauw and, later, Robertson, tirelessly vilified the New World with accusations that everything good that was introduced there was doomed to decay and degeneration, equal to that in which the inhabitants of the land were to be found. The old engravings of cannibalism and social disorder were re-utilized in the service of this slanderous propaganda, which had much to do with the backlash against the Spaniards.

A response was not long in coming. People of both the Old and New Worlds, including the Jesuits who had been expelled from New Spain and now lived in Italy, were to become involved in the evolving picture of this land. However, in terms of illustrations and images, even those that Clavijero utilized in his *Historia Antigua de México* (Ancient History of Mexico), carried on

with the same interpretation of indigenous history, in the hope that a glorious past would vindicate the present. It seemed that the misery and poverty of the inhabitants of these lands was such that its current image would not serve to convince anyone of what had once been; rather, the place would be shunned. The absence of modern images, that could be considered defamatory in light of the current conditions facing the native inhabitants, was to last until the voyage by von Humboldt.

Von Humboldt, being both a modern scientist and a foreigner, was interested in what was occurring in the present and the degree to which advances had been made in these lands, recording his findings in an outstanding body of work. He also possessed a refined human sense that permitted him insight and understanding as to the state in which he found the spirit of the residents of New Spain in view of the European attacks, leading him to criticize those implicated in the Dispute and sympathize with those who wrote only about ancient history. To the first group he responded: "It is worth noting how the mestizos and the Indians, employed in the carrying of ore on their shoulders and who have been given the name *tenateros*, are carrying loads of from 225 to 350 pounds for periods of six hours, in high temperatures, and climbing up eight or ten times in a row without a rest, stairways of 1800 steps. The sight of these laborious and robust men would have been able to change the opinions of the Reynals, the Pauws and the great number of authors, otherwise estimable, who have so much declaimed about the degeneration of our species in the torrid zone."[6] To the second group he directed: "How, then, can one judge from these miserable remains that which was once a powerful people, and the degree of culture they had achieved between the twelfth and sixteenth centuries and, much less, the intellectual progress which can be perceived? If one day nothing were to remain of the French or German nation but the poor of the countryside, could it be read from their physiognomy that they were part of a people that had produced men such as Descartes, Clairaut, Kepler and Leibnitz?"[7] In this way von Humboldt, in spite of the fact that he himself continually spoke from the point of view of a scientist on the situation of the contemporary natives, justified an entire literature that spoke of the indigenous past, evading its current situation and its graphic image. The expelled Jesuits, as well as von Humboldt, in their capacity as enlightened men, knew the cause of the situation: the lack of freedom that had impeded the natives in a proper development. It is significant that the

Laguna y canal de Texcoco.

A la amable y virtuosa Srita Joaquina de la Cortina dedica, su atento amigo y servidor Pelegrín Clavé

Méjico 11 Abril de 1850.

PELEGRÍN CLAVÉ
LAKE AND CANAL AT TEXCOCO [131]

publication of the extensive writings by von Humboldt coincided with the freedom movements in the Americas, proof that his accounts captured a situation that was both politically and socially unbearable for any longer.

Once independence had been achieved, the situation changed markedly. Permission for entry by foreign travelers became common and not limited to just a select few. Descriptions of these new countries filled the pages of diaries and memoirs, the inexhaustible curiosity about that which Spain had so jealously guarded was sated and new images of the inhabitants of these lands began to be diffused.

Why, one might ask, only now and within the span of just a few years did the graphic images multiply and spread so? Had the material and moral poverty of the indigenous peoples instantly mutated so as to now be so proudly presented? It is evident that, materially, this was not so, but that their worth or repre-

sentative status had radically changed. No longer vassals, much less abstract allegories or proof of the degeneration of the human species in specific regions, or even the historical model that had been the only dignified representation, now the inhabitants of these lands could be represented as free men, and to this new status could also be added another identity, that of being Mexican.

Two things resulted from this new double status. Their new position as free men made them profoundly attractive to travelers who, as children of the Enlightenment and the French Revolution, perceived this state to be the essential element. As Mexicans and as having formed a new country, an extra connotation was added that was significant for the Europeans who were living through revolutions of nationalistic origins during the mid-eighteenth century. In becoming free men with a new nationality, they formed part of the amalgam of different populations

DANIEL THOMAS EGERTON
ANGELS WITH SYMBOLS OF THE PASSION [132]

DANIEL THOMAS EGERTON
CHRIST CARRYING THE CROSS WITH THE VIRGIN BEHIND [133]

that had satisfied, in great measure, the incipient nationalism that was emerging in Europe.

The curiosity surrounding these people was, therefore, multifaceted. The Europeans were motivated by the surroundings, the new flora and fauna, the customs, etc., as well as the living laboratory in which they could observe the direction that the new libertarian and nationalistic ideals would take in the hands of nineteenth-century man. Thus, the traveler-artist captured not only the indigenous people, as had always been done, but also the mestizo, the Creole and whomever else he found to be inhabiting these lands. Illustration was not limited to one sector of the population that sought recognition or vindication. Rather, it encompassed all the social, racial, political and economic groups pertaining to this new nationality and granted unto each one its own ethnic features, illustration in a sense becoming as varied as the inhabitants.

We can distinguish two forms of representation of Mexico's inhabitants in the nineteenth century: that which isolated and described the subject and that which placed the subject within a landscape or a narrative description. Both forms had been utilized earlier, the former during the sixteenth century, when a few draftsmen had been fortunate enough to have before them a native of these lands and the latter at various times throughout the three centuries of the Kingdom of New Spain, generally within the context of historical narrative. The incorporation of the landscape was a response to new motivations and is discussed in other sections of this catalog.

The differences between the images from the nineteenth century and those of earlier times was that now the traveler had come face to face with the subject of his portrait and, in the case of the narrative image, the setting was folkloric rather than historical, thus forming part of the new picturesque and nationalistic currents of European romanticism.

In order to understand the artist who abstracted and isolated his subject and portrayed him with a series of characteristics of ethnicity and dress, neither curiosity nor the search for romantic exoticism nor the existence of a scientific stance provide sufficient explanation. Although it is evident that many of the travelers that came to Mexico were looking for images to complement works of a scientific nature and that many were even sponsored by men such as von Humboldt, the depiction of subjects with their particular features, in their own clothes and placed within a given framework, implied a necessary reflection on man in general since one such in particular was to be described. The study and depiction of man carried out by the traveler-artists in the nineteenth century did not lie far from a general reflection, which we could consider anthropological, that was occurring at the time.

Beginning with the Enlightenment, and even more so during the nineteenth century, man's accomplishments were being reappraised in the light of reason. In the same way, reflection on man and his relationship with his surroundings, as well as his manner of transforming them, were subjects that occupied the minds of everyone interested in culture including, of course,

DANIEL THOMAS EGERTON
SOLDIERS AND TABOR [134]

DANIEL THOMAS EGERTON
PILATE [135]

many of these travelers. The mere act of leaving one's circle in order to travel to and observe another environment demonstrated that they were neither naive nor indifferent. The undertaking of the voyage meant coming into contact with the "others," obliging the careful analysis of new situations, as well as the description, evaluation and compilation of data that many of the travelers carried out. Such undertakings should be considered within the larger context of the general discussion taking place relative to man and his development. In fact, many of the travelers were charged with the compilation of data and the furnishing of examples that would illustrate the origins, institutions and significance of other societies.

The scientific expeditions mounted during the eighteenth century (which are discussed in another essay within this catalog) supplanted, in great part, the labor of individual travelers, as they were organized undertakings with specific goals. However, the work of the lone traveler cannot be seen as diminished in that his mobility and freedom provided him with the possibility of assembling data that not even the most organized scientist who formed part of an expedition could possibly acquire, an acknowledgment that von Humboldt reiterated as to the work by these spirited adventurers.

In a sense, these independent and avant-garde travelers were doing no more with their drawings than was being undertaken at the desks of the European men of science, which was the interpretation of data that the region provided, thus gaining a greater perspective on man in general. The desire that such data

become useful had provoked the publication of such works as *L'Instruction generale aux voyageurs* (General Instructions to Voyagers), elaborated by the Société Ethnologique of Paris which had been founded in 1839. Societies such as this began to provide grants, curiously, in the beginning for travelers and only later for government officials. Likewise, in 1843, England founded an Ethnological Society which also published a guide for working in the field. In Germany, in 1869, the Gesellschaft für Anthropologie, Ethnologie und Urgeschichte was founded while in 1842, the American Ethnological Society had been founded in the United States. The creation of these societies and others exemplifies the awakening interest in the reflection on man, not only within the philosophical context that had existed earlier but also within the realm of science. At the same time, driven by scientists interested in the new sciences, chairs in anthropology and ethnology began to be created in the universities, such as in Paris, in 1855. It was evident that with all this latent interest in the condition of man and his societies, the descriptions provided by the travelers needed to change their focus from the curious, strange and, as yet, uncommon to culturally valid descriptions.[8]

In the nascent anthropology of the nineteenth century, the idea that was to remain dominant until at least the last decade of the century was that known generically as the "comparative method," from which developed a concept of evolution. This wasn't a new method, yet it now began to take on a scientific air and became governed by laws and, although not explicitly outlined in any text until the point at which it became criticized

JOHANN SALOMON HEGI
INTERIOR OF A HOME IN ELOTEPEC. MAKING TORTILLAS [136]

and, finally, displaced, it explained in a concise manner the idea of the development of man. According to this theory, mankind had passed from savagery through barbarism to civilization and these three stages were inarguably linked in a sequence of natural progression in the same direction. All human groups had followed the same path in a parallel and regular manner. Cultural evolution took place in a series of stages, the first several of which could be documented with ethnographic data collected from within the society under study, in whatever state of evolution, or through data provided by travelers from other societies. The later stages could be analyzed via historical data that was interconnected with the European institutions of the nineteenth century.[9]

An element of great importance in the development of this theory was the existence of "survivors." These were identified as the institutions which had carried over from one stage to another and that could provide evidence as to the origin of the previous stage. Another supposed basic element was that of the "physical unity" of humanity. The unity of human nature explained the fact that even in populations that were geographically distant from each other, some of the same customs could be observed. The tendency was, especially among the later adherents to the comparative school, to interpret cultural similarities in terms of independent parallel development rather than as a result of a historical process of diffusion, which was the school of thought which became predominant in later years, finally supplanting the theories of the comparative method.

Such ideas found easy acceptance since, in conformity with the mind-set of the "enlightened" man of the eighteenth century, the encounter with the New World presented not only landscapes, animals and an atmosphere which might have been those of Europe in its infancy but also the very important reflec-

tion that, upon describing the inhabitants of the Americas, they found that they were describing themselves, exactly as Todorov had described the encounter with "otherness" by saying, "the *others* are *now* as *we* were *before.*" [10]

The ideas of liberty and equality that emanated from the French Revolution infused the painter and the draftsman with a respect for representation that was individualized, specific, faithful and objective as to the inhabitants of a new nation. Of equal importance was their depiction as a whole, with all their varied ethnicity, customs, rituals, class distinctions, etc., and not merely a select group or stratum. The scientific approach isolated humans, in a certain sense, as if they were specimens to be studied objectively and by means of direct observation of the model.

The new theories of ethnology and anthropology placed the inhabitants of the American continent within their own history, as a living example of their past. Upon examining drawings such as those mentioned at the beginning of this arti-

cle, we can see the desire on the part of Waldeck to individualize his portraiture and, thus, escape the generalizations that had been produced before; hence, his inclusion of the name and age of his subject. At the same time we can observe the scientific keenness for classification in some of his other plates, such as the one in which he places a skull, a sculpture of a head from the ruins at Palenque and various heads of contemporary men and women, the women being depicted with careful attention to their particular style of knotting or coiling their hair at the back. The result is not only a specific cranial typology but an examination of the ritual deformation typical of the region's past.

In other plates, also from Palenque, he drew the inhabitants with a certain Apollonian touch that reminds us of classical sculpture. This is particularly evident in the drawing on page 230 of his album, now found in the Newberry Library, in which a masculine figure is supporting on his shoulders what appears to be an architectural grotesque from the Palenque ruins. His

Jean-Frédéric Waldeck
NICTE-TAC, NUDE YOUNG LACANDON GIRL [138]

Jean-Frédéric Waldeck
AZTEC PRINCESS [139]

left arm is curved above his head in order to grasp the upper part of the mask, framing the face. His right hand is placed on his hip and the left foot is firmly planted, creating an axis of support which contrasts with the right foot, which is extended behind him and seems to be barely touching the ground. Such details create an image that is strongly reminiscent of the classical figures by Praxiteles. This image, along with many others executed by travelers, represents the encounter between modern man and that which forms his past, the classical world, inaugurating a new manner in which to make comparisons with classical antiquity. Any European who was to see this image, filled with dignity and elegance, could proudly exclaim: "This is how we were! Surely the men of our classical past were like this!"

Elsewhere in this same album are two images very similar to each other. In one, a nude woman is seated on a rock and, in the other, a woman is seen among the ruins of a pre-Hispanic palace, where she approaches a fountain of water. Both images are drawn according to what we might consider canons of neoclassicism in the style of David or Ingres. We know for certain that Waldeck had contact with this school and the fact that he painted an indigenous woman from the Palenque region with such characteristics of form, shadowing, proportion, etc., mark his connection to this artistic style, even more so when this plate is compared to Ingres' famous work, *The Fountain*. Beyond simply signifying his artistic creed, the work demonstrates that Waldeck was steeped in neoclassicism, believing that the recovery of the values of Antiquity could achieve bliss in a state of primitive purity, as well as believing in a utopian world, in a true Arcadia that was within reach. It was here that Waldeck's neoclassical dream seemed to materialize, in a trace of the past that could be used to construct a future. Near a fountain—symbolic of purity, birth and origin—he places an indigenous Mexican whose characteristics are represented in the neoclassical style, sending the message that "this is how we were," and at the same time suggesting what could be created in the New World based on the principles of Antiquity. Nothing could be more neoclassical and revolutionary than this. Certainly this is an image of what the mind can make of reality, perhaps indicating the "how it should be" and in doing so becoming a political thought. For the neoclassicists, Waldeck was evidently providing a classical model with this image, assuming an ethical-ideological character that is identified with the ideal solution to the conflict of liberty, necessity and duty.

With the same scientific and attentive stance, as witness to the "present antiquity," he painted his observation (dated 1832, in Palenque) of a ritual involving the *caballeros jaguares* (jaguar noblemen), a scene which he carefully described and annotated as to the characters who participated as well as the surroundings in which the action took place. In another work he isolated one of the *caballeros*, endowing him with majestic posturing and gestures, a manifestation of dignity that is comparable to the works by David and which would make anyone proud who could claim him as an ancestor.

Although the nascent anthropological theories in combination with a neoclassical mind-set resulted in Europe's recognizing itself in the New World, other elements such as narration, a nationalistic sense, the values of the local colors in distinguishing a personality, and the advances in the study of the geographical territory in union with its inhabitants provided another type of representation that influenced the increased value placed on genre painting in Europe. In this type of genre representation the subjects may be isolated (capturing genre as well as the anthropological past) or may be placed within a landscape (of great interest to the nineteenth-century traveler-artist). In the latter example, in spite of the combination of man and geography (significant in that at this time the universities in Europe were beginning to lend importance to the concept of "human" geography), the scenes remain genre studies in that human types and related elements are superimposed on the surroundings or exist only as depictions of the human subjects represented within, that is, when the human figure is neither part of the landscape nor human filler for the geography.

The genre scenes captured by the travelers are varied even though the subjects and the landscapes are often repeated, perhaps because the artists were attracted by the sharp contrasts to those found in Europe. The coloring of the works also varied, the result of attempts to represent the diversity and originality of the peoples depicted. William Bullock's work, *Hog Skin for Holding Pulque*, now found in the British Museum, is an example of the many depictions of the characters who transported pulque in wineskins. Countless depictions of water vendors appear, such as those by Pingret, as well as the market scenes that had so attracted von Humboldt. On viewing these distinctive characters from nineteenth-century Mexico, we are reminded that the travelers belonged to a generation that had lived through the nationalistic wars in Europe and, following in the footsteps of writers such as Herder, were sensitive to any regional or nationalistic characteristic and, therefore, found any representation of such to be significant.

An important feature of this nationalism was the attention given to scenes in which religious themes were predom-

EDOUARD PINGRET
FRUIT WATER STAND [142]

inant. Realism and precision mark works such as that by Waldeck of the interior of a humble home in which the Virgin of Guadalupe, Christ and two religious engravings dominate the image. Egerton captured Holy Week processions in which each of the participants was depicted with attention to his distinctive dress. It is evident that these scenes attracted the travelers in the same way that they had impressed von Humboldt who wrote: "The religious festivities, the fireworks that accompany them, and the processions that mix dance and extravagant costumes are, for the common Indian people, a rich source of amusement. It is in these festivities that they display their national character as much as their individuality."

As to the scenes in which folkloric subjects are set within a landscape, outstanding are those which possess a theme (that is, when the composition makes evident certain attitudes or actions on the part of the subjects) which lends an intensity to the whole that goes beyond a simple descriptive quality. On some occasions the author has not left us any clue as to the interpretation of the theme, yet the intensity remains. One such example is the *Pico de Orizaba*, by J.M. Rugendas, in which, despite its straightforward descriptive title, our interest in the landscape is supplanted by the scene which is unfolding. We see a multitude of villagers dressed in a variety of styles under the shade of a tree, gathered around a person dressed in black and wearing a straw hat. In his hands he holds what appears to be an idol. Nearby is what appears to be a recent excavation (archaeological?). A man on horseback, evidently of a different social class, approaches the group. What is Rugendas narrating here? We aren't sure. Perhaps the man at the center of the group is speaking to them about the nature of their past as represented in the stone fragments. Or is he a missionary? In spite of our lack of

understanding, the fact that "something" is happening grants a certain vitality to what might have been a mere descriptive landscape of a volcanic peak. We find the same situation in another of Rugendas' works, this one titled *Marktszene in Mexiko*, now found in the Hamburger Kunsthalle, in which a group is gathered around a white man who is conversing or exchanging something with a tall indigenous man. Surrounding this scene is a representation of society in general, clerics and civilians of every social class, who are seen milling around a market stall. The coloring is similar to the tones utilized by other European travelers. What is going on in these scenes? Obviously it is difficult to understand, but they provide an excellent representation of the society at the time and the enigma of the narration at least forces us to focus more closely on the characters who are depicted.

Doubtless, through this process the Mexicans discovered their landscapes and their surroundings, as well as their value, with the help of the traveler, just as a new nation recognized its individuality as captured in these images executed by foreigners. It was they who isolated the personage in order to achieve a more finished model of his autonomous personality and who blended both customs and geography in their paintings. Through these works the Mexican was, for the first time, able to see himself as he was: a heterogeneous, mestizo mix of many elements. Not just a segment was depicted, as had earlier been done with the indigenous, but the mixture of great diversity that made up a new whole. Paradoxically, the Europeans looked at the inhabitants of the New World as a mirror of their own identity and diversity, yet they were the ones who, in turn, effected the new image of the Americas.

Johann Moritz Rugendas
pico de orizaba [144]

p. 182. Jean-Frédéric Waldeck
reconstrucción ideal de una
ceremonia (detail) [145]

THE ANTIQUARIAN THEME AMONG THE TRAVELER-PAINTERS

ELENA ISABEL ESTRADA DE GERLERO

Beginning with Mexico's independence in 1821, a spirit of opening prevailed in which politicians, such as the Minister of Internal and External Relations, Lucas Alamán, in 1823, and, a bit later, the Oaxacan deputy Carlos María Bustamante, headed the group that attempted to present unto other nations the roots of Mexico's splendid antiquity as one of the foundations of solidity on which the institutions of the new country should be appraised. Undoubtedly, "enlightened" Bourbon reformist policy, initiated during the reign of Charles III, had, as one of its goals, to face and rebut the detractors of Spain, demonstrating to them certain expressions of the reality of her dominions. Part of this reform became evident in the fomentation of research and antiquarian collection, consolidated by the previous record of Charles III and his sponsorship of the excavations at Pompeii and Herculaneum.

If in Spain, Hispanic-Roman antiquity went hand in hand with the rebirth of "good taste" proclaimed in the neoclassical ideals of the Real Academia de San Fernando and disseminated, by means of the twenty volumes of the *Viage de España* (Voyage from Spain), by Antonio Ponz (1772-1792), throughout New Spain the tradition of the pre-Columbian civilizations, although aesthetically foreign to the classical model, represented a glorious past that not even Madrid itself could deny. What is more, it was the Crown, via the Supremo Consejo de Indias (Supreme Council of the Indies), and its official chronicler Juan Bautista Muñoz, that initiated the systematic fomentation of antiquarian research in New Spain. The repercussions of the Crown's cultural policy in these lands were to, among other things, present the antiquarian vestiges as evidence of the grandeur of many of the indigenous American cultures prior to the Conquest, placing them on a par with the ancient civilizations of the West. Thus, the Spanish scientist Antonio de Ulloa, supported by the Minister of the Indies, José de Gálvez, was to include a meticulous antiquarian section in his questionnaire for *Relaciones Científicas de la Nueva España* (Scientific Accounts from New Spain) of 1777.[1]

From early on, it was normal for many of the questionnaires from the Supremo Consejo de Indias to require, as an indispensable part of the methodology, the inclusion of faithful drawings to complement the explanations, in addition to duplicate or even triplicate reports of the complete results. It is for this reason, in great part, that more than one version of these reports have been located, on various occasions, in different repositories. During the period of the Enlightenment, the drawing and the engraving had been turned into indispensable tools for the diffusion of the sciences and the arts.

This questionnaire had direct and indirect repercussions on a great quantity of the reports on the material vestiges of American antiquities, among which the outstanding were those by José Antonio Calderón (1784), the architect Bernasconi (1786) and Antonio del Río (1787), which were undertaken at Palenque, in Guatemala. The latter two efforts included an abundance of architectural and sculptural drawings. The same holds true of the drawings of the site at Mitla by the architect for the Real Academia de San Carlos, Luis de Martín; the studies of Xochicalco by José Antonio Alzate—made known in Europe, together with the studies on Papantla, by P. Márquez, in 1804; the text, illustrated with engravings by Antonio León y Gama on the colossal sculptures discovered in Mexico City's central plaza, in 1790; and, finally, the monumental work by the retired

Flemish military officer Guillermo Dupaix who in his tireless antiquarian travels covered an enormous expanse of New Spain after his arrival in 1790, including a trip to Palenque during the third phase of the Royal Expedition (1805-1809), in addition to many other prior reports on sites of lesser importance that provided the model for much of the research mentioned.

This "enlightened" spirit did not die with Mexico's independence. Rather, in great measure, it continued well beyond it. For his part, the *Essai politique sur le royaume de la Nouvelle Espagne...* (Political Essay on the Kingdom of New Spain...) of 1811, by the German scientist Alexander von Humboldt, was pivotal in opening the eyes of Europeans to the enormous cultural, economic and commercial potential of this part of the Americas. Unfortunately, they converted it into a sort of private domain for the acquisition, licit or illicit, of antiquarian treasures. Other works by von Humboldt also stimulated an interest in New Spain among the Europeans, particularly his *Vues de Cordillères et Monumens de peuples indigenes de L'Amérique* (Views of the Mountain Ranges and Monuments of the Indigenous Peoples of America), illustrated with engravings of antiquarian drawings provided by Martín, Dupaix and Castañeda, among others. These graphic representations of antiquarian vestiges profoundly impressed the Europeans and spurred the arrival of throngs of traveler-painters after 1823. Alexander von Humboldt even supported some of them, such as Carl Nebel and Johann Moritz Rugendas, in their artistic projects of registry.

It is necessary, however, to underline that as much as von Humboldt saw the antiquities of the Americas as simply a tool for history, by contrast, some of the "enlightened" colonists that he met during his stay in Mexico in 1803, as well as other "enlightened" Mexicans from the first decade after the birth of independence, appreciated the objects for their unquestionable artistic value[2] and wanted that they be considered incontestable proof in the "defense of America" against its European detractors.

Just after the fall of the ephemeral Mexican Empire of Agustín Iturbide, Lucas Alamán, in his annual reports to the Congress (1823, 1825, 1830, 1831 and 1832), stood firm on the necessity of implementing indispensable reforms, with a series of initiatives relative to the restructuring of education through the Academia de las Nobles Artes, "the fountain of the good taste of our nation," as well as the Botanical Garden, the Archivos del Virreinato (Viceregal Archives), and the antiquities of the Museo Nacional, which represented an undoubted possibility of prosperity and progress for the country.[3]

As to concern for the antiquities, the first report of 1823 made clear the recent and deplorable disappearance of invaluable documents, the great part of them belonging to the Boturini Collection, noting the urgent need to gather them into a library, and properly catalog them, within the Museo Nacional. This was to finally be established in 1825, under the direction of Ignacio Icaza. Luciano Castañeda, who had earlier collaborated with Guillermo Dupaix on the Royal Antiquarian Expedition sponsored by Charles IV (1805-1809), worked in the library as official draftsman. As an important feature of this cultural policy, Lucas Alamán proposed the protection and publication, as soon as possible, of the library's collection of drawings. Toward

1831, the initiatives continued to be discussed. In the meantime, however, the Museo Nacional had been considerably increasing its collection, due not only to the fortuitous discovery of many pieces during excavations for new construction but also because various collections had been donated and another important one purchased. At this point, a board of directors for the museum was established, with Lucas Alamán as president, and an interest was re-ignited for a new and exhaustive expedition to the ruins at Palenque, which was to be directed by Frédéric Waldeck.[4]

For his part, Carlos María Bustamante published an annotated second edition of the work by León y Gama of 1794, *Descripción histórica y cronológica de las dos piedras que en ocasión del empedrado que se está formando en la plaza principal de México, se hallaron en ella el año de 1790* (Historical and Chronological Description of the Two Stones Found during the Paving of the Principal Plaza of Mexico City in the Year 1790), which he felt compelled to dedicate to Lucas Alamán, in 1832. The political ambitions of this edition were certain as, with it, Bustamante hoped to accentuate the memory of the founder of the Museo Nacional. Likewise, in 1828, Bustamante presented before the Congress the initiative for a law of patrimonial protection, deploring the antiquarian plundering that Mexico had suffered at the hands of pillaging foreigners and which continued toward 1836 due to the ease in the corrupting of minor officials in a time of many political and social difficulties:

Since the opening of our ports to free trade with Europe, it has been noted on the part of many of these travelers, a consistent dedication to the study of our History, the seeking out of our origins, the gathering of the wretched remains of what had been our antiquities, the copying of our vistas, and the prodigal examination of the celebrated ruins at Palenque, Mictlan, Xochicalco, Caverna de Cacahuamilpa, Uxmal in Yucatán, and other objects that capture curiosity of the lovers of the arts. They have captured views of Puebla, Mexico City, the Popocatepetl volcano, to where they have conducted expeditions in order to measure its height, as well as many magnificent, towering mountains. They have purchased the rarest productions of the three kingdoms, with which to enrich their cabinets ... a multitude of ancient paintings, though from the houses of individuals that the majority of people viewed, while not with disdain, at least with indifference, when met by the eyes of the intelligent they are marvelous works of the

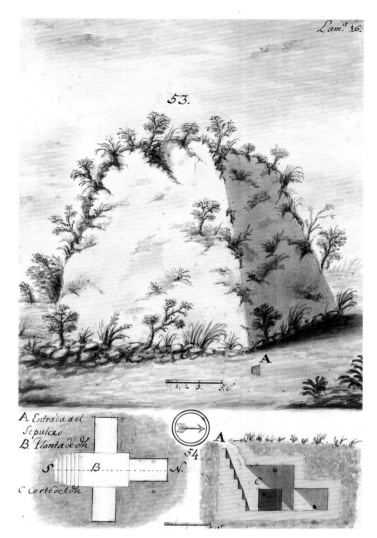

LUCIANO CASTAÑEDA / GUILLERMO DUPAIX
PYRAMID, PLAN AND CROSS SECTION [147]

painting of the best professors of Europe of the preceding centuries; but, the most sensitive is, that they have taken a portion of the maps of Mexican antiquity, made of maguey paper, palm paper or on cotton mantas, onto which was consigned the true ancient History, which were its backup ... [for] they have taken manuscripts stolen from archives or that have been cheaply sold. This sacking and pillage has not been able to be impeded by the Ley del Soberano Congreso (Law of the Sovereign Congress), initiated by me, and that has not been applied because the gold which has been paid ... holds greater power than the laws and the love of country.[5]

Bustamante added that at the Archivo de la Audiencia de México, the paper—which is to say, the valuable manuscripts—had

Luciano Castañeda / Guillermo Dupaix
relief at xochicalco [148]

Jean-Frédéric Waldeck
sketch of the pyramid at xochicalco [149]

JEAN-FRÉDÉRIC WALDECK
RECONSTRUCCIÓN IDEAL DE UNA CEREMONIA [150]

been frequently sold to makers of fireworks, shopkeepers and druggists, even though don Ignacio Cubas, the archive's director and longtime member of the Junta de Antigüedades para la Real Expedición (Council on Antiquities for the Royal Expedition), had defended the works as much as possible,[6] this during a period of "enlightened" longings yet one pressed by anarchy, hunger and constant epidemics.

It is quite possible that Bustamante's initiative derived from a Royal Order similar to that from the period of Charles III, dated October of 1779, published and precisely annotated by Antonio Ponz, whose itineraries of artistic and antiquarian registry in Spain were widely known in the Americas. Ponz commented on the pillage suffered by Seville at the hands of foreign buyers:

> With the same motive as the Italians, many Flemish houses established themselves in Seville so that the paintings they brought, and continued to receive from their countries, filled Seville with beautiful Italian and Flemish paintings, from the year 1560 until 1660, causing the period to come to be called the century of Fine Arts, of which remain precious few signs in private homes and in churches, with the feeling that nearly everything has been removed during the present century to England, Germany, Holland, Italy, along with much of the production of such Sevillians as Murillo, Velázquez, etc.[7]

In such a way that:

> In order to impede that from today onward the paintings of the Kingdom are plundered by foreigners, Paintings by the hand of authors no longer living, the King ordered me—as Floridablanca noted—to write to the Syndic of Seville, D. Francisco Domenzain the letter whose contents I am going to copy for His Highness. It has come to the notice of the King our Lord, that some foreigners are buying in Seville all the paintings that they can by Bartolomé Murillo, and by other celebrated painters, to remove them

187

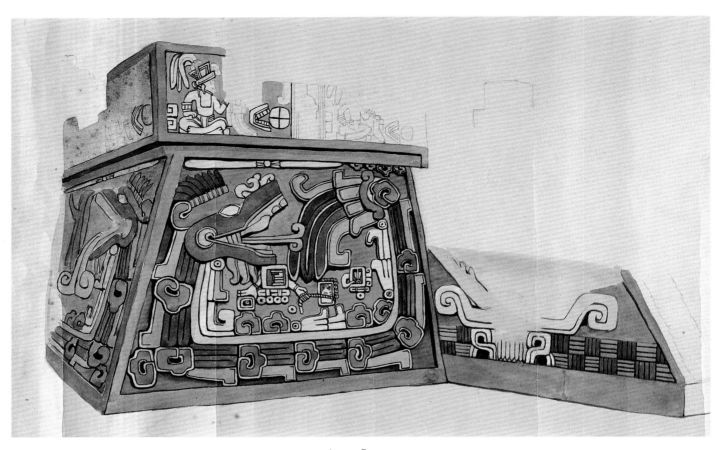

ADELA BRETON
STUDY OF THE RELIEF WORK AT XOCHICALCO [151]

JEAN-FRÉDÉRIC WALDECK
THE PYRAMID AT XOCHICALCO [152]

PÁL ROSTI
XOCHICALCO [153]

from the Kingdom under cover or surreptitiously against the order of His Majesty on the subject in view of the inveterate and pernicious abuse that was experienced in the sacking of Spain. The tarnishing and detriment that resulted from it as to the concept of instruction, and good taste of the same, motivated this just resolution by the King, who so providently and generously promotes the Fine Arts.[8]

It is justly within the framework mentioned earlier by Carlos María Bustamante that this brief outline is inserted relative to the traveler-painters that visited Mexico and made the antiquities one, but doubtless not the only, of the important themes of their work. Efforts that were not limited to drawing, painting or lithographing them—frequently with the help of tools

like cameras lucida and cameras obscura[9]—but, in many cases, to acquiring them by any means at their disposal. For this reason, nearly all of the traveler-painters were also considered among the foreign collectors and speculators, it being impossible to divorce one occupation from another: the zeal to possess pre-Columbian pieces, to sell them with a certain keenness for profit, and to exchange them among each other to be translated to paper. Likewise, it is difficult to present these painters of greatly varying artistic aptitudes in terms of only one of their special inclinations toward portraiture, decoration, scenography, "picturesque-ism," genre painting, landscapes, cartography or antiquities. The great majority of them, in accordance with their imperative and undeferable economic urgencies, recorded what they perceived of Mexican reality, indistinguishably, in all

BARON DE COURCY
THE RUINS AT XOCHICALCO [154]

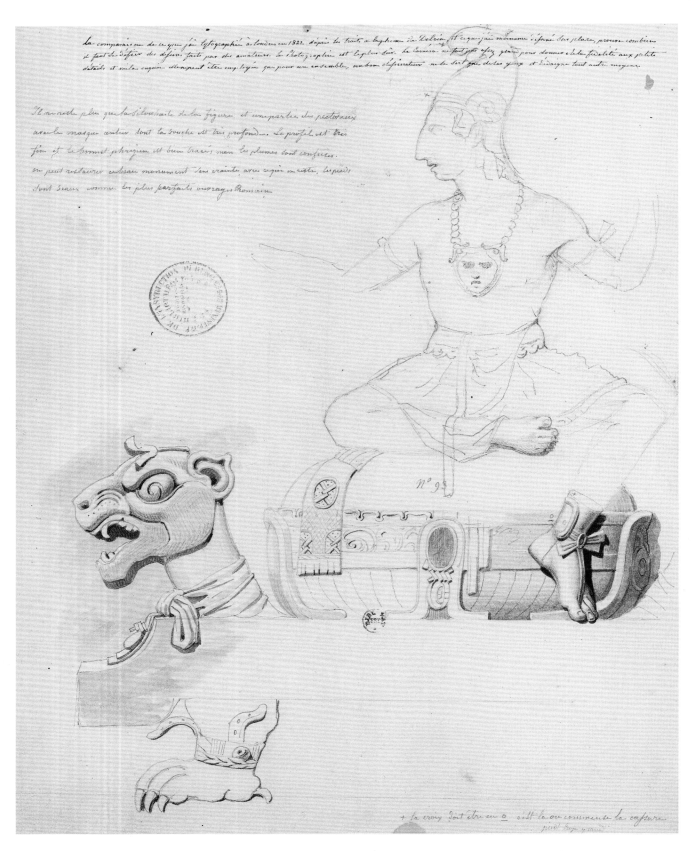

JEAN-FRÉDÉRIC WALDECK

PALENQUE, STUDY OF A RELIEF OF A SEATED DEITY [155]

JEAN-FRÉDÉRIC WALDECK
PALENQUE. VIEW OF A FAÇADE OF A PALACE [156]

MAXIMILIAN FRANCK
JARRÓN DE ARCILLA [157]

of these mediums. The traveler-artists obtained, within some of these genres, either private or governmental sponsorship, or else turned to productions popular with local or foreign investors, to pay for their most ambitious projects. Additionally, on occasion they would collaborate on a project.

The beginning of 1823 marked the arrival of two of the initial visitors, William Bullock and his son. The first was a miner and businessman who dabbled in antiquities, who wrote *Six Months' Residence and Travels in Mexico...*, and the second a not very deft draftsman, who illustrated the text with a certain profusion and who years later died in this country of yellow fever. This publication included, among many others, three antiquarian plates of vistas of Teotihuacan and various figures of idols. Bullock's project to obtain support from Lucas Alamán in publicizing the virtues of Mexico in London, with the exhibition at the Egyptian Hall in Piccadilly, in 1824, was successful in that the Mexican government not only lent him manuscripts from the Boturini Collection and original pieces, but also authorized him to make molds of the Aztec Calendar and the Sacrificial Stone. He also

copied many of the plates that Luciano Castañeda had elaborated for the Real Expedición Anticuaria conducted with Guillermo Dupaix, which were still to be found in the Real Seminario de Minería where they had been left the year before by Fausto de Elhuyar, executor of the Flemish antiquarian's estate. Bullock had the opportunity of meeting Castañeda personally and affirmed that he possessed various of the original drawings from the expedition.[10]

The arrival in Mexico of the draftsman and lithographer Claudio Linati, in 1826, marked the introduction of a new form of graphic impression that facilitated the reproduction of a series of a drawing. His arrival had been sponsored by the innovative spirit of Lucas Alamán, who allowed him to install his presses at the Ministry of Relations. Linati's work is principally known through his *Costumes Civils, Militaires et Religieux du Mexique* (Civil, Military and Religious Dress from Mexico), printed in Brussels by Jobard, in 1828, the result of his journeys through diverse parts of Mexico. Contained within the work, plate no. 29, *Muchacha de Palenque* (Girl from Palenque), has as its backdrop a stepped pyramid. In the same way, the corresponding explanation puts in evidence the heated topic that Palenque was within the gatherings of the day, inasmuch as Linati speaks with familiarity of that which at the time was being argued with relation to the origins of American man and of that which the "learned" were lucubrating on the subject of this civilization, among them Latour-Allard, of whom we shall speak a few paragraphs further on. Frédéric Waldeck was to establish a solid friendship with him and later, upon Linati's departure from the country in 1827, to utilize his presses in conjunction with his fellow Frenchman, Robert. The Mexican government entrusted Linati with Ignacio Icaza's 1827 project, *Colección de Antigüedades que existen en el Museo Nacional* (Collection of Antiquities Existing in the National Museum), through which it is certain that Alamán hoped to fulfill his longing to publish the work of Dupaix. Linati had never been associated with antiquarian work, but Waldeck mentions in his diary that the Parmesan lithographer had given him a work depicting the Cross of Palenque that he had elaborated from the original. Added to this is that the drawing in no way resembles that which Waldeck himself copied a few years earlier in lithography for the London publication by Berthoud (1822) of the account of Palenque by Antonio del Río. It is notable that the work by Linati is lacking the hieroglyphs at the sides, with the exception of seven that, to

ANNIE HUNTER
STUDY OF EIGHT ARCHAEOLOGICAL OBJECTS [158]

Waldeck, seem very curious.[11] In reality, after Waldeck's sojourn to the mines at Tlapujahua, Fiorenzo Galli, a partner of Linati's at the magazine *Iris,* informed him that the lithographer proposed to leave the country and suggested to him the possibility of taking charge of the lithography for the government, which the Italian was willing to leave him.[12]

It is through the diaries that Frédéric Waldeck kept of his life in Mexico (1826-1837) that one can catch a glimpse of the local antiquarian commerce and the interest demonstrated by a considerable group of painters and draftsmen in the topic. Insistently, time and again, the impact of the expeditions from the eighteenth and early nineteenth century by Del Río and Dupaix appears.

Waldeck visited Mexico City for the first time in July of 1826. As has been stated, and noted by Galli, he immediately forged a friendship with Claudio Linati. Additionally, he met Lucas Alamán, the English minister Ward and the consul O'Gorman. He began regularly attending meetings of the York Society[13] and met the French painter and antiquarian from Louisiana, Latour-Allard who showed him his collection of pre-Columbian objects shortly before his return to Paris, where he was to exhibit them with great success.[14] Latour-Allard was also to take with him to Paris a version—certainly unofficially—of the drawings by Luciano Castañeda, which he later sold in London to Lord Kingsborough and which were to later be published in *Antiquities of Mexico* (1834). Waldeck, on seeing the drawings of Palenque in the collection of Latour-Allard, noticed that they were the same that he had copied for the edition of the incomplete report by Antonio del Río, for Berthoud, in 1822, but that those that he was now examining had been done by the hand of Luciano Castañeda.[15]

Years later, in January of 1831, General Anaya visited him and presented him with the greatest description of Palenque that Waldeck had ever heard, not only showing him an infinity of drawings—certainly bad—but lending him the work of Del Río, by Berthoud, that Waldeck himself had lithographed in

Alfred P. Maudslay
SERPENTS' HEADS. MOUND 14, CHICHÉN-ITZÁ [159]

Alfred P. Maudslay
THE CASTLE AT CHICHÉN-ITZÁ. BASE OF THE NORTH STAIRCASE WITH ELEMENT
IN THE FORM OF A SERPENT'S HEAD [160]

1822, as well as the complete original manuscript, with all the ink drawings that corresponded to the plates missing in the English edition[16] and that—I think—Anaya probably removed from the archives of the Ciudad Real de Chiapa, and which originally had belonged to Ramón Ordóñez.

Waldeck was introduced to the circle of the German antiquarian Uhde, and a short while later was to gain access to his collection in order to copy various pieces, which had to have occurred prior to the opening of the pre-Columbian exhibition hall in the Museum of Berlin. Also at this time, he met another antiquarian artist, Frank, with whom he would later collaborate.

His relationship with Ignacio Icaza, from the Museo Nacional, and with the antiquarian Carlos María Bustamante turned out to be exceedingly advantageous, even if conflictive (all of Waldeck's relationships were, by nature, conflictive). Icaza went as far as to periodically lend him pieces from the museum which Waldeck would then draw at home. It is at about this time that he began his own antiquarian collection which would come to compare advantageously with that of Luciano Castañeda, who not only offered him further data on Palenque but went as far as to, a short while later, request him to impart some classes on color and present him with a copy of his best piece, entitled *Basalta*. Certainly, Waldeck's opinion of Castañeda's artistic aptitudes, who at this time was the draftsman for the Museo Nacional, was never favorable.

As a result of the promulgation of a law of patrimonial protection of 1828, the travelers had to be duly authorized to undertake excavations and to export antiquarian pieces. The Frenchman, Baradère, obtained such permission and committed himself to leaving in Mexico that which he found "worthy of figuring in a museum, half of the collection that he assembled at his expense." Of the 1400 pieces collected, the explorer—whose principal goal was Palenque, to which he never managed to arrive—received in exchange, in a decision by the Mexican government, one of the official series of the drawings by Luciano Castañeda and an authenticated copy of the Itinerary of Dupaix.

The agreement was signed between the conservator of the Museum, Icaza and by Baradère, on November 7, 1828, and took two years in being approved. The aim was that everything was to be published, thus fulfilling the longing that Lucas Alamán had expressed since 1823. The reality was that, in 1825, the Société de Géographie of Paris had offered a prize to the traveler who could present authentic, irrefutable proof of the existence Palenque. In part, this provoked the obsession this site held for many traveler-painters, collectors and antiquarians, and spurred more than one expedition to the zone. In 1832, said prize was finally awarded to Baradère who, in his "Dedication to the Congress of the Mexican Nation," in *Rélation des Trois Expéditions du Capitaine Dupaix ordonnés en 1805* (Account of Three Expeditions by Captain Dupaix Undertaken in 1805), published by the Bureau des Antiquités Mexicaines in 1834, made public his debt of gratitude to the country.[17] Curiously, Waldeck makes no reference whatsoever to Baradère in his diaries.

He does, on the other hand, make reference to Carl Nebel, whose sojourn in Mexico began in 1829. His attraction to the country was born, apparently, upon reading the chapters on antiquarian monuments in *Vues de Cordillères...*, by von Humboldt, to whom he later dedicated his lithographic work, *Voyage Pittoresque et Archeologique dans la partie le plus intéressante du Mexique pendant les annés 1829 et 1834* (Picturesque and Archaeological Voyage Through the Most Interesting Part of Mexico During the Years 1829-1834), which ponders the eagerness of the painter in making known the genius of the people of Aztlán and the beauty of the physiognomy of the tropical vegetation that embellished the country. The French edition appeared in 1834 and the Spanish, in 1840.

Moreover, like so many other traveler-painters, Nebel, too, felt himself irredeemably attracted to collecting. His friendship and collaboration with Waldeck on a government project involving the registration of antiquarian pieces, in December of 1829[18]—during which there was to be, however, a surge of discord between the two artists—was complemented by the mutual borrowing of pieces in their possession for copying, as well as travels together and visits to other local collectors such as Uhde and Vischer, to delineate the pieces in their collections. Toward the end of 1829, Waldeck made drawings of Xochicalco and, with the passage of time, he became more associated with Palenque. He also made a copy of the sixteenth-century canvas at the Ayuntamiento de Miacatlán in which, at the center, appears a

pyramid, as well as the execution of four drawings of a sculpture, from his collection, of a plumed serpent.[19] A short while later, Waldeck lent Nebel his coyote so he could draw it.[20] Faced with the anarchic situation in the country, the two friends decided to pack their collections and send them to London,[21] though it seems that in the end they were acquired by the German, Uhde and the Swiss, Vischer. Not completely in vain, during these years Lucas Alamán and Ignacio Icaza had attempted the impossible in trying to convince the collectors, both foreign and national, to cede their pieces to the Museo Nacional. Waldeck flatly refused their petition.[22] I don't know of the responses by Nebel, Frank, Uhde or Vishcer... the only thing certain is that the Marquise de Sierra Nevada did cede two pieces.

In July of 1830, a deal was initiated between Alamán and Waldeck regarding a new expedition to Palenque, in spite of the agreement that had been established with Baradère. Due to a total lack of funds, the project was to be supported by private donations. Thus, Waldeck approached Uhde, who did not offer him the necessary support. Time passed and Waldeck began to suspect that Nebel, with Uhde's support, instead of going to Papantla had headed for Palenque, and that he would beat him to the goal and, to top it off, obtain the post of draftsman at the museum.[23] He fervently wish a fever to befall Nebel.... In reality, Uhde had sponsored through his own means—even while Waldeck was receiving official support—the expedition to Palenque by the private copier, Calfous.[24]

About October of 1831, Waldeck's Palenque project had taken a more certain shape; the government was resolute and a number of sponsors had lent their support. Waldeck went to Teotihuacan to draw the pyramids. Months later, mention appears of his friendship with Rugendas and of the latter's excursion to Xochicalco in January of 1832. It is interesting to note Waldeck's opinion of Rugendas' work, which he pronounced as picturesque, undefined and lacking true value for antiquarians.

Finally, in February of 1832, Frédéric Waldeck left Mexico City and headed for Palenque, with a badly chosen human team that was to continue separating from the expeditionary group until ending up alone. Once in Palenque, in his astonishment at the ruins, he criticized the drawings by Del Río as much as those of Castañeda for their imprecision and complete lack of the picturesque. He worked with zeal, but the funds became grievously scarce, to the point where, beginning in July of the same year, he directed a series of letters to Lord Kingsborough[25] and to the Société de Géographie in Paris—perhaps in the hope that the prize had still not been awarded—in order to salvage the expedition. Finally, after months of waiting, in May of the following year he received encouraging news of generous support from Kingsborough.

He left Palenque in July of 1833 and, after a stay of several months in Tabasco, arrived in Mérida on December 25, 1834. One month earlier, Waldeck, perhaps protecting himself in light of his uncertain sponsorship by the Mexican government, had decided to send to London not only the diaries that he had been entrusted with regarding Palenque, but the rest of his Mexican work, as well. Once in Mérida, he was to receive from Kingsborough, in two shipments, Baradère's publication, in addition to Kingsborough's own work on the expedition by Dupaix.

In December he received word that the Mexican government had named Pédrauville as explorer of antiquities for the republic and considered that his own position had been annulled.[26] In the end, his worst fears were realized when on January 16, 1836, the mayor, Félix Guerrero, accompanied by his assistants Cobián, Escalera, and the notary Badillo, with an order from the government of Mexico, arrived to decommission him of his papers and drawings. Additionally, General Gil Pérez received an order to confiscate the drawings of Palenque, which Waldeck had quickly attempted to duplicate. The antiquarian painter preferred not to put up a resistance but decided to recover his work.[27] The suspicion was that he had trafficked in and had hidden various antiquities. Even under the threat of arrest, however, he received support in going to draw the ruins at Uxmal, Mayapan.

The beginning of 1837 found Waldeck back in Paris with the hope of receiving royal sponsorship for the publication of his work. With the death of Kingsborough, in March, his hopes again fell. However, in 1838 his *Voyage Pittoresque et Archeologique dans la province Yucatan (Amérique Centrale) pendant les annés 1834 et 1836* (Picturesque and Archaeological Voyage in the Province of Yucatán [Central America] During the Years 1834-1836) appeared, dedicated to his unrestrictive patron, Lord Kingsborough, while *Monuments anciens du Mexique: Palenque...* was to wait several years, until 1866, for its publication, which included an introductory study by Brasseur du Bourbourg.

Lastly, Frederick Catherwood, in 1834, interested John Lloyd Stephens in an joint exploration of the ruins at Palenque that

PÁL ROSTI
PIEDRA DEL SOL [162]

had been previously investigated by Del Río and Dupaix. Perhaps the reading of publications on these expeditions had inspired them. In 1841 they published *Incidents of Travel in Central America, Chiapas and Yucatán* and, two years later, *Incidents of Travel in Central America*. In 1844, Catherwood published twenty-five lithographs of the ruins at Copán, Palenque, Uxmal, Kabah, Sabaché, Labná, Bolonchén, Chichén Itza, Tulum and Izamal in *Views of Ancient Monuments in Central America, Chiapas, and Yucatán*. Included, apart from the use, now widespread, of cameras obscura and lucida, was the introduction of the daguerreotype as one more of the technical mediums within the reach of the dissemination of the arts and sciences.

All of the traveler-artists mentioned herein were to have a decided impact on the development of the antiquarian theme among the Mexican lithographers of the second half of the nineteenth century and on artists of the stature of José María Velasco.

pp. 200-201. JOHANN MORITZ RUGENDAS
RUINS AT CENTLA, VERACRUZ [163]

IMAGES OF PALENQUE

MARÍA CONCEPCIÓN GARCÍA SÁIZ

In 1784, José Antonio Calderón, the deputy mayor of Palenque, toured the ruins of the site known as Casas de Piedra (Stone Houses) and wrote a succinct report, accompanied by highly schematic drawings in which he attempted to represent the human figures, appearing in stucco relief, that decorated some of the panels covering the façades of many of the buildings and pilasters. His visit was in response to an order by the President of the Captaincy General of Guatemala, José de Estachería, who thus initiated an official investigation that was to make known the archaeological ruins of the Mayan city of Palenque.

Knowledge of the existence of the ruins had not yet reached beyond the immediate region although it had been approximately fifty years since visitors had been coming, each time gaining more momentum, thanks to the endeavors of people such as Ramón Ordóñez y Aguiar, who was able to communicate his interest to various relatives and friends who themselves later traveled to the site and provided him with information he used to write the various texts in which are included descriptions of the ruins, part of a more general work, pompously titled *Historia de la creación del cielo y de la tierra* (History of the Creation of Heaven and Earth).

The drawings accompanying Calderón's report are the first visual representation that we have of images from Palenque. In these four rapidly made sketches, the author had merely intended to show some of the architectural details, such as a tower, and the existence of human representations. The following year, a new examination was made by the architect Antonio Bernasconi, also sent by Estachería, to complete the work begun by Calderón. This time, the attention given to the architecture was greater, with the execution of plans and elevations of various buildings to which he added the reproduction of "some figures and decorations from the ruins," which served to somewhat amplify the site's iconographic lexicon.

In 1787, a third official expedition toured the site, made up of Captain Antonio del Río and an artist named Ricardo (or Ignacio?) Armendáriz. This time the initiative had been taken directly by the Spanish Crown, based on an interest in information that had arrived in Madrid. The historian Juan Bautista Muñoz, of Spain's Real Academia de la Historia, tried to focus future work on the aspects that he considered of special importance, such as the construction systems and materials, objects and instruments of all types, and the "description and drawings of the figures." The results were much more comprehensive than in the previous expeditions, mostly in terms of the figures, which were represented in greater number and with much more attention. Of the thirty images that were collected on the twenty-five plates that are known of, the majority are dedicated to the decorations in relief, and in them the personages appear to have been treated with the necessary detail. A desire for faithfulness of representation can be observed in the attention paid to the attitudes of the figures, the details of their headdresses and garments, and the glyphs, all of which remained incomprehensible only because of the difficulty in understanding what they depicted.

The originals and clean copies made from them were sent to Spain while the rough drafts and duplications made from having viewed them remained in Guatemala. There they were studied by local scholars, led by the aforementioned Ramón Ordóñez, who elaborated theories on the presence of Romans,

F. Catherwood / H. Warren
PRINCIPAL PATIO OF THE PALACE AT PALENQUE [164]

Figure 1.

WALKER/CADDY EXPEDITION
STUDY OF A MAYAN RELIEF [165]

Carthaginians, English, etc., in these lands prior to the arrival of the Spanish, determining that they had been responsible for a culture that, in their opinion, was alien to that of the contemporary inhabitants of the region. The analysis of one of the drawings, made on the expedition by Del Río and Armendáriz, led José Miguel de San Juan, participating in a discussion group on Palenque with Ordóñez and Félix Cabrera, to some specific conclusions:

> the plate ... is that of the upper chapel in which Proserpina is seen seated upon a two-headed animal, as if ready to be able to travel to one place or another (as the Romans had painted her), which seems to allude to an ability to live half the year on Earth and the other half in Hell. In her beaded necklace can be seen the little points of the tau of the Hebrews, a mysterious sign revered by the Egyptians, as well as that of the Holy Cross, many years before our Redemption, whose images were also not lacking within this Lighthouse, made clear by the paintings that Río executed and remitted on this occasion. Seated to one side of Proserpina we see Ceres presenting her with a wicker tray of fruit, and a glass of water, symbolized by the hieroglyphic rising above the tray.

This image had been reproduced by Bernasconi and described with the brief note: "This stone bed, with the circular figure of a low-relief portrait, is found in the front patio, that faces toward the South, beneath the vaults, of which there are five." Two years later, Del Río limited himself to saying that it "apparently represents one of their gods seated effeminately on an animal in the state expressed by this same [plate]. One might believe it to show the god of water, in the same way that the ancients used to depict Pegasus in the proper manner."

It is evident that none of the members of the various commissions sent to Palenque prior to this period at the end of the eighteenth century had any specific interest in the study of the indigenous ruins, though they nevertheless developed adventurous interpretations of them. All were concise in their descriptions—at times excessively so—and cautious in their appraisals.

For this reason the drawings acquired great importance, taking on a life of their own apart from the texts that accompanied them, permitting anyone who contemplated them to make their own deductions, taking the type of liberties we saw in the case of José Miguel de San Juan. The artist, who interpreted what he saw in the images as being culturally recognizable, provided

DEL RÍO / ARMENDÁRIZ EXPEDITION
STUDY OF A MAYAN RELIEF [166]

the first step in an identification with a past that formed part of his own tradition. Only when he ventured to reproduce what he didn't comprehend, without adapting it to his own formal vocabulary, did he leave the door open to other possibilities. The incomprehensibility of the aesthetic principles of the indigenous cultures led many Europeans of the sixteenth century to consider that such images that did not conform to Western canons were demonic works and that they should be destroyed. Toward the end of the eighteenth century, the more common recourse was to transform the images into acceptable models. This was a very common transgression within the production of the scientific expeditions, affecting the principles of direct observation and the faithful reproduction of reality.

In such a case, the images captured by Armendáriz became so identified with Palenque that it came to be represented without regard to its own reality. Similarly, when an expedition in the nineteenth century visited the ruins—or boasted of having visited them—they limited themselves to reproducing Armendáriz rather than Palenque. The most resonant case was that of a team formed by Guillermo Dupaix and José Luciano Castañeda, the first chief head of the Real Expedición de Antigüedades de la Nueva España which, under the sponsorship of King Charles IV, toured various archaeological sites throughout the colony while collecting an extensive amount of information. Between 1805 and 1808 they made three voyages and, on the last of these, during 1807 and 1808, they arrived at Palenque.

Although they mention nothing of it in their memoirs or reports, if we compare these drawings with those made by Armendáriz, it is plain that Castañeda—an artist trained at the Real Academia de San Carlos in New Spain, inseparable companion of Dupaix and illustrator for the entire project—unashamedly reproduced the work of Armendáriz and included it within his portfolio as his own work while Dupaix endeavored to praise his skillfulness in the representations and testified to the veracity of all of the work of his companion. Thus, when he reproduced the throne that had provoked such peculiar commentaries from San Juan, he was tripped up by one small detail: one of the feet had been in Madrid since 1787, where it had been sent along with the report and the objects collected on the expedition by Del Río and Armendáriz and which, therefore, could not have appeared in an image intended to represent an object exactly as it had been found in the moment. A carelessness that was repeated on various occasions.

From this point on, the images, created by an inexpert artist who seemed obliged to represent some models that, to him, were alien when contemplated for the first time, took on a prestige that transcended even that of their copier, an accomplished, academic artist who had dedicated years to dealing with these themes. And although the name of the author may have disappeared from all official references, the work followed an independent path to which we alluded earlier on.

Years later, in 1822, a new event occurred in the life of our images of Palenque. The English publisher Henry Berthoud decided to publish a selection of images accompanied by a text by Félix Cabrera, one of the members of the discussion group mentioned earlier, as well as a translation of the report made by Antonio del Río. Berthoud hired Frédéric Waldeck to take charge of the lithographs based on the drawings by Armendáriz. Waldeck

was limited to reproducing the models which had been delivered to him and did so with sufficient fidelity to the substance of the work, however simplifying some of the details. In this edition, the text by Del Río appears incomplete and badly translated and that of Cabrera, pretentious and confusing, not worthy of any great attention among possibly interested parties. However, the publication was reviewed in specialized magazines and summaries were made that were promptly translated into French and German, at the same time that some of the plates were being reinterpreted by the new illustrators of these editions. From this point on, interest in Palenque became accentuated among the "Americanists" in Europe and the English publication served as much in making known the existence of the ruins as it did in demonstrating how much remained unknown about the site and its inhabitants. A work indispensable to the baggage of any explorer of the area, it was kept quiet by many who played at being discoverers.

In 1826, the Société de Géographie of Paris announced a competition that offered a prize for the best description of Palenque. Desire to achieve this international recognition turned Palenque into the focal point for a great number of adventurer-travelers, in the best sense of both words, who turned their lives to the goal of gaining direct knowledge of the ruins and the elaboration of corresponding reports. Six years later, the prize remained unawarded and, paradoxically, it was Dupaix and Castañeda who had received the greatest exposure, due to a reevaluation of their work by Baradère, with the publication of *Antiquités Mexicaines*, in which appeared, among others, the drawings that Castañeda had plagiarized from Armendáriz, forming the major part of the drawings related to Palenque.

At the same time, in the period after the initiation of the competition, Waldeck had begun receiving news in Paris about the activities taking place in Mexico and Central America. In May of 1832, he arrived himself to the site he had seen ten years earlier when he transcribed the works of Armendáriz into the language of lithography, in preparation for their publication. Months later, he met François Corroy, another French traveler interested in archaeological antiquities who had executed his own, personalized version of the antiquity of Palenque by means of repeated descriptions, accompanied by the now inevitable drawings, elaborated after many visits. Logically, he also had aspirations as to the prize offered by the French institution.

Jean-Frédéric Waldeck
INTERPRETATION OF THE MYTH OF ARIADNA BEFORE THE RUINS OF PALENQUE [167]

JEAN-FRÉDÉRIC WALDECK. STUDY OF A MAYAN RELIEF [168]

Waldeck and Corroy weren't the only Europeans who traveled to the ruins during this period.

One year earlier, Juan Galindo had made his appearance on the scene, a complex man who, in spite of his multiple efforts, did not receive the attention of the circles of Americanist Europeans to which he directed part of his work on Palenque.

The period between 1839 and 1840 saw another series of visits to Palenque, the last of true importance before the close of the first half of a century in which the image had played a much more valuable part than writings. These were not individual expeditions such as those just described. Rather, they were carried out in pairs, with a division of duties, in the manner of Del Río/Armendáriz or Dupaix/Castañeda. The most important was, without doubt, that formed by John Lloyd Stephens and Frederick Catherwood, although one cannot discount the role, however more modest, played by Patrick Walker and John Herbert Caddy, of the United States.

Artistically, the lead taken by Waldeck and Catherwood is far above that of any other artist. Apart from their capacity to reproduce, with greater or lesser accuracy, the constructive and ornamental details on which, at last, a scientific archaeology could be based, both artists incorporated other aspects of no less importance. The first of these was to situate the ruins in a geographic context, representing and even "manipulating" with great skill the communication of the complexity of emotions that they hoped the spectator might share with the artist-explorer. Catherwood explained without reservations that on different occasions he modified his own landscapes in order to give greater visibility to the buildings, in the same way that he reconstructed the decoration of some of them from the elements that were to be found about the grounds. Waldeck, who never confessed to supposed caprices of this type, also maintained a balance between description and creation.

In addition, they achieved the introduction of man into their scenes, something absent in the early representations of Palenque from the eighteenth and early nineteenth centuries, product of a classical formation. They were also the first to rise from anonymity, attesting with their presence to the veracity of what they exhibited, with an obsession for the representation of the reality that in numerous cases hid an idyllic recomposition, much closer to what the author believed that it should be than what it was. It was here where a sampling of characters was situated that had nothing to do with the inhabitants of the ruins, and where the illustrator had surrendered to the artist.

In the approximately fifty years covering the period of these explorations, Palenque had played the part of a symbolic representation of the American continent in its relationship with Europe, and its images had acted as an emblematic reflection of prestige: that of the Enlightened monarchy that sought prosperity through knowledge; that of a society in formation that needed a past in which to reaffirm its personality; and that of individuals that looked to the New World, once again, for fame, money and social consideration. And to each had been given an answer.

DUPAIX / CASTAÑEDA. STUDY OF A MAYAN RELIEF [169]

THE PICTORIAL-DESCRIPTIVE FOCUS IN THE LITERATURE OF TRAVELERS

JOSÉ ENRIQUE COVARRUBIAS V.

The nineteenth century was noteworthy in terms of the curiosity that burned within Europeans as to the Americas and the desire for an interchange between them. Proof of this is to be found in the enormous quantity of accounts of voyages that appeared in the Old World during this century, greater than that of any previous epoch. If any period in modern history has looked to books by travelers as a means of acquiring knowledge of other places and peoples it is, without doubt, the past century, a time before the telegraph, the daily press and scientific specialization had begun to sift and sort the type of information that had, until then, appeared in a delicious whole in the writings by travelers. The apex of this literary form is, therefore, a topic of primary importance in the history of the interchanges between Europe and the Americas.

Among the cultural elements that help to explain the zenith of these writings from the period in question, noteworthy was the growing scientific curiosity about man as both a social and economic being, in addition to a notable perfecting of general geographic knowledge. A summary of the writings of Europeans who traveled to Mexico in the nineteenth century serves to illuminate the broad range of interests and curiosity that gave birth to works of this type. This is not, however, the theme of this article. Among the diverse variations in the literature created by travelers to Mexico, we will focus on those works by authors who combined the use of images and of writing in order to transmit the experience of their sojourns in Mexico, a modality of primary importance within the genre. This pictorial-descriptive focus contributed greatly to the forging of the European perception of Mexico during this entire period.

Any attempt to approach the writings by Europeans on the subject of Mexico that appeared in the nineteenth century must begin with Alexander von Humboldt and his widely known descriptions of the landscapes and flora and fauna, as well as the folklore and customs, collected in the extensive French edition of his travels and studies in the Americas (Paris, 1805-1834). Among the works which deal with Mexican subjects within von Humboldt's vast production, two stand out for the influence and stimulus they provided the later European writers. The celebrated *Essai politique sur le royaume de la Nouvelle Espagne...* (Political Essay on the Kingdom of New Spain...) from 1811, as well as *Vues de Cordillères et Monumens de peuples indigenes de L'Amérique* (Views of the Mountain Ranges and Monuments of the Indigenous Peoples of America) from 1810, sparked an ongoing flurry of imitation and continuance that wasn't to subside until the second half of the century. *Vues de Cordillères...*, particularly, represented a model for those who sought to develop their talents with the brush and the pen, in the face of a public interested in knowing of the beauty and exuberance of a world forbidden to the Europeans for three centuries by the lack of accessible passage. Among the first to produce literary and visual accounts must be mentioned Carl Nebel, the German author of *Voyage Pittoresque et Archeologique dans la partie le plus intéressante du Mexique pendant les annés 1829 et 1824* (Picturesque and Archaeological Voyage Through the Most Interesting Part of Mexico During the Years 1829-1834), originally published in French, in 1836, and shortly after, at the wish of the author, in Spanish (1840).

With clear acknowledgment to von Humbolt, who he considered the definitive precursor to his work and from whom he

JOHANN SALOMON HEGI
THE HOUSE AT THE HACIENDA EL MIRADOR [171]

p. 210. JOHANN MORITZ RUGENDAS
VIEW OF THE HACIENDA EL MIRADOR
AND THE PICO DE ORIZABA (DETAIL) [170]

JOHANN SALOMON HEGI
FULL MOON AT THE HACIENDA EL MIRADOR AND HUTS [172]

JOHANN MORITZ RUGENDAS
VIEW OF THE HACIENDA EL MIRADOR AND THE PICO DE ORIZABA [173]

received resolute support, Nebel strove to communicate to the reader what he judged to be most worthy of visual admiration in Mexico: the beautiful styles of dress, the venerable indigenous antiquities, and the picturesque landscapes. His effective means to this end were to combine his beautiful plates with commentary relative to the themes that each plate represented. With the aim of providing the greatest reach to what was being transmitted visually and to complete the portrait of life being communicated, Nebel included within the textual accompaniment the peculiarities of the citizenry as well as the natural placement of many of the related sites and archaeological monuments. Notwithstanding his obvious debt to von Humboldt, who, incidentally, wrote the prologue to the book, it must be pointed out that Nebel's intention was to, above all, engage and entertain the reader, something that cannot be said of the writings of his mentor.

Nebel was not merely passing through Mexico. Rather, he actually resided in the country from 1829 until 1834. His vision, therefore, can be considered more profoundly grounded than those of von Humboldt and the other writers who were only visiting the new republic. Such a writer can steep his documentation in personal experiences, forming, as Nebel did, the basis for a personal vision of Mexico. The same can be said of Frédéric de Waldeck, a native of Prague, whose work came to be known throughout Europe with his *Voyage Pittoresque et Archeologique dans la province Yucatan (Amérique Centrale) pendant les annés 1834 et 1836* (Picturesque and Archaeological Voyage in the Province of Yucatán [Central America] During the Years 1834-1836), the original version of which was published in Paris, in 1838. Waldeck had moved to Mexico during the previous decade and his resulting literary work combines the rich artistic, social and political

experiences he gained during his long cohabitation with the Mexican people, kept in the diary of his travels in the Yucatán.

Waldeck combined his interests in art and science, and these he infused with the compilation of statistics and archaeological considerations. In his work we touch upon one of the peculiarities of the literature of travelers which give it a special charm, something lacking in much of contemporary cultural works: an integral personality. Although the author was, above all, interested in enlightening the European public as to the little-known archaeological riches of the country, the expressive diary of his travels informs the reader as to statistical aspects of Tabasco and the Yucatán, as well as the natural, social, ethnographic and cultural idiosyncrasies of the region. Waldeck's primary motivation, however, was to depict the mysterious character of the ruins of southeast Mexico and to reveal "the serious questions connected

to these nations [that] have until now remained in the sphere of enigmas." The clarification of these questions implied, on various occasions, the comparison between archaeological relics from Mexico and those from the ancient nations of the Orient. However, beyond this effort, the sheer emotion of discovering ancestral mysteries and the penetration into the hidden tropical forest guaranteed the enjoyment of the reader as he alternately consulted the plates and the text of this beautiful book. Undoubtedly, the work has been appreciated more for its archaeological contributions than for the sociological reflections contained within the impressions noted during the author's travels which, although scattered throughout, begin to awaken the interests of the historian and the social scientist. Waldeck left us a wealth of data, including even information as to the monetary situation in the Yucatán.

William Bullock
view of the city and valley of mexico [175]

ANTHONY CAREY STANNUS
CONVENT OF SANTO DOMINGO [176]

ANTHONY CAREY STANNUS
STUDY OF A BAROQUE WINDOW [177]

A.E. WALTER BOODLE
FRUIT VENDOR [178]

A.E. WALTER BOODLE
VIEW FROM BOODLE'S WINDOW (8 CINCO DE MAYO [STREET])
TOWARD THE CATHEDRAL [179]

As has been noted, the most celebrated contribution made by this book has been in the area of archaeology. It deals, most directly, with the Mayan city of Uxmal. Given the length of his visit to this site, Waldeck was in a position to correct and amplify observations by von Humboldt, Del Río, Dupaix, Buchon, Saint-Priest and other scholars who had previously disseminated imprecise information regarding the ruins. Another work by Waldeck later appeared, this time dedicated to the ruins at Palenque, published, in French, by an abbot named Brasseur de Bourbourg, in 1866. This late date, however, does not coincide with the peak of the pictorial-descriptive current reviewed herein, as will be seen. Rather, it

was between 1830 and 1855 that this species of author was most comfortable with the composition of such works and was able to spark an enthusiasm on the part of the European public. In addition to Nebel and Waldeck, the early part of the aforementioned period marks the productive years of Daniel Thomas Egerton, an equally important exponent of this genre, although the first to portray the new republic with illustrations and text had been William Bullock, another Englishman, in his book *Six Months' Residence and Travels in Mexico...*, first published in London, in 1824.

From a thematic point of view, perhaps it was the work by Egerton, *Views in Mexico*, originally published in London, in

MEXICO. MAY.7. Old Spanish Drinking Fountain. San

A.E. WALTER BODDLE
FOUNTAIN AT SAN COSME [180]

1840, which most revealed the interest which began to dominate the genre toward the middle of the century. Now it was no longer so much the archaeological aspect but the folklore and, more so, the landscapes that became increasingly important to the authors, who endeavored to integrate these two new aspects into an artistic form. The plates and lithographs from these books demonstrate aspects that other travelers and residents had been fascinated by for the previous two decades. Giacomo C. Beltrami and Henry George Ward, to mention only two examples, had been painstaking in pointing out the extent and magnificence of the geographical expanse of Mexico in their works *Le Mexique* (Paris, 1827) and *Mexico in 1827* (London, 1828). This natural reality had now been eloquently expressed in the splendid landscapes included by Egerton in his compilation of Mexican vistas.

The interest in the geological peculiarities of the country is also very representative of the curiosity dominant in the middle of the century, as evidenced by the representation of the interior of a mine by the English painter. The itinerary of these chroniclers rarely left out an expedition to the grottoes of Cacahuamilpa, a perfect occasion for meditation on natural history and the seeming eternity of the stone formations housed in this gigantic terrestrial cleft.

Thus, a notable contrast arose between the picturesque quality of the landscapes and the sinister darkness of the mines or of the grottoes and, equally, between the gentle climate found in the greater part of the country as opposed to the violence of the terrestrial revolts that occurred in the form of earthquakes and volcanic eruptions. This reality of extremes and gray areas literally fascinated the artists, as well as the rest of the authors and the readers of the descriptions of Mexico made around 1850. A new challenge arose and stimulated the descriptive inspiration of the Europeans: to communicate the majestic unity that included elements which at other latitudes, such as Europe, would appear dissimilar.

Among the authors who went the farthest in demonstrating the intimate cohesion of phenomena at apparent extremes we find Carl Christian Sartorius, whose book, *Mexico. Landscapes and Popular Sketches*, was first published in German (Darmstadt, 1852). This book is notable for the doubly descriptive integration it achieved whereby the descriptive and folkloric outlines of Sartorius are accompanied by lithographs by the painter Johann Moritz Rugendas, also German and a friend of

DESIRÉ CHARNAY
IZAMAL, PYRAMID AT HUNPINTOK [181]

the writer. As much as the work intends to follow in the footsteps of von Humboldt, there is no doubt that Sartorius went
much deeper than his eminent predecessor in delineating the
basic features of the Mexican character. His writing reveals a
clear sense of the ultimate link between the moral profile of
the diverse human types and their geographic location. This
geographic-descriptive skill conforms excellently with that of the
painter, various of whose illustrations reflect the atmosphere of
tranquillity and sweet indolence that impregnated life in Mexican cities, while in others we can observe scenes of the for-
midable vitality that made up the landscape of the interior of
the country. Sartorius points out with precision, in his text,
the contrast between the sloth of life in the city and the harsh-
ness of the agricultural and pastoral labor on the broad Mexican *altiplano*.

This combination of pictorial and ethnological description by Sartorius and Rugendas appears to mark the zenith of

the joint use of image and text that we set out to review.
Although the plates by Rugendas included in the book include
no archaeological topics, such themes cannot be entirely
excluded from the contributions by Sartorius. In all fairness,
Sartorius relied deeply on his twenty-five years of life in
Mexico as a foundation for the variety of descriptions that he
presented.

In the notable decade between 1850 and 1860 we may also
place various of the most finished works, in terms of the general characterizations of the moral countenance of the country, a time in which a certain decline in the interest in archaeology can be perceived among the authors. On one hand we
have writings by people who had resided for long periods in
the country, such as Sartorius and the Frenchman, Mathieu de
Fossey, author of *Le Mexique* (Paris, 1857), who also recounted
the personal experiences of his twenty-five years in Mexico.
On the other hand, it is evident that William Prescott, John L.

DESIRÉ CHARNAY
MITLA. PATIO OF THE FRETS [182]

Stephens and other scholars of ancient Mexican cultures had already inaugurated a new pre-Columbian current of study among the North Americans which appears to have had a repercussion on the attention that Europe had begun to focus on the political and social situation in Mexico. The question as to whether Mexico—and her foreign allies—would be better served by a republican regime or a monarchy began to fill the pages written in Europe. At any rate, some Europeans continued to tour the important archaeological sites. The traveler Desiré Charnay some decades later published his *Voyage to the Yucatán at the End of 1886*. It was in these later years, however, that photography was becoming the principal resource for the communication of the most notable personal experiences.

Based on the review just completed we can permit ourselves some reflections on the value of the pictorial-descriptive current herein presented. In a period in which Mexico still lacked an organized scheme of institutions and scholars with which to undertake the recognition and survey of the country's archaeological wealth, the earlier works in the genre provided an important contribution to the enterprise: the *in situ* description that documented not only the ruins and existing monuments. Additionally, given that the pictorial translation of the nature and the customs found in Mexico demanded a relatively prolonged stay in the country, the texts in question offer us a profound and colorful appreciation of the physical and moral realities. The writings by travelers on brief tours, or entangled in business dealings, cannot be compared to those who, drawn by the beautiful and captivating presence of the country, were compelled to seek out, live, and expound on the totality of its folkloric and geographic background. In this manner, the idea that this pictorial-descriptive focus represents an apex in the history of artistic creation on the theme of Mexico would not at all seem to be preposterous.

p. 224. L. FALCONETT
SAN LUIS POTOSÍ. PROCESSION DE N.D. DEL CARMEN (DETAIL) [183]

THE CAPTURE AND REPRODUCTION
OF THE DECISIVE INSTANT
IN THE NINETEENTH CENTURY

AURELIO DE LOS REYES

Falconnet, André-Toussaint Petitjean and an anonymous third party, soldiers in the French army that traveled to Mexico to shore up Maximilian's empire, left behind graphic testimonies of their sojourns in Mexico in the form of albums elaborated with love, care and nostalgia which, when viewed as a whole, demonstrate the rich variety of techniques used in the production and reproduction of images during the nineteenth century.[1] Falconnet and Petitjean assembled their albums in France after returning while the anonymous soldier's album was compiled in Mexico. The former two incorporated drawings, watercolors, engravings, lithography and photography while the latter limited himself to photography. This array of techniques was complemented by cinematography, introduced to Mexico thirty years later by Gabriel Veyre, a traveling cameraman.

Falconnet was in Mexico from 1865 until 1867 and from the note at the bottom of his photographic portrait, made in a visiting card format and placed at the beginning of the album, we know that he was attached to the Emperor's cabinet. We can deduce that he spent the better part of his stay within Mexico City and that he traveled with a notebook and a small case that contained sheets of paper, brushes, colors, pens, and both black and colored pencils for making drawings. Likewise it can be deduced that he possessed a curious and sensitive spirit and was keen to observe and better know the country to which he had traveled.

He began his album with a thought on Mexico:

Pays du Nopal et du Maguey, terre de Montezuma et de Malinche! Son souvenir me domine! Les annés puvent finir, ma main se dessech-

er, mon cour viellir, mais moi vivant je ne s'enblierai jamais. Pour rien au monde je ne voudrai s'effacer de ma memoire.

He ordered the images according to his itinerary so they could be read like a diary. He set sail from Gibraltar (of whose cliffs he made a watercolor) on May 4, 1865, aboard the *Tarn,* passing by Santa Cruz de Tenerife in the Canary Islands, a port he also captured in a magnificent watercolor. The ship reached Veracruz on June 16th. Falconnet returned home from the same port on February 17, 1867, aboard the *Yvonne,* just prior to the execution of Maximilian. He arrived in Havana on the 25th, later passing Florida and the Azores until arriving in Brest on April 8th and disembarking the next day. His album includes 37 photographs; 2 charcoal drawings; 3 gouaches; 24 watercolors; 4 maps; 3 lithographs, one in color; 8 woodcuts; and a sample of embroidered cloth made by prisoners in Mexican jails.

The quality of the images is in proportion to the time invested in the creation of each one. If he stayed in a location more than a day, he made better ones; if he were on the move, he simply made sketches. His best were executed in Mexico City by virtue of his having been stationed there for the majority of his stay. He captured a vendor of lottery tickets, an indigenous woman selling onions and another smoking, a hat vendor, the interior of an inn and market scenes, among others.

The obvious care taken with the composition and coloring in the drawings of the hat vendor and the ticket seller lead me to assume that he convinced them to pose. Those of a charcoal vendor and a seller of rebozos reflect his having been under pressure, as though they had been unwilling to pose. He was impressed by the *paso del viático,* as well as the market scenes in

L. Falconett

environs de puebla [184]

L. Falconett

san luis potosí. procession de n.d. del carmen [185]

Mexico. — Scène d'intérieur.

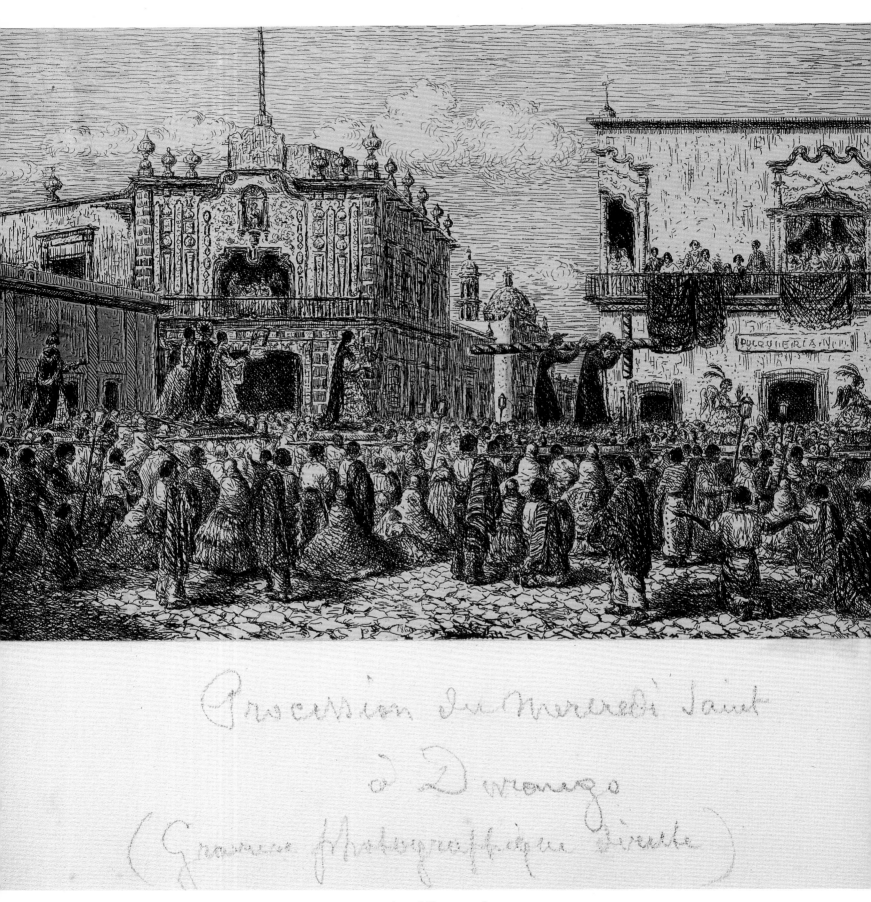

André-Toussaint Petitjean
procession du mercredi saint a durango [187]

Mexico City and the Holy Week procession in San Luis Potosí. The first he observed carefully in order to best depict it. By contrast, the image of the Holy Week procession is of surprising quality considering that he observed it on only one day. Also of note is the apparent rapidity of the strokes in his market scenes, in spite of his having observed them on a daily basis as in the case of the *paso del viático.*

If he hadn't time to draw he would purchase photographs to copy from, as in the example of the two young black girls from Martinique, their bosoms exposed, copied from photographs in the visiting card format from the endless gallery of "national types," the folkloric creations expressed first in lithography and later in photography. He applied this same solution to his image of a vendor of pulque, one of a *tlachiquero,* and another of two Mexican night watchmen, in these incorporating three tints of watercolors. His image of the central plaza in Veracruz also appears to have been copied from a photograph.

On the way from Veracruz to Mexico City he drew *Montée de la cordilliere de Chiquihuite,* depicting a point along the mountain range called Cumbres de Maltrata, to which he later added watercolors. Again, pressured strokes can be perceived in the ink drawings of the ranch at San Bartolo, the parish of San Antonio Acultzingo and the approach to Mexico City from Puebla, leading me to assume that he executed them during brief stops along the way.

The alternating valleys and mountain ranges along the route, by way of Orizaba and Puebla, captured his attention and he included in his album an orographic cross section noted "*travail executé en fevrier 1865 par MM. A. Dolffus et E. de Monserrat.*" His curiosity led him to cut out lithographs of pre-Columbian sculpture from magazines, including the goddess Coatlicue, the Calendar of the Sun, idols and ceramic fragments. In Mexico City he collected photographs, some of them signed (I would guess that they were sold to tourists and perhaps the French soldiers provided a market for this commercial angle in photography). He would include notations at the feet of the images pointing out such details as the fine quality of the pulque at San Bartolo; that the pulque from San Martín Texmelucan was very popular; that the vendor of lottery tickets would shout, "Raffle in benefit of the children of the foundling hospital! Three-hundred-peso jackpot this afternoon!"; and that the candy vendor would shout, "Young ladies! Cinnamon candy! Almonds! Caramels!"

From his return trip are included a lithographed map and two views of Havana—one aerial, probably made from a bal-

L. Falconett
la cebollera [188]

loon—as well as a *pour les dames* flyer and a photograph of Funchal, Madeira.

In spite of his having left Mexico before the execution of Maximilian, he added an appendix that he titled *Souvenir à toutes les personnes appelés au palais de Mexico,* which includes a collection of portraits of some of the personalities from Imperial Mexico such as Maximilian and Carlota, Bazaine, Josefa de la Peña, Miramón and others, as well as the members of the execution squad, the bullet-ridden jacket worn by Maximilian, the site of the execution and a photograph of a drawing of the execution. He also included a photograph of the allegory of Carlota's madness. These images he certainly bought in Europe, where they were widely circulated, and utilized them to express the pain he felt about the epilogue to his Mexican adventure.

ANONYMOUS
BAZAINE'S HOUSE, PLAZUELA BUENAVISTA [189]

While Falconnet spent nearly all his time in Mexico City, André-Toussaint Petitjean traveled to the country, where he captured landscapes in drawings, watercolors, engravings and photographic experiments. He also left two exceptional leaves depicting watercolored scenes of military life, on both sides of the paper, that include narrative texts of a corrosive humor. His stay in Mexico covered the years from 1862 until 1866.

His watercolors of Pachuca stand out for their attempt to capture the light rather than the colors, using a technique similar to that of the impressionists. The results are attributable to his European roots, which had sensitized him to the perception of the hues of light, and to the pace of the march of the military through the country which, as Falconnet had experienced, limited the amount of time that could be spent depicting such scenes, leading to his use of rapid brushstrokes. Unlike Falconnet, he attempted to resolve the problem by carrying a camera but was plagued by

having to prepare the plates with dry collodion and spent considerable time in making the exposures and in developing the negatives. In October, 1864, he apologized to his commander for the poor photographic quality of a landscape, taken between Patos and Parras, that he had sent him, citing the difficulty in finding products of good quality in San Luis Potosí, another of the problems involved in his photographic experiments.

He made exposures of Parras and of the hacienda of Patos and its surroundings, which suffered from the same problems of darkness and poor definition. To overcome the lack of quality of this type of photography he took to drawing the landscapes directly onto the plates with engraving instruments, calling them "photographic engravings." The most interesting is called *Procession du mercredi Sait a Durango*. However, more than an adequate solution, it is now a curiosity.

In my judgment, the most interesting works correspond to

ANONYMOUS
SCHOOL OF MINING [190]

his impressions of his sojourn in Durango, dated December 29, 1862. The two letter-size sheets are divided into three horizontal sections of equal size. In the center frame of one sheet he drew a campsite which he titled *Triste exile sur la terre extrangere...*, below which he wrote the lyrics to a song that the soldiers had sung on leaving for Mexico:

Suivez moi, castillans, le Mexique vous appele; Cortez va vous conduire a des succés nouveaux, a des succés... ès nou-ou-ouveaux Pas d'écho triste- ! Triste!! TRISTE!!!

In the upper section he depicted scenes of army life, one of them footnoted with: "*avant de se mettre en route on singurgite une légère tasse de moka.*"

The reverse side of the sheet is divided in the same manner.

The upper section is divided into two parts. On the left side is an overloaded mule, whose mountain of cargo is topped by a turkey, "*On n'a jamais pu savoir au juste le maximum du poids que peut porter un mulet d'infanterie.*" On the right side is an equally overloaded mule, topped with picks and shovels of seemingly bone-crushing weight, "*le mulet des sapeurs tout son corps et couvert de pointes menaçantes.*" Just below, in the center section, is a Zouave infantryman, as overloaded as the mules (a self-portrait?), and written below: "*tous les courriquots ne sont pas quadrupedes: 60 cartouches, 4 jours de viores, de l'eau et du bois pour le gran halte, la marmite de l'escuadre, armes, capote, couverture, tente abri ¡voilà! avec quelques autres légeres bibelots—et asor—de qui se compose le bagage du fans assin francais.*" To the *bibelots* should be added the photographic camera and the paintbox of the traveling painter.

The other sheet is also divided into three horizontal sections, each subdivided at the center. On the left side of the center section, of the front of this sheet, is a landscape captioned at the bottom with, "*Une heure de retard dans l'arrivée des éclaireurs de la colonne à l'Encarnación, et les chinacos achevaient de couper les talus qui retiennent l'eau de l'unique mare du pays et vôtre serviteur avoila pepier!!!*" Opposite this drawing, on the right side, three men are urinating into the cap of the man in the middle, footnoted, "*Le troupier, tojours ingenieuse, filtre l'eau des mares dans son couvre-nuque et se procure par ce moyen: 1o. un plat de grenouilles; 2o. une fritture de poissons; 3o. quelques anguilles; 4o. une demi douzaine de sangouves qu'il compete offrir a son cirugien major.*"

The richness of the variety of techniques in the albums of Falconnet and Petitjean was occasioned by the limited photographic technique to which they had access, as we will see in the album by the anonymous soldier. The limitations in capturing transitory scenes, in stopping or freezing time onto a plate of glass or a piece of paper, stimulated the pictorial skills of both travelers.

The last album is composed of 86 photographs (24 x 31 cm) taken about 1863, mostly of buildings and plazas in various parts of Mexico City. The photos are characterized by an absence of people or animals in motion, lending a ghostly, strange air to the city. The Zocalo, the city's main plaza, generally filled with people and carriages, both stationary and in motion, looks desolate. Why the solitude? A consequence of the French Intervention? Photographic problems? The intention of this soldier to communicate a strange image of Mexico City? It seems to me that this loneliness is the result of all three elements. One of the photos of the Zocalo clearly reveals the latter two elements. The photographer chose an angle of the Palacio Nacional in which can be noted three carts, some people and some horses, blurred because of their movement. Another, of a horse-drawn cannon, is also blurred due to the animal's movement while the soldier was exposing the photograph. If he had been experiencing these problems, it is logical that he looked for the moment in which his locations were devoid of moving objects.

This anonymous soldier took various photographs in the garden of Bazaine's house, his human subjects posing motionless on a bench. His photos of the Ciudadela, the boulevard Paseo de la Reforma, Juárez Avenue and the tiny plaza of Guardiola are characterized by a lack of people or animals in motion, unmistakable proof that he sought an empty city due to the limitations

of the photographic techniques to which he had access. At the time, other photographers were having no problems in capturing urban scenes that included the movement of people, animals and vehicles. As early as 1859, E. Anthony had published, in the United States, a view of a rainy day on Broadway.

In light of such photographic limitations, Falconnet y Petitjean opted for traditional techniques such as engraving, lithography, drawing and watercolors. Doubtless, had they had access to snap cameras they would have captured the folkloric scenes, landscapes and the local flavor at their every whim. The invention of such cameras, however, was not achieved until the 1880's, thanks to which they left us with their beautiful albums.

Gabriel Veyre, a traveling cameraman in the employ of the Lumière Brothers, was to be the first to introduce Mexico, in August of 1896, to cinematography. Surpassing snap photography, it not only captured motion but could reconstruct and transmit its illusion:

...is a type of magic lantern that projects its luminous cone onto a white screen placed in front of the spectators [where] scenes filled with life andmovement unfold.... All ... which are most marvelous.

In *Llegada del tren* (Arrival of the Train), the advance, with its natural movements, of the engine and its wagons of passengers can be seen, and then their hurried disembarkation and going away.

The scene is so natural that it seems one can perceive the noise of the trainand the murmur of the passengers.

In *Las montañas rusas* (The Roller Coasters), a scene shown is similar to that which we saw in the pantomime *Un bautizo en el carnaval* (A Baptism at the Carnival) at the Circo Orrín (Orrín Circus): a small boat that descends a ramp and breaks the water's surface, causing a light shower that envelopes, for a moment, the vessel....

In all of these scenes, the movements are perfectly photographed: there is natural life and animation in them, and they all produce an excessively marvelous effect.[2]

p. 233. ANDRÉ-TOUSSAINT PETITJEAN
MES IMPRESSIONS DE VOYAGE PAR DURANGO [191]

pp. 234-235. PEDRO GUALDI
VIEW OF MEXICO CITY [192]

MES IMPRESSIONS de voyage

Durango, le 25 9bre 1864

Triste exilé sur la terre étrangère ....

Dès l'aube du jour, une douce harmonie produite par une douzaine de tambours et tout autant de clairons prévient le troupier qu'en sa qualité d'homme vertueux on l'invite à se lever pour voir lever l'Aurore.

Avant de se mettre en route on s'ingurgite une légère tasse de moka.

Le chant du départ.

Suivez-moi, Castillans, le Mexique vous appelle ;
Cortez va vous conduire à des succès nouveaux,
à des succès .... ès .... nou-ou-ouveaux.

Pas d'écho — triste ! triste !! triste !!!

Vera Cruz, Mexique

Bordó
5 avril 18

ADVENTUROUS EUROPE, 1800-1899. GUADALUPE JIMÉNEZ CODINACH

NOTES

[1] Jacques Haudaille, "Gaetan Souch d'Alvimart, The Alleged Envoy of Napoleon to Mexico, 1807-1809," in *The Americas* XVI (1969), pp. 109-131.

[2] "Causa instruida contra el Generalísimo D. Ignacio de Allende," May 10 to June 29, 1811, in *Documentos históricos mexicanos*, ed. Genaro García (México, INEHRM, 1985) Vol. I, pp. 17, 43-44.

[3] *Ibid.*, p. 44.

[4] "Declaración del cura Hidalgo, en ochenta y nueve fojas," Cuaderno No. 13, in *Colección de documentos para la historia de la guerra de independencia de México de 1808 a 1821*, ed. Juan Hernández y Dávalos (México, INEHRM, 1985) Vol. I, p. 26.

[5] Justino Fernández, *Arte moderno y contemporáneo de México*, 2 vols. (México, UNAM, 1993) Vol. I, p.26.

[6] *Ibid.*

[7] *Ibid.*, p. 26.

[8] *Ibid.*, p. 27.

[9] W. D. Gunn, *Escritores norteamericanos y británicos en México* (México, Fondo de Cultura Económica, 1977) p. xi.

[10] Archivo General de Simancas, *Estado*, 8173 (Despacho 62).

[11] Guadalupe Jiménez Codinach, *La Gran Bretaña y la independencia de México, 1808-1821* (México, Fondo de Cultura Económica, 1991) p. 38.

[12] "Carta de Agustín Iturbide a Nicolás B. de la Gándara," February 3, 1822, in *La correspondencia de Iturbide después del Plan de Iguala* 2 vols. (México, Archivo General de la Nación, 1945) Vol. I, p. 180.

[13] "Statement by General Wavell, Envoy to Great Britain," in the British Library, Ms. Add. 38296. ff. 85-86 v.

[14] Guadalupe Jiménez Codinach, *op. cit.*, p. 314.

[15] Justino Fernández, *op. cit.*, pp. 29-30.

[16] *Ibid.*, p. 30.

[17] Henry George Ward, "México en 1827. Selección," in *Lecturas Mexicanas* (México, Fondo de Cultura Económica, 1981) No. 73, pp. 8-9.

[18] Guadalupe Jiménez Codinach, "*La Confédération Napoléonnie*. El desempeño de los conspiradores militares y las sociedades secretas en la independencia de México," in *La Revolución de Independencia*, coord. Virginia Guedea (México, El Colegio de México, 1995) pp.130-155.

[19] René Albrecht Carrie, *Europe After 1815* (Totowa, Adams and Company, 1968) p.12.

[20] "Guerra y paz en tiempos de revolución. 1793-1830," in Universidad de Cambridge. *Historia del mundo moderno* (Barcelona, SOPENA, 1979) IX, 374.

[21] *Ibid.*

[22] René Albrecht Carrie, *op. cit.*, p. 43.

[23] J. A. S. Grenville, *La Europa remodelada, 1848-1878* (México, Editorial Siglo XXI, 1980) p. 239.

[24] Alexis de Tocqueville, "On the Latent Revolution," January 27, 1848, in *Metternich's Europe*, ed. Mark Walker (London, Macmillan, 1968) p. 341.

[25] Carlton J. H. Hayes and Charles Woolsey Cole, *History of Europe Since 1500* (New York, The Macmillan Co., 1959) p. 317.

[26] *Ibid.*, pp. 318-319.

[27] *Ibid.*, pp. 354-355.

[28] *Ibid.*, p. 358.

[29] Cited by J. A. S. Grenville, *op. cit.*, p. 309.

ALEXANDER VON HUMBOLDT'S EXPEDITION THROUGH MEXICO. FRANK HOLL

NOTES

[1] Alexander von Humboldt, *Reise auf dem Río Magdalena, durch die Anden und Mexico. Aus den Reisetagebüchen zusammengestellt und erläutert durch Margot Faak* (Berlin, Akademie-Verlag, Vol. I, 1986 and Vol. II, 1990) I, 316.

[2] *Ibid.*, I, 358.

[3] Alexander von Humboldt, *Essai politique sur le royaume de la Nouvelle Espagne. Avec un atlas physique et géographique du royaume de la Nouvelle. Espagne, fondé sur des observations astronomiques, des mesures trigonométriques et des nivellementes barométriques*, 2 Vols. plus an atlas (Paris, Schoell, 1811).

[4] von Humboldt, *Reise auf dem Río Magdalena...*, I, 319.

[5] Alexander von Humboldt, *Vues de Cordillères et Monumens de peuples indigenes de L'Amérique*, (Paris, Schoell, 1810) [Vol. I, illustrations and Vol. II, text] I, plate 9 and II, 37-41.

[6] *Ibid.*, I, plates 49 ff. and II, 270-273.

[7] von Humboldt, *Reise auf dem Río Magdalena...*, I, 322.

[8] *Ibid.*, I, 323.

[9] *Ibid.*, I, 330.

[10] *Ibid.*, I, 331.

[11] *Ibid.*, I, 333.

[12] von Humboldt, *Vues de Cordillères...*, I, plates 21,23,29.

[13] von Humboldt, *Reise auf dem Río Magdalena...*, II, 366.

[14] von Humboldt, *Vues de Cordillères...*, II, 125-195.

[15] von Humboldt, *Reise auf dem Río Magdalena...*, I, 355.

[16] *Ibid.*, I, 324.

[17] *Ibid.*, I, 342.

[18] *Ibid.*, I, 348.

[19] *Ibid.*, I, 352.

[20] von Humboldt, *Vues de Cordillères...*, I, plate 22.

[21] *Ibid.*, I, plate 64.

[22] von Humboldt, *Reise auf dem Río Magdalena...*, I, 365.

[23] *Ibid.*

[24] *Ibid.*, I, 375.

[25] von Humboldt, *Vues de Cordillères...*, I, plate 43.

[26] von Humboldt, *Reise auf dem Río Magdalena...*, I, 375.

[27] Alexander von Humboldt, *Atlas géographique et physique du royaume de la Nouvelle Espagne, fondé sur les observations astronomiques, des mesures trigonométriques et des nivellements barométriques*, (Paris, Schoell, 1811), plate 29.

[28] von Humboldt, *Vues de Cordillères...*, I, plate 43.

[29] *Ibid.*, I, plate 52 ff. and II, 275.

[30] *Ibid.*, I, plate 7 ff.

[31] *Ibid.*, II, 27.

[32] *Ibid.*, II, 35.

[33] *Ibid.*, I, plate 34.

[34] von Humboldt, *Atlas...*, plate 17.

[35] Alexander von Humboldt, *Mexico-Werk. Politische Ideen zu Mexico. Mexicanische Landeskunde*, ed. and with notes by Hanno Beck, in collab. with Wolf-Dieter Grün, et al (Darmstadt, Wissenschaftliche Buchgesellschaft, 1991) p. 85.

[36] von Humboldt, *Reise auf dem Río Magdalena...*, I, 391.

PHILLIPE RONDE

SAN JUAN DE ULÚA AND VERACRUZ (DETAIL) [193]

PROFILE OF THE TRAVELER-ARTIST IN THE NINETEENTH CENTURY. Pablo Diener

NOTES

[1] Hans Becher, ed., *Lukas Vischer (1780-1840). Künstler - Reisender - Sammler* (Hanover, Völkerkundliche Abhandlungen, 1967) II, 20-21.

[2] Jean Baptiste Louis Gros, *Ascension du Grand Volcan de Mexico*, Printing proof dated March, 1866 (Paris, Archives Nationales, F 17, 2914, 2).

[3] María de Fátima Costa and Pablo Diener, *Viajando nos Bastidores. Documentos de Viagem da Expedição Langsdorff* (Cuiabá, Ed. UFMT, 1995) p. 58.

[4] Jean-Frédéric Waldeck, *Journal d'Amérique 1829-1839* (British Museum, Add. Ms. 41684).

[5] Gertrud Richert, *Johann Moritz Rugendas. Ein Deutscher Maler des XIX Jahrhunderts* (Berlin, Rembrandt Verlag, 1959) p. 12.

[6] Pablo Diener, *Rugendas. Bilder aus Mexiko,* Catalog (Augsburg, Wissner Verlag, 1994) p. 109.

FRANÇOIS MATHURIN ADALBERT, BARON DE COURCY. Katherine Manthorne / Pablo Diener

NOTES

[1] For more on the relationship between de Courcy and Rugendas refer to: Pablo Diener, "Rugendas y sus compañeros de viaje," within the collection of articles "El viajero europeo del siglo XIX," *Artes de México*, XXXI (1996) 26-36.

HUBERT SATTLER. Nikolaus Schaffer

BIBLIOGRAPHY

Faszination Landschaft. Exhibition catalog. Salzburg, Residenzgalerie, 1995. p. 110.

Hyde, Ralph. *Panoramia! The Art and Entertainment of the "All-Embracing" View*. Exhibition catalog. London, Barbican Art Gallery, 1988.

Oettermann, Stephen. *Das Panorama: Die Geschichte eines Massenmediums*. Frankfurt, Sydikat, 1980. p. 230.

Sehsucht: Das Panorama als Massenunterhaltung des 19. Jahrhunderts. Exhibition catalog. Bonn, Kunst- und Ausstellungshalle der Bundesrepublik Deutschland, 1993.

Stopfer, Beate. "Hubert Sattler - Materialien zur Monographie eines Reisemalers," in *Salzburger Museum Carolino Augusteum*, Yearbook 22/1976, 103 ff.

Wieder, Wolfgang. "Kino des 19. Jahrhunderts. Das Panorama: Schule der Seh(n)sucht," in *Von Menschen und Masken*. Vienna/Munich, 1987. pp. 52-60.

JULIUS HOFFMANN, ARCHITECT TO MAXIMILIANO. Ferdinand Anders

THE ARCHITECTURAL PROJECTS OF ARCHDUKE FERDINAND MAXIMILIAN AND EMPEROR MAXIMILIAN I

1) Maxing. Villa ("Schlößl", or "little castle") and garden in the surroundings of the castle Schönbrunn (Vienna)

2) Projects for "Neu-Maxing." One project among this series conceived the building as a residence for the Commander in Chief of the Austrian Navy in Vienna.

3) Villa Lazarovich. Mansion and garden in Trieste, residence of the Commander in Chief of the Austrian Navy in Vienna.

4) Castelleto. Located in the park of Miramare. First residence of Maximilian and Carlota after their wedding.

5) Gardens in the Lombardo-Venetian kingdom (Milan, Monza, Venice).

6) Miramare. Palace and garden in the surroundings of Trieste.

7) Lacroma. Near Ragusa (Dubrovnik), castle (reconstructed monastery) and garden.

8) Palacio Nacional. Residence of the Emperor en Mexico.

9) Calzada del Emperador. Boulevard (today's Paseo de la Reforma) in Mexico City.

Die Bauschöpfungen des Erzherzogs Ferdinand Maximilian und Kaisers Maximilian I.

10) Borda Garden. Emperor's residence in Cuernavaca.
11) Olindo. In Acapatzingo (Cuernavaca). Mansion and garden.

12) Alcázar de Chapultepec (Miravalle)
Castle and garden, Emperor's residence.

BIBLIOGRAPHY

Anders, Ferdinand. *Erzherzog Ferdinand Maximilian und das Segundo Imperio Mexicano. Wissenschaft / Münzen & Medaillen / Ordenswesen / Philatelie.* Hardegg, 1974.

—"Il secondo imperio messicano." in *Massimiliano da Trieste al Messico.* Trieste, 1986. pp. 101-104.

—"Scienziati ed artisti austriaci al servizio dell'imperatore Massimiliano." in *Massimiliano da Trieste al Messico.* Trieste, 1986. pp.105-108.

—*Die Gärten Maximilians.* Vienna, Bezirksmuseum Hietzing, 1987.

—"Erzherzog Ferdinand Max als Schloß- und Gartenschöpfer." in *Massimiliano. Rilettura di un'estistenza.* Trieste, 1992. pp. 235-250.

Anders, Ferdinand., and Klaus Eggert. *Maximilian von Mexiko. Erzherzog und Kaiser.* St. Pölten, 1982.

Drewes, Michael. *Projekte Carl Gangolf Kaysers für Kaiser Maximilian von Mexiko.* Vienna, ARX/1980. pp. 3-18.

"Un Giardino in Riva al Mare." in *Il Parco di Miramare ieri e domani: vicende storiche e prospettive culturali.* Trieste, 1986.

Wilcek, Felix. *Finanzen der Familie Habsburg-Lothringen unter besonderer Berücksichtigung von Erzherzog Ferdinand Max. Versuch einer Darstellung (bis zur 2. Republik).* Vienna, Doctoral thesis, University of Vienna, 1991.

NOTES

[1] Thieme-Becker, *Allgemeines Lexikon der bildenden Künstler* (Leipzig, 1924) s.v. "Hoffman," Vol. XVII.

[2] Manuel Payno, "Obras en el palacio de México y en Chapultepec," in *Cuentas, Gastos, Acreedores y otros asuntos del tiempo de la Intervención francesa y del Imperio del 1861 a 1867* (Mexico City, 1868) p. 713.

[3] Egon Caesar Conte Corti, *Maximilian und Carlota von Mexiko* (Vienna, 1924) II, 30.

[4] Payno, *op. cit.*, p. 713.

[5] Simon Leo Reinisch, "Reise nach Mexiko (Tagebuch)," in Ferdinand Anders, "Im Schatten des Kaiserreiches – Österreichisch-mexikanische Miszellen (1864-1870)" in *Wiener Völkerkundliche Mitteilungen* (Vienna, 1993) Vol. 35, 39-184.

[6] Conte Corti, *op. cit.*, II, 108.

[7] José Luis Blasio, *Maximiliano íntimo. El emperor Maximiliano y su corte. Memoria de un secretario particular* (Paris, 1905) p. 191.

[8] *Ibid.*, p. 177.

[9] *Ibid.*

[10] Felix Wilcek, *Erzherzog Ferdinand Maximilian Joseph, Kaiser Maximilian I. von Mexiko (1832-1867). Seine Unternehmungen und deren finanzielle Hintergründe.* (Vienna, Thesis, University of Vienna, 1988) p. 117.

WILLIAM BULLOCK: SHOWMAN. Jonathan King

BIBLIOGRAPHY

Alexander, E.P. "William Bullock: Little-Remembered Museologist and Showman." in *Curator*, 28, 1985, II, 117-147.

Bullock, William. *A Companion to the Liverpool Museum...* 5th ed. Liverpool, G. F. Harris, 1807.

—*A Companion to Mr Bullock's Museum...* 8th ed. London, Henry Reynell, 1810.

—*A Companion to Mr Bullock's Museum... now open for public inspection in the Egyptian Temple...* 10th ed. London, 1812.

—*The narrative of Jean Hornn, military coachman to Napoleon Bonaparte.* 2nd edition. Bristol, Bennett for the London Museum, Piccadilly, 1816.[a.]

—*A description of the costly and curious military carriage of the late Emperor of France, taken on the evening of the Battle of Waterloo... now exhibiting (by permission) at the London Museum.* London, Whittingham and Rowland, 1816. [b.]

—*Catalogue... of the Roman Gallery of Antiquities and Works of Art, and the London Museum of Natural History... Which will be Sold by Auction... by Mr Bullock... On Thursday, the 29th of April, 1819, And continue every Tuesday, Wednesday, Thursday, and Friday, till the whole is sold....* London, 1819.

—*An account of the family of Laplanders... now exhibiting at the Egyptian Hall, Piccadilly.* London, printed for W. Bullock, 1822.

—*Six Months' Residence and Travels in Mexico...* London, John Murray, 1824. [a.]

—*Catalogue of the exhibition called Modern Mexico...* London, J Bullock, 1824. [b.]

—*A description of the unique exhibition, called Ancient Mexico...* London, James Bullock, 1824. [c.]

—*A descriptive catalogue of the exhibition, entitled Ancient and Modern Mexico...* London, James Bullock, 1824. [d.]

Burford, J. and R. *Description of a view of the City of Mexico...* London, J. and C. Adlard, 1826.

Graham, Ian. "Three Early Collectors in Mesoamerica" in *Collecting the Pre-Columbian Past.* ed. Elizabeth Hill Bonne. Washington DC, Dumbarton Oaks, 1993. pp. 49-80.

Mayes, Stanley. *The Great Belzoni.* London, Putnam, 1959.

Saxon, A. H. *P. T. Barnum. The Legend and the Man.* New York, Columbia University Press, 1989.

Wainwright, Clive. *George Bullock Cabinet-Maker.* London, John Murray and H. Blairman & Sons, 1988.

[1] While some of Bullock's antiquities are in the British Museum, his casts have not been fully researched. One may be in Edinburgh, in the Royal Museum of Scotland: "Plaster cast, painted to represent dark grey andesite, of the central medallion of the calendar stone. Diameter (sight size 29 inches approx.)" [Information from Maureen Barrie, letter of 11.10.1993]. Another may also have been recorded in Edinburgh, in the then Museum of the Society of Antiquaries, in about 1870, by A. W. Franks. In one of the series of his small notebooks in the archives of the Department of Ethnography, British Museum, is a drawing of a serpent's head captioned: "H c 1 ft 9 ins." [A. W. Franks. "Museum of the Soc. of Antiquaries Edinburgh," Small Notebook 25: f 7].

[2] Bullock's Elmwood was, in 1991, a series of design studios called Gaither's, at 244 Forest Avenue, Ludlow, KY 41016.

THE PANORAMA OF LEICESTER SQUARE. Scott Wilcox

NOTES

[1] The major works on the phenomenon of the panorama are: Stephan Oettermann, *Das Panorama: Die Geschichte eines Massenmediums* (Frankfurt, Syndikat, 1980); Ralph Hyde, *Panoramania! The Art and Entertainment of the "All-Embracing" View,* exhibition catalogue (London, Barbican Art Gallery, 1988); and *Sehsucht: Das Panorama als Massenunterhaltung des 19. Jahrhunderts,* exhibition catalogue (Bonn, Kunst- und Ausstellungshalle der Bundesrepublik Deutschland, 1993).

[2] Fuller accounts of Barker and the early history of the panorama are given in Scott Wilcox, "The Early History of the Panorama," in *Das Panorama in Altötting: Beiträge zu Geschichte und Restaurierung* (Munich, Bayeriches Landesamt für Denkmalpflege, 1990); and Scott Wilcox, "Erfindung und Entwicklung des Panoramas in Grossbritannien," in *Sehsucht.* A complete listing of the panoramas exhibited at Leicester Square can be found in Scott Wilcox, *The Panorama and Related Exhibitions in London* (University of Edinburgh, unpublished M.Litt. thesis, 1976).

[3] *The Repertory of Arts and Manufactures: Consisting of Original Communications, Specifications of Patent Inventions, and Selections of Useful Practical Papers from the Transactions of the Philosophical Societies of All Nations, &c. &c.* (London, 1796) pp. 165-67.

[4] *The Edinburgh Evening Courant,* December 29, 1787.

[5] *Morning Chronicle, and London Advertiser,* March 14, 1789.

[6] Letter from John Constable to John Dunthorne, Senior, May 23, 1803, *John Constable's Correspondence,* ed. R. B. Beckett, vol. 2 (Ipswich, Suffolk Record Society, 1964) p. 34.

[7] *Morning Chronicle,* April 21, 1801.

[8] *Ibid.,* March 14, 1789.

[9] *The Diary; or, Woodfall's Register,* June 10, 1789.

[10] *Repository of Arts,* third series, 28 (1826) p. 297.

[11] *Blackwood's Edinburgh Magazine,* 15 (1824) pp. 472-73.

[12] *Description of a View of the City of Mexico, and Surrounding Country, now Exhibiting in the Panorama, Leicester Square* (London, J. and C. Adlard, 1825) p. 5.

[13] Although it seems likely that the panorama of Mexico City exhibited in 1863 was the same one shown a decade earlier, that this was the same actual panorama exhibited in 1825 seems less likely.

LANDSCAPE PAINTING AMONG THE TRAVELER-ARTISTS. Pablo Diener

NOTES AND BIBLIOGRAPHY

[1] Barbara Novak, *Nature and Culture. American Landscapes and Painting, 1825-1875* (New York and Toronto, Oxford University Press, 1980; paperback 1981) p. 36 [Church's annotation dated July 11, 1856].

Additional information can be found in:

Bullock, William. *Description of a View of the City of Mexico, and Surrounding Country, Now Exhibiting in the Panorama, Leicester Square.* London. 1826.

Gros, Jean Baptiste Louis. *Ascension du Grand Volcan de Mexico.* Paris, Archives Nationales, F 17, 2914, 2. (Printing proof dated March, 1866).

Harkort, Eduard. Correspondence found in the Westfälisches Wirtschaftsarchiv. Dortmund, Germany. (Portions of the text have been published in Pablo Diener, *Rugendas. Un pintor aluscinado con el paisaje de Colima.* Colima, Universidad de Colima, 1995).

Moyssén, Xavier. "Eugenio Landesio. Teórico y crítico de arte." in *Anales del Instituto de Investigaciones Estéticas,* 32, p. 69-91. Mexico City, UNAM, 1963.

Rugendas, Johann Mortiz. *Voyage Pittoresque dans le Brésil.* Paris, Engelmann & Co. (Published in installments beginning in 1827).

Waldeck, Jean-Frédéric. *Journal d'Amérique 1829-1839.* (British Museum, Add. Ms. 41684).

ETHNOGRAPHY AND GENRE IN THE IMAGES OF THE TRAVELERS. Juana Gutiérrez Haces

NOTES

[1] Antonio del Río, *Description of the ruins of an ancient city discovered near Palenque, in the Kingdom of Guatemala in Spanish America, translated from the original manuscript report of Captain Antonio del Río, followed by Teatro crítico americano, a critical investigation and research into the history of americans, by Dr. Felix Cabrera, of the city of Guatemala,* (London, Henry Berthoud, 1822). The original images from this expedition had not been published apart from one that appeared, incorrectly described, in the work by von Humboldt, *Vues des Cordillères....* Regarding this topic and the various copies that existed of these drawings, see: Ma. Concepción García Sáiz, "Antonio del Río y Guillermo Dupaix. El reconocimiento de una deuda histórica," in *Anales del Museo de América* (Madrid, 1995) II, 99-119.

[2] Roger Barta, *El Salvaje en el espejo* (Mexico City, UNAM-ERA, 1992).

[3] Hugh Honour, *The New Golden Land. European Images of America from the Discoveries to the Present Time* (New York, Pantheon Books, 1975).

[4] *Ibid.,* pp. 84-117.

[5] Benjamin Keen, *La Imagen azteca en el pensamiento universal* (Mexico City, Fondo de Cultura Económica, 1984) p. 185.

[6] Alexander von Humboldt, *Ensayo político sobre el reino de la Nueva España,* facsimile edition, Paris, 1822 (Mexico City, Instituto Cultural Helénico/Miguel Angel Porrua, 1985) I, p. 137.

[7] *Ibid.* pp. 172-173.

[8] Paul Mercier, *Historia de la Antropología* (Madrid, Ed. Península) Serie Universitaria No. 41, p. 31.

[9] *Enciclopedia Internacional de las ciencias sociales,* dir. David L. Sills (Madrid, Aguilar, 1975) I, 394 *et seq.*

[10] Tzvetan Todorov, *Los morales de la historia* (Barcelona, Ediciones Paidos) p. 28.

THE ANTIQUARIAN THEME AMONG THE TRAVELER-PAINTERS. Elena Isabel Estrada de Gerlero

NOTES

[1] "Cuestionario para la formación del completo conocimiento de la Geografía Física, Antigüedades, Mineralogía y Metalurgia de este Reino de Nueva España e Instrucción sobre el modo de formarlas. Veracruz, 22 de enero de 1777," in the index of documents to *Antonio de Ulloa y la Nueva España,* by Francisco de Solano (Mexico City, Universidad Nacional Autónoma de México, 1979) p.CXLIV (Found in the Archivo General de la Nación: Bandos, Vol. X, fols. 17-20v; in Biblioteca Nacional de México: Ms. 138/3, fols. 457-460V; and in RAH: Correspondencia Bucareli, Vol. 72, Ms. 9/4379.)

[2] Elena Isabel Estrada de Gerlero, "La labor anticuaria novohispana en la época de Carlos IV: Guillermo Dupaix, precursor de la historia del arte prehispánico," in *XVII Coloquio Internacional de Historia del Arte. Arte, Historia e Identidad en América: Visiones Comparativas,* 3 volumes, ed. Gustavo Curiel, Renato González Mello and Juana Gutiérrez Haces, (Mexico City, Universidad Nacional Autónoma de México, Instituto de Investigaciones Estéticas, 1994) I, 191-205, 199.

[3] "Memorias de la Secretaría y del Despacho de Relaciones Exteriores e Interiores," in *Documentos diversos, inéditos y muy raros,* ed. and introduction and notes by Rafael Aguayo Spencer (Mexico City, Editorial Jus, 1945-1947) *passim,* pp. 39-391.

[4] *Ibid.,* p. 390.

[5] Carlos María Bustamante, *Mañanas de la Alameda de México,* 2 volumes (Mexico City, INBA and the Instituto Nacional de Estudios Históricos de la Revolución Mexicana, de la Secretaría de Gobernación, 1986) I, "Prólogo," p. xii.

[6] *Ibid.,* "Prólogo," p. xiii.

[7] Antonio Ponz, *Viage de España,* a facsimile of the edition published in Madrid by the Viuda de Ibarra, Hijos y Compañía, 1787 (Madrid, Ediciones Atlas, 1972) IX, 269.

[8] *Ibid.,* IX, 289.

[9] Frédéric Waldeck, *Journal 1825-1829,* Newberry Library, Ayer Manuscript 1261, p.35 and *Journal d'Amérique 1829-1839,* British Museum, Add. Ms. 41684, p. 74.

[10] William Bullock, *Seis meses de residencia y viajes en México,* translated by Gracia Bosque de Ávalos, with preliminary study and notes by Juan A. Ortega y Median (Mexico City, Banco de México, 1983) p. 180-186. Also recommended: *A Description of the Unique Exhibition Called Ancient Mexico: Collected on the Spot in 1823, with the Assistance of the Mexican Government, and Now Open for Public Inspection at the Egyptian Hall, Piccadilly,* by W. Bullock, F.L.& S. &c &c, London, Printed by the Proprietor, 1824.

[11] Frédéric Waldeck, *Journal 1825-1829,* Newberry Library, Ayer Manuscript 1261, p. 81. No one has mentioned this drawing by Linati, perhaps found in one of Waldeck's portfolios.

[12] *Ibid.,* p. 98, 102.

[13] *Ibid.,* p. 49.

[14] *Ibid.,* p. 103.

[15] *Ibid.,* p. 133.

[16] Waldeck, *Journal d'Amérique 1829-1839,* British Museum, Add. Ms. 41684, p. 33.

[17] Baradère, *"Dedicación al Congreso de la Nación Mexicana,"* UTBLAC, G434, Guide No. 683, 7 fols.

[18] Frédéric Waldeck, *Journal d'Amérique 1829-1839,* British Museum, Add. Ms. 41684, p. 33.

[19] *Ibid.,* p. 3, 4.

[20] *Ibid.,* p. 17.

[21] *Ibid.,* p. 6.

[22] *Ibid.,* p. 18.

[23] *Ibid.,* p. 51.

[24] *Ibid.,* p. 24.

[25] *Ibid.,* p. 233.

[26] *Ibid.,* p. 402.

[27] *Ibid.,* p. 405.

IMAGES OF PALENQUE. María Concepción García Sáiz

BIBLIOGRAPHY

Alcina Franch, J. *Arqueólogos o Anticuarios. Historia antigua de la Arqueología en la América Española.* Barcelona, Ediciones del Serbal, 1995.

Ballesteros Gaibrois, M. "Nuevas noticias sobre Palenque en un manuscrito del siglo XVIII." in *Cuadernos del Instituto de Historia. Serie Antropológica.* No.II. Mexico City, UNAM, 1960.

Baudez, Claude-François. *Jean-Frédéric Waldeck, peintre. Le premier explorateur des ruines mayas.* Paris, Ed. Hazan, 1993.

Berlin-Neubart, H. "Miscelánea Palencana." in *Journal de la Société des Americanistes.* N.S. 59 (1970), 107-128.

Brasseur de Bourbourg, Charles E. *Monuments anciens du Mexique. Palenque et autres ruines de l'ancienne civilisation du Mexique. Collection de Vues, Bas-Reliefs, Morceaux d'Architecture, Coupes, Vases, Terres cuites, Cartes et Plans dessinés d'aprés nature et relevés par M. de Waldeck.* Paris, Arthus Bertrand, editeur, 1866.

Brunhouse, R. L. *In Search of the Maya. The First Archaeologist.* Albuquerque, University of New Mexico, 1973.

Cabello, P. *Política científica de la época de Carlos III en el área maya.* Madrid, Ediciones de la Torre, 1992.

Castañeda Paganini, R. *Las ruinas de Palenque. Su descubrimiento y primeras exploraciones del siglo XVIII.* Guatemala City, Ministerio de Educación Pública, 1946.

Dupaix, Guillermo. *Dupaix: Expediciones acerca de los Antiguos Monumentos de la Nueva España. 1805-1808.* Introduction and notes by José Alcina Franch. Madrid, Ed. Porrua, 1969.

García Sáiz, María C. "Antonio del Río y Guillermo Dupaix. El reconocimiento de una deuda histórica." in *Anales del Museo de América.* Vol.II, 99-120. Madrid, 1995.

Greene Robertson, M. *The Sculpture of Palenque.* 4 Volumes. Princeton, Princeton University Press, 1983-1991.

Hagen, V. W. von. *Maya Explorer. John Lloyd Stephens and the Lost Cities of Central America and Yucatan.* Norman, University of Oklahoma Press, 1948.

Pendergast, D. M. Palenque: *The Walker-Caddy Expedition to the Ancient Maya City, 1839-1840. The American Explorations and Travel Series.* Norman, University of Oklahoma Press, 1967.

Río, Antonio del. *Description of the ruins of an ancient city discovered near Palenque, in the Kingdom of Guatemala in Spanish America, translated from the original manuscript report of Captain Antonio del Río, followed by Teatro crítico americano, a critical investigation and research into the history of americans, by Dr. Felix Cabrera, of the city of Guatemala.* London, Henry Berthoud, 1822.

—*Descripción del terreno y población antiguamente descubierta en las inmediaciones del pueblo de Palenque jurisdicción de la provincia de Ciudad Real de Chiapa una de las del reino de Goathemala de la América Septentrional.* Madrid, Edición de Manuel Ballesteros Gaibrois, 1939.

Waldeck, Frédéric de. *Voyage Pittoresque et Archeologique dans la province Yucatan (Amérique Centrale) pendant les annés 1834 et 1836. dedié à la memoire de peu le vicomte de Kingsborough.* Paris, Bellizard Dufour et Ca. éditeurs, 1838.

THE PICTORIAL-DESCRIPTIVE FOCUS IN THE LITERATURE OF TRAVELERS.
José Enrique Covarrubias

BIBLIOGRAPHY

Beltrami, Giacomo C. *Le Mexique.* 2 Volumes. Paris, Crevot, 1830.

Bullock, William. *Seis meses de residencia y viajes en México.* Translated by Gracia Bosque de Ávalos. Mexico City, Banco de México, 1983.

Charnay, Desiré. *Viaje a Yucatán a fines de 1886.* Translated by Francisco Cantón Rosado. Mérida, Imp. de la Revista de Mérida, 1888.

Egerton, Daniel Thomas. *Vistas de México.* Translated by Manuel Romero de Terreros. Mexico City, F. Zamora Millet, 1966.

Fossey, Mathieu de. *Le Mexique.* Paris, Henri Plon, 1857.

Nebel, Carl. *Viaje pintoresco y arqueológico sobre la parte más interesante de la República Mexicana, en los años transcurridos desde 1829 hasta 1834.* Mexico City, Librería de Manuel Porrúa, S.A., 1963.

Sartorius, Carl Christian. *México. Paisajes y bosquejos populares.* Translated from the English by Mercedes Quijano Narezo. Mexico City, Centro de Estudios de Historia de México - CONDUMEX, 1988.

Waldeck, Frédéric de. *Viaje pintoresco y arqueológico a la provincia de Yucatán durante los años 1834-1836.* Translated by Manuel Mestre Ghiagliazza. Mérida, Compañía Tipográfica Yucateca, S.A., 1930.

Ward, Henry George. *México en 1827.* Translated by Ricardo Haas. Mexico City, Fondo de Cultura Económica, 1981.

THE CAPTURE AND REPRODUCTION OF THE DECISIVE INSTANT IN THE NINETEENTH CENTURY.
Aurelio de los Reyes

NOTES

[1] I wish to thank Frances Terpak, Director of Special Collections at the Getty Center Library, for having made known to me these three albums, valuable documents relating to the French Intervention in Mexico that communicate the personal experiences of the soldiers who came to do combat.

[2] "El cinematógrafo Lumière," *El Monitor Republicano*, August 16, 1896, p. 3.

Eugenio Landesio
ON THE WAY TO SANTA MARÍA REGLA (DETAIL) [194]

LIST OF ILLUSTRATIONS

PAUL FISCHER
STUDY OF PLANTS (DETAIL) [195]

15. Ignacio Castera
Plan ignográfico de la hacienda de Mazapa; Texcoco
1787
watercolor on paper
27 × 32.5 cm
Archivo General de la Nación
Mexico City
Civil: vol. 2043, exp. 12, f. 10, cat. 4180

16. Tadeo Hanke
Systema colorum tabulare atque comparativum pro expeditione in itinere cum hispanis navibus circa globum terraqueum annis 1789-1793
1789-1793
Real Jardín Botánico
Consejo Superior de Investigaciones Científicas
Madrid, Spain

17. Tadeo Hanke
Systema colorum tabulare atque comparativum pro expeditione in itinere cum hispanis navibus circa globum terraqueum annis 1789-1793
1789-1793
Real Jardín Botánico
Consejo Superior de Investigaciones Científicas
Madrid, Spain

18. Anonymous
Map of the Curacy of Orizaba
1771
watercolor on paper
40 × 31 cm
Archivo General de la Nación
Mexico City
Clero regular y secular: vol. 51, fc. 95

19. Anonymous
Herbariums for the transport of plants
1779
engraving on paper
24 × 20 cm
Archivo General de la Nación
Mexico City
Bandos: vol. 11, fc. 140

20. Atanasio Echeverría
Ascensión al volcán de San Andrés Tuxtla
1793
watercolor on paper
29.5 × 32.5 cm
Archivo General de la Nación
Mexico City
Historia: vol. 558, exp. 7, f. 19, cat. 452

21. Fernando Brambila
View of the Town and Port of Acapulco as Seen from the Frontón del Grifo
gouache, with ink retouching, on paper
41 × 62 cm
Museo de América
Madrid, Spain
Inv. 2.234

22. Hubert Sattler
The Port of Veracruz (detail)
1862
oil on canvas
98.5 × 127 cm
Salzburger Museum Carolino Augusteum
Salzburg, Austria
Inv. 9063/49

23. Daniel Thomas Egerton
The Pico de Orizaba
1831-1842
oil on canvas on masonite
33 × 41 cm
Collection of Banco Nacional de México, S.A.
Mexico City

24. Johann Moritz Rugendas
The Volcano at Colima
1834
oil on canvas
48 × 67 cm
Collection of Banco Nacional de México, S.A.
Mexico City

25. José Arpa
Popocatépetl
19th century
oil on canvas
42 × 57 cm
Private collection
Courtesy of Agustín Cristóbal
Mexico City

26. Octaviano D'alvimar
Main Plaza of Mexico City
1823
oil on canvas
78 × 96 cm
Private collection
Photo: Courtesy of the Instituto de Investigaciones Estéticas-UNAM
Mexico City

27. Phillipe Ronde
Miners at the San Pedro Mine, Chihuahua
1849
pencil and watercolor on paper
29.1 × 23 cm
Bibliothèque Nationale de France
Paris, France
Inv. 198b-d/ii-40

28. Alexander von Humboldt
Plate 34: *Coffre de Perotte*, from *Vues de Cordillères et Monumens des Peuples Indigènes de l'Amérique. Planches.*
Paris, Schoell, 1810
Bibliothèque de l'Institut Royal de France

29. Alexander von Humboldt
Plate 7. *Pyramide de Cholula* (detail), from *Vues de Cordillères et Monumens des Peuples Indigènes de l'Amérique. Planches.*
Paris, Schoell, 1810
Bibliothèque de l'Institut Royal de France

30. Alexander von Humboldt
Plate 22. *Rochers Basaltiques et Cascade de Regla*, from *Vues de Cordillères et Monumens des Peuples Indigènes de l'Amérique. Planches.*
Paris, Schoell, 1810
Bibliothèque de l'Institut Royal de France

31. José de Gorostieta and Juan Antonio de Ayerde
Bellows Machine Used to Extract Metals with Fire
1818
watercolored drawing on paper
33 × 21.5 cm
Archivo General de la Nación
Mexico City
Minería: vol. 134, exp. 1, f. 5, cat. 2786

32. C. Rochussen
Costumes of the Indians of Michoacán
1806
watercolor on paper
22 × 28 cm
Collection of Renato Mazzoni
Paris, France

33. Daniel Thomas Egerton
Mine Shaft at La Valenciana
1831-1842
oil on canvas
33 × 40 cm
Collection of Banco Nacional de México, S.A.
Mexico City

34. Baron de Courcy
The "La Gallega" Mine near Zacatecas
1832
pencil and watercolor on paper
27.5 × 22.3 cm
Collection of Eduardo Uhart
Paris, France

35 y 36. Ph. Simonneau
Estampa 2ª en la que van representados en grande los hornos que sirven para separación del azogue. Estampa 3ª utensilios, en el expediente sobre la habilitación de la mina de azogue en Tlalchiapa, Axuchitlán, obispado de Valladolid
1778
watercolored drawing on paper
31 × 22 cm
Archivo General de la Nación
Mexico City
Correspondencia de virreyes: 1ª serie, vol. 109, exp. 28, f. 238.

37. Eugenio Landesio
The "La Purísima" Mine at Real del Monte (detail)
1857
oil on canvas
45.6 × 63.3 cm
Musée du Louvre
Paris, France
Inv. MNR 342
Photo: Réunion des Musées Nationaux

38. Eugenio Landesio
View of the Hacienda de Sánchez
1857
oil on canvas
45.3 × 63.4 cm
Musée du Louvre
Paris, France
Inv. MNR 339
Photo: Réunion des Musées Nationaux

39. Adela Breton
Caryatids or Atlantes in the Upper Hall of the Jaguars at Chichén Itzá
late 19th century
hand-colored photograph
18.2 × 24 cm
Bristol City Council. Bristol Museums and Art Gallery
Bristol, England
Inv. Ea 11079

40. Adela Breton
Study of Caryatid IX in the Upper Temple of the Jaguars at Chichén Itzá
late 19th century
pencil and watercolor on paper
37.3 × 51.2 cm
Bristol City Council. Bristol Museums and Art Gallery
Bristol, England
Inv. Ea 8189a IX

41. Adela Breton
Jambs with Relief in the Interior Hall of the Upper Temple of the Jaguars at Chichén Itzá
late 19th century
hand-colored photograph
32 × 50.5 cm
Bristol City Council. Bristol Museums and Art Gallery
Bristol, England
Inv. Ea 8191e

42. Desiré Charnay
Mitla. Hall of the Columns from *Album of Archaeological Monuments*
19th century
photograph
52 × 70 cm
Mapoteca Orozco y Berra
Centro de Estadística Agropecuaria-SAGAR
Mexico City

43. Brecht
Studies of Soldiers
1862
crayon and watercolor on paper
20 × 10 cm
Musée de l'Armée
Paris, France
Inv. E01084

44. Pál Rosti
Real del Monte from the album *Memories of a Voyage Through America*
1856-1859
photograph
National Széchényi Library
Budapest, Hungary

45. Pelegrín Clavé
Landscape in Durango
1846-1868
oil on pasteboard
15.5 × 41 cm
Collection of Arq. Luis Ortiz Macedo
Mexico City

46. Jean Baptiste Louis, Baron Gros
Popocatépetl and Pico del Frayle
1834
oil on paper on canvas
34 × 46 cm
Collection of Banco Nacional de México, S.A.
Mexico City

47. Pelegrín Clavé
Study of the Grotto at Cacahuamilpa
1846-1868
oil on bristol board
22 × 28 cm
Collection of Banco Nacional de México, S.A.
Mexico City

48. Jean Baptiste Louis, Baron Gros
Teotihuacan. The Pyramid of the Sun
1832
oil on pasteboard on canvas
33.8 × 46.4 cm
Private collection
Munich, Germany

49. Lukas Vischer
Typical Character in *Carnet de Voyage en Mexico*
1828-1832
pencil and watercolor on paper
18.6 × 14.6 cm
Collection of Anthony Guy Vischer
Basel, Switzerland

50. Lukas Vischer
Typical Character in *Carnet de Voyage en Mexico*
1828-1832
pencil and watercolor on paper
18.6 × 14.6 cm
Collection of Anthony Guy Vischer
Basel, Switzerland

51. Johann Moritz Rugendas
Portrait of Lukas Vischer
1831-1833
pencil and watercolor on paper
23.5 × 32 cm
Staatliche Graphische Sammlung
Munich, Germany
Inv. 15822

52. Baron de Courcy
Calle [street] *del Presbiterio in Jalapa*
1832
watercolor on paper
20 × 27.1 cm
Collection of Eduardo Uhart
Paris, France

53. Paul Fischer
Xochimilco
late 19th century
watercolor on paper
28 × 49 cm
Private collection
Mexico City

54. Johann Moritz Rugendas
*View of the Slopes of Popocatépetl and Iztaccíhuatl
with the Valley of Mexico in the Background*
1831
oil on pasteboard
28 × 80.9 cm
Staatliche Graphische Sammlung
Munich, Germany
Inv. 18555

55. Anonymous
Camera lucida
ca. 1800
24.6 × 5.2 × 2.1 cm
Deutsches Museum
Munich, Germany
Inv. 75273

56. Anonymous
Camera obscura
ca. 1800
15.7 × 15.7 × 15.7 cm
Deutsches Museum
Munich, Germany
Inv. 08/13075

57. *Plate IV. "Dessein, chambre obscure",* in
*Dictionnaire Raisonné des Sciences,
des Arts et des Métiers -Encyclopédie de Diderot et
D'Alembert*
Paris. Plates. Vol. 3, *Recueil de Planches,
sur les Sciences et les Arts Seconde Partie*
1751-1772
printed
40 × 25.7 cm

58. *Plate V. "Dessein, chambre obscure",* in
*Dictionnaire Raisonné des Sciences,
des Arts et des Métiers -Encyclopédie de Diderot et
D'Alembert*
Paris. Plates. Vol. 3, *Recueil de Planches,
sur les Sciences et les Arts Seconde Partie*
1751-1772
printed
40 × 25.7 cm

59. Edouard Pingret
Kitchen in Puebla
1851-1855
oil on canvas
41 × 58 cm
Private collection
Mexico City

60. Daniel Thomas Egerton
San Agustín de las Cuevas
1842
oil on canvas
41.5 × 52 cm
Private collection
Mexico City

61. Daniel Thomas Egerton
Crater of Popocatépetl
1834
oil on canvas on masonite
33 × 41 cm
Collection of Banco Nacional de México, S.A.
Mexico City

62. Johann Salomon Hegi
Marketplace
1850-1860
pencil and watercolor on paper
43.5 × 53.8 cm
Collection of Salomón y Brigitte Schärer
Zurich, Switzerland

63. Johann Salomon Hegi
Self-portrait
After 1840
pencil and watercolor on paper
31.5 × 24.2 cm
Collection of Salomón y Brigitte Schärer
Zurich, Switzerland

64. Johann Salomon Hegi
Muleteers
1850-1860
pencil and watercolor on paper
39.5 × 50 cm
Collection of Salomón y Brigitte Schärer
Zurich, Switzerland

65. Johann Salomon Hegi
Good Friday
1850-1860
pencil and watercolor on paper
34.2 × 47.5 cm
Collection of Salomón y Brigitte Schärer
Zurich, Switzerland

66. Johann Salomon Hegi
Picador
1850-1860
pencil and watercolor on paper
46 × 62.3 cm
Collection of Salomón y Brigitte Schärer
Zurich, Switzerland

67. George Henry White
San Juan de Ulúa, Veracruz
1862-1863
watercolor on paper
22.4 × 30.6 cm
ING Baring Holdings, Limited
London, England
Inv. DR 11.02

68. George Henry White
The Pico de Orizaba as Seen from the Sea
1862-1863
watercolor on paper
15.6 × 22.9 cm
ING Baring Holdings, Limited
London, England
Inv. DR 11.93

69. George Henry White
Xochimilco
1862-1863
watercolor on paper
19.8 × 27.6 cm
ING Baring Holdings, Limited
London, England
Inv. DR 11.30

70. George Henry White
Popocatépetl and Iztaccíhuatl as Seen from Tacubaya
1862-1863
watercolor on paper
23.3 × 95 cm
ING Baring Holdings, Limited
London, England
Inv. DR 11.49a

71. Baron de Courcy
The Pyramid of the Sun. Teotihuacan
1832
watercolor on paper
21 × 27.9 cm
Collection of Eduardo Uhart
Paris, France

72. Baron de Courcy
Church at Teotihuacan
1832
watercolor on paper
16.9 × 23.4 cm
Collection of Eduardo Uhart
Paris, France

73. Johann Moritz Rugendas
Portrait of Baron de Courcy
1832
pencil and watercolor on paper
20.1 × 19.3 cm
Collection of Eduardo Uhart
Paris, France

74. Baron de Courcy
Watchtower Overlooking Corn Fields
1832
watercolor on paper
24 × 19.4 cm
Collection of Eduardo Uhart
Paris, France

75. Hubert Sattler
Sketch for *View of Mexico City*
1853
pencil and watercolor on paper
34 × 89.5 cm
Salzburger Museum Carolino Augusteum
Salzburg, Austria
Inv. 12523/49

76. Hubert Sattler
View of Mexico City with Popocatépetl and Iztaccíhuatl
1854
oil on canvas
103 × 132 cm
Salzburger Museum Carolino Augusteum
Salzburg, Austria
Inv. 9059/49

77. Hubert Sattler
Labnah
1836
oil on canvas
99 × 126 cm
Salzburger Museum Carolino Augusteum
Salzburg, Austria
Inv. 5654/49

78. Julius Hoffmann
Palace at Cuernavaca. Bedroom of Maximilian. Decoration of walls
1853
pencil and ink on paper
20.8 × 20.6 cm
Graphische Sammlung Albertina
Vienna, Austria
Inv. Az. 5082 (79/5/13)

79. Julius Hoffmann
Palace at Cuernavaca. Bedroom of Maximilian. Decoration of walls
1853
pencil and ink on paper
21.1 × 36.1 cm
Graphische Sammlung Albertina
Vienna, Austria
Inv. Az. 5083 (79/5/14)

80. Julius Hoffmann
Palace at Cuernavaca. Front view
1853
gouache on paper
17.8 × 25.3 cm
Graphische Sammlung Albertina
Vienna, Austria
Inv. Az. 5080 (79/5/11)

81. Julius Hoffmann
Chapultepec. Remodeling project
1853
pencil and ink on paper
52.5 × 33.5 cm
Graphische Sammlung Albertina
Vienna, Austria
Inv. Az. 5101 (79/3/3)

82. Julius Hoffmann
Palace at Cuernavaca. Ground floor
1853
pencil and ink on paper
25 × 25.3 cm
Graphische Sammlung Albertina
Vienna, Austria
Inv. Az. 5081 (79/5/12)

83. William Bullock
Water Carrier (detail)
1823
pencil and watercolor on paper
13.5 × 18.6 cm
The British Museum. Department of Ethnography. Museum of Mankind
London, England
Inv. KUD (BUL-) 6759

84. William Bullock
Xochimilco
1823
pencil on paper
13.5 × 22 cm
The British Museum. Department of Ethnography. Museum of Mankind
London, England
Inv. KUD (BUL-) 6759

85. William Bullock
Water Carrier and Man with Coat of Leaves
1823
pencil and watercolor on paper
13.5 × 18.6 cm
The British Museum. Department of Ethnography. Museum of Mankind
London, England
Inv. KUD (BUL-) 6759

86. William Bullock
Pulque Carrier
1823
pencil and watercolor drawing on paper
13.5 × 18.6 cm
The British Museum. Department of Ethnography. Museum of Mankind
London, England
Inv. KUD (BUL-) 6759

87. William Bullock
View of the City and Valley of Mexico
1823
pencil on paper
13.2 × 37.5 cm
The British Museum. Department of Ethnography. Museum of Mankind
London, England
Inv. KUD (BUL-) 6759

88. William Bullock
Teotihuacan. The Pyramid of the Sun
1823
pencil on paper
13.5 × 22 cm
The British Museum. Department of Ethnography. Museum of Mankind
London, England
Inv. KUD (BUL-) 6759

89. Félix Eloin
Panoramic View of Mexico City Seen from the Roof of La Enseñanza
1867
pencil on paper
71 × 118 cm
Musée Royal de l'Armée et d'Histoire Militaire
Brussels, Belgium
Inv. 506874

90. Robert Mitchell
Cross Section of the Rotunda at Leicester Square, in *Plans and Views in Perspective of Buildings Erected in England and Scotland*
1801
aquatint on paper
36.8 × 54.3 cm
Yale Center for British Art. Paul Mellon Collection.
New Haven, Connecticut, U.S.A.
Inv. 86.2 FoB

91. J. y R. Burford
Pamphlet *"Panorama of the City of Mexico"*, in *Description of a View of the City of Mexico*.
London, J&C Adlard
1826
print
30.5 × 45 cm
Private collection
Mexico City

92-96. Dante Escalante
Reconstruction of the *"Panorama of the City of Mexico"* by *William Bullock*
1996
acrylic on linen
90 × 770 cm

97. August Lohr
Iztaccíhuatl
1869
oil on canvas
32 × 22 cm
Private collection
Mexico City

98. Jean Baptiste Louis, Baron Gros
The Valley of Mexico as Seen from Lake Texcoco
ca. 1832-1834
oil on canvas
36 × 45 cm
Collection of Banco Nacional de México, S.A.
Mexico City

99. Jean Baptiste Louis, Baron Gros
View of Texcoco (detail)
ca. 1833-1834
oil on canvas
35 × 58.5 cm
Private collection

100. Pál Rosti
Popocatépetl from the album *Memories of a Voyage Through America*
1856-1859
photograph
National Széchényi Library
Budapest, Hungary

101. Pál Rosti
Iztaccíhuatl from the album *Memories of a Voyage Through America*
1856-1859
photograph
National Széchényi Library
Budapest, Hungary

102. Pál Rosti
Cathedral from the album *Memories of a Voyage Through America*
1856-1859
photograph
National Széchényi Library
Budapest, Hungary

103. Pál Rosti
Fountain of Arcos de Belén from the album *Memories of a Voyage Through America*
1856-1859
photograph
National Széchényi Library
Budapest, Hungary

104. Pedro Calvo
Valley of Mexico. El artista con cámara obscura
1825
oil on canvas
115 × 172 cm
Ibero-Amerikanisches Institut
Preussischer Kulturbesitz
Berlin, Germany
Inv. F 6713 a

105. Daniel Thomas Egerton
San Juan Teotihuacan
1831-1842
pencil and gouache on paper
15.5 × 21 cm
Private collection
Mexico City

106. Daniel Thomas Egerton
San Juan Teotihuacan, Late Afternoon
1831-1842
pencil and gouache on paper
16 × 21 cm
Private collection
Mexico City

107. Daniel Thomas Egerton
San Juan Teotihuacan at Sunset
1831-1842
pencil and gouache on paper
23.5 × 28 cm
Private collection
Mexico City

108. Jean-Frédéric Waldeck
The Valley of Mexico from the Bishop's Garden in Tacubaya from the album *Antiquités Mexicaines*
ca. 1829-1830
pencil and watercolor on paper
39 × 56.3 cm
Bibliothèque Nationale de France
Paris, France
Inv. Gd 50 c-e

109. Johann Moritz Rugendas
Gorge of the Río Grande de Santiago
1834
oil on pasteboard
24.5 × 38 cm
Museum für Völkerkunde
Staatliche Museen zu Berlin
Preussischer Kulturbesitz
Berlin, Germany
Inv. VIII E 2598

110. Anthony Carey Stannus
Veracruz
ca. 1865
watercolor on paper
29.9 × 64.8 cm
Private collection
Munich, Germany

111. Anthony Carey Stannus
La Alameda and Façade of the Hospital de San Juan de Dios
ca. 1865
pencil and watercolor on paper
25 × 52 cm
Collection of Juan D. Béistegui
Mexico City

112. Daniel Thomas Egerton
The Basaltic Formations and Cascade at Regla
1831-1842
pencil and watercolor on paper
22 × 16.6 cm
Private collection
Mexico City

113. Adela Breton
The Basaltic Formations and Cascade at Regla
1894
watercolor on paper
60.3 × 42.4 cm
Bristol City Council. Bristol Museums and Art Gallery
Bristol, England
Inv. Ea 8412

114. José Gutiérrez
The Hacienda de Regla
pencil, ink and gouache on paper
27.5 × 44 cm
Museo Naval
Madrid, Spain
Inv. 1723(27)

115. Johann Moritz Rugendas
The Basaltic Formations and Cascade at Regla
1832
oil on pasteboard
25.5 × 39.8 cm
Museum für Völkerkunde
Staatliche Museen zu Berlin
Preussischer Kulturbesitz
Berlin, Germany
Inv. VIII E 2539

116. Baron de Courcy
The Basaltic Formations and Cascade at Regla
1832
watercolor on paper
20.6 × 26.9 cm
Collection of Eduardo Uhart
Paris, France

117. Pál Rosti
Santa María Regla from the album *Memories of a Voyage Through America*
1856-1859
photograph
National Széchényi Library
Budapest, Hungary

118. Adela Breton
Palms in Colima
1896
watercolor on paper
36.3 × 39 cm
Bristol City Council. Bristol Museums and Art Gallery
Bristol, England
Inv. Ea 8377

119. Eduard Hildebrandt
View of Acapulco
1864
watercolor on paper
27.7 × 37.5 cm
Kupferstichkabinett
Berlin, Germany
Inv. SZ 506

120. John Th. Haverfield
San Blas. Houses next to the Sea
1887
pencil and watercolor on paper
25.3 × 35.5 cm
Private collection
Courtesy of Ángel Cristóbal
Mexico City

121. Johann Moritz Rugendas
Sunset at Laguna de Cuyutlán
1834
oil on pasteboard
39.1 × 71.6 cm
Staatliche Graphische Sammlung
Munich, Germany
Inv. 18604

122. Johann Moritz Rugendas
Market in Mexico City (detail)
ca. 1848-1853
oil on canvas
56 × 70 cm
Hamburger Kunsthalle
Hamburg, Germany
Inv. 3494

123. Lukas Vischer
Water Carrier in *Carnet de voyage en Mexico*
1828-1832
pencil and watercolor on paper
18.6 × 14.6 cm
Collection of Anthony Guy Vischer
Basel, Switzerland

124. Anonymous
Water Vendor in Mexico City
19th century
gouache on paper
17 × 10 cm
Museo de América
Madrid, Spain
Inv. 2.238

125. Claudio Linati
Water Vendor and Other Vendors
1828
watercolor on paper
18 × 22 cm
Museo Soumaya
Mexico City

126. Phillipe Ronde
Water Vendor in Mexico City
1850
pencil and watercolor on paper
40.6 × 25.7 cm
Bibliothèque Nationale de France
Paris, France
Inv. 198b-d/1-12 DC, 198B tome 2, p. 12

127. Jean-Frédéric Waldeck
Fiesta de los cinco días
1832
oil on pasteboard
39.1 × 58.8 cm
The Newberry Library
Chicago, Illinois, U.S.A.
Inv. E-4/NC296

128. Claudio Linati
Atigrado de Carnestolendas at Palenque
1828
watercolor on paper
19 × 12 cm
Museo Soumaya
Mexico City

129. Jean-Frédéric Waldeck
Dancer Dressed in Tiger Skin
1832
pencil and gouache on paper
28.3 × 23.3 cm
The Newberry Library
Chicago, Illinois, U.S.A.
Inv. B-1/248

130. Jean-Frédéric Waldeck
Mecapalero
1829
pencil and gouache on paper
40 × 20 cm
Collection of Gabriel Terrades Pujol
Paris, France

131. Pelegrín Clavé
Lake and Canal at Texcoco from the album *Liber Amicorum* by Joaquina de la Cortina
1850
22.3 × 30.3 cm
Collection of Guillermo de Osma Galería
Madrid, Spain

132. Daniel Thomas Egerton
Angels with Symbols of the Passion
1831-1842
pencil and watercolor on paper
17 × 21.6 cm
Private collection
Mexico City

133. Daniel Thomas Egerton
Christ Carrying the Cross with The Virgin Behind
1831-1842
pencil and watercolor on paper
16.7 × 21.7 cm
Private collection
Mexico City

134. Daniel Thomas Egerton
Soldiers and Tabor
1831-1842
pencil and watercolor on paper
17 × 21.6 cm
Private collection
Mexico City

135. Daniel Thomas Egerton
Pilate
1831-1842
pencil and watercolor on paper
17 × 21.6 cm
Private collection
Mexico City

136. Johann Salomon Hegi
Cartulina: Río de Coatzacoalcos, Minatitlán and Chinameca, 3. Interior of a Home in Elotepec. Making Tortillas
1858
pencil and watercolor on paper
31 × 47 cm
Collection of Salomon y Brigitte Schärer
Zurich, Switzerland

137. Jean-Frédéric Waldeck
Making Tortillas
1825
watercolor on paper
30 × 42 cm
The Newberry Library
Chicago, Illinois, U.S.A.
Inv. D-2/110

138. Jean-Frédéric Waldeck
Nicte-tac, Nude Young Lacandon Girl
watercolor on paper
50.6 × 39.7 cm
The Newberry Library
Chicago, Illinois, U.S.A.
Inv. D-7/247

139. Jean-Frédéric Waldeck
Aztec Princess
1833
watercolor on paper
29.5 × 22 cm
The Newberry Library
Chicago, Illinois, U.S.A.
Inv. B-3/29

140. Daniel Thomas Egerton
El tlachiquero
1831-1842
pencil and watercolor on paper
16.5 × 21.8 cm
Private collection
Mexico City

141. Adalbert Schönowsky
Tlachiquero, in *Diary of Voyage*, Volume 10
1866
pencil and watercolor on paper
29.5 × 23.5 cm
Österreichisches Staatsarchiv Nachlässe und Sammlungen
Vienna, Austria
Inv. B/510, vol 10, p. 89

142. Edouard Pingret
Fruit Water Stand
1851-1855
pencil and watercolor on paper
Collection of Arq. Luis Ortiz Macedo
Mexico City

143. Johann Moritz Rugendas
Market in Mexico City
ca. 1848-1853
oil on canvas
56 × 70 cm
Hamburger Kunsthalle
Hamburg, Germany
Inv. 3494

144. Johann Moritz Rugendas
Pico de Orizaba
ca. 1848-1853
oil on canvas
56 × 70 cm
Hamburger Kunsthalle
Hamburg, Germany
Inv. 3492

145. Jean-Frédéric Waldeck
Reconstrucción ideal de una ceremonia (detail)
ca. 1867
oil on canvas
91 × 135 cm
Museo Soumaya
Mexico City

146. Luciano Castañeda / Guillermo Dupaix
Title page from the *Álbum de dibujos originales de los monumentos de la Nueva España*
early 19th century
pencil and watercolor on paper
41.2 × 30 cm
Collection of Juan D. Béistegui
Paris, France

147. Luciano Castañeda / Guillermo Dupaix
Plate 16. Pirámide, planta y corte transversal, in *Álbum de dibujos originales de los monumentos de la Nueva España*
early 19th century
pencil and watercolor on paper
72 × 53 cm
The British Museum. Department of Ethnography. Museum of Mankind
London, England
Inv. 15.502

148. Luciano Castañeda / Guillermo Dupaix
Plate 15. Relieve de Xochicalco, in *Álbum de dibujos originales de los monumentos de la Nueva España*
early 19th century
pencil and watercolor on paper
72 × 53 cm
The British Museum. Department of Ethnography. Museum of Mankind
London, England
Inv. 15.502

149. Jean-Frédéric Waldeck
Sketch of the Pyramid at Xochicalco
19th century
pencil and ink on paper
33 × 54 cm
The Newberry Library
Chicago, Illinois, U.S.A.
Inv. D-1/13

150. Jean-Frédéric Waldeck
Reconstruccion ideal de una ceremonia
ca. 1867
oil on canvas
91 × 135 cm
Museo Soumaya
Mexico City

151. Adela Breton
*Study of the Relief Work at Xochicalco: North
Section of the East Side of the Temple of the
Plumed Serpent*
late 19th century
pencil and watercolor on paper
45.3 × 30.1 cm
Bristol City Council. Bristol Museums
and Art Gallery
Bristol, England
Inv. Ea 8271f

152. Jean-Frédéric Waldeck
The Pyramid at Xochicalco from the album
Antiquités Mexicaines
ca. 1829
watercolor on paper
44.7 × 60.8 cm
Bibliothèque Nationale de France
Paris, France
Inv. Gd 50 c-e

153. Pál Rosti
Xochicalco from the album *Memories of a Voyage
Through America*
1856-1859
photograph
National Széchényi Library
Budapest, Hungary

154. Baron de Courcy
The Ruins at Xochicalco
1832
pencil and watercolor on paper
14.1 × 23.2 cm
Collection of Eduardo Uhart
Paris, France

155. Jean-Frédéric Waldeck
Palenque. Study of a Relief of a Seated Deity
from the album *Antiquités Mexicaines*
1832-1836
pencil and watercolor on paper
29.2 × 23.1 cm
Bibliothèque Nationale de France
Paris, France
Inv. Gd 50 c-e

156. Jean-Frédéric Waldeck
Palenque. View of the Façade of a Palace from
the album *Antiquités Mexicaines*
1832-1836
oil on pasteboard
35.6 × 43.7 cm
Bibliothèque Nationale de France
Paris, France
Inv. Gd 50 c-e

157. Maximilian Franck
Drawing No. 9 "Jarrón de arcilla"
1829
pencil on paper
The British Museum. Department of
Ethnography. Museum of Mankind
London, England

158. Annie Hunter
Study of Eight Archaeological Objects
last quarter of the 19th century
watercolor on paper
30.5 × 45 cm
Victoria and Albert Museum
London, England
Inv. E 431-1935

159. Alfred P. Maudslay
Serpents' Heads. Mound 14. Chichén Itzá. in
Biologia Centrali-Americana, vol. III
1889-1902
photograph

160. Alfred P. Maudslay
*The Castle at Chichén Itzá. Base of the North
Staircase with Element in the Form of a Serpent's
Head*
1885
photograph

161. Desiré Charnay
Palenque. Panel of the Cross in *Album of
Archaeological Monuments*
photograph
52 × 70 cm
Mapoteca Orozco y Berra
Centro de Estadística Agropecuaria, SAGAR
Mexico City

162. Pál Rosti
Piedra del Sol from the album *Memories of a
Voyage Through America*
1856-1859
photograph
National Széchényi Library
Budapest, Hungary

163. Johann Moritz Rugendas
Ruins at Centla, Veracruz
1831
oil on pasteboard
22.5 × 31 cm
Museo Nacional de Historia, INAH
Mexico City
Inv. 230079

164. F. Catherwood / H. Warren
*Stephens/Catherwood Expedition. Principal Patio
of the Palace at Palenque*
lithograph by H. Warren from the original by
Catherwood for the 1844 edition of *Views of
Ancient Monuments in Central America, Chiapas
and Yucatan*
1839-1840
lithography

165. *Walker / Caddy Expedition*
Photograph of Caddy's original, now destroyed
1839-1840
Museum of the American Indian
New York, New York, U.S.A.

166. *Del Río / Armendáriz Expedition 1787*
copy from 1789
Palacio Real
Madrid, Spain

167. Jean-Frédéric Waldeck
*Interpretation of the Myth of Ariadna before the
Ruins at Palenque*

168. *Jean-Frédéric Waldeck Expedition (1832-1834)*,
lithograph by Gilbert from the original by
Waldeck for the 1866 edition of *Monumens
Anciens du Mexique, Palenque, Ocosingo et Autres
Ruines de l'Ancienne Civilisation du Mexique*

169. *Dupaix / Castañeda Expedition 1808*
copy from 1820
Laboratorio de Arte. Universidad de Sevilla
Seville, Spain

170. Johann Moritz Rugendas
*View of the Hacienda El Mirador and the Pico de
Orizaba* (detail)
1831-1832
oil on canvas
70 × 92 cm
Collection of Irma Stallforth
Augsburg, Germany

171. Johann Salomon Hegi
*Cartulina: Hacienda El Mirador, 1. The House at
the Hacienda El Mirador*
1850-1860
pencil and watercolor on paper
22 × 29.5 cm
Collection of Salomon y Brigitte Schärer
Zurich, Switzerland

172. Johann Salomon Hegi
Cartulina: Hacienda El Mirador, 14. Full Moon at the Hacienda El Mirador and Huts
1850-1860
pencil and watercolor on paper
31 × 47 cm
Collection of Salomon y Brigitte Schärer
Zurich, Switzerland

173. Johann Moritz Rugendas
View of the Hacienda El Mirador and the Pico de Orizaba
1831-1832
oil on canvas
70 × 92 cm
Collection of Irma Stallforth
Augsburg, Germany

174. Paul Fischer
Baroque Façade
late 19th century
watercolor on paper
39 × 58 cm
Private collection
Mexico City

175. William Bullock
View of the City and Valley of Mexico in *Six Months' Residence and Travels in Mexico with Plates and Maps,* London, John Murray
1824
engraving
13 × 37 cm
The British Museum. Department of Ethnography. Museum of Mankind
London, England
Inv. KUD (BUL-)M6759

176. Anthony Carey Stannus
Convent of Santo Domingo
ca. 1865
watercolor on paper
47.5 × 38.5 cm
Victoria and Abert Museum
London, England
Inv. 5731

177. Anthony Carey Stannus
Study of a Baroque Window
ca. 1865
watercolor on paper
47 × 33.2 cm
Victoria and Albert Museum
London, England
Inv. 5730

178. A.E. Walter Boodle
Fruit Vendor
1881
pencil and watercolor on paper
21.6 × 13 cm
Collection of Jesús González Vaquero
Mexico City

179. A.E. Walter Boodle
View from Boodle's Window (8 Cinco de Mayo [Street]) Toward the Cathedral
1884
pencil and watercolor on paper
13 × 21.6 cm
Collection of Jesús González Vaquero
Mexico City

180. A.E. Walter Boodle
Fountain at San Cosme
1884
pencil and watercolor on paper
13 × 21.6 cm
Collection of Jesús González Vaquero
Mexico City

181. Desiré Charnay
Izamal, Pyramid at Hunpintok in *Album of Archaeological Monuments*
19th century
photograph
52 × 70 cm
Mapoteca Orozco y Berra
Centro de Estadística Agropecuaria-SAGAR
Mexico City

182. Desiré Charnay
Mitla. Patio of the Frets in *Album of Archaeological Monuments*
19th century
photograph
52 × 70 cm
Mapoteca Orozco y Berra
Centro de Estadística Agropecuaria-SAGAR
Mexico City

183. L. Falconnet
"San Luis Potosí. Annonce de la Procession de N.D. del Carmen", in *Album of Mexico* (detail)
1865
20 × 30 cm
The Getty Center fot the History of Art and the Humanities
Santa Monica, California, U.S.A.
Inv. 93.R.20

184. L. Falconett
"Environs de Puebla. Le mayordomo" in *Album of Mexico*
1865
20 × 30 cm
The Getty Center for the History of Art and the Humanities
Santa Monica, California, U.S.A.
Inv. 93.R.20

185. L. Falconett
"San Luis Potosí. Procession de N.D. del Carmen", in *Album of Mexico*
1865
20 × 30 cm
The Getty Center for the History of Art and the Humanities
Santa Monica, California, U.S.A.
Inv. 93.R.20

186. L. Falconett
"México, Scène d'Intérieur", in *Album of Mexico*
1865
20 × 30 cm
The Getty Center for the History of Art and the Humanities
Santa Monica, California, U.S.A.
Inv. 93.R.20

187. André-Toussaint Petitjean
"Procession du Mercredi Saint a Durango", in *Album of Sketches, Watercolors, Clichés-verre and Photographs of México*
1864-1866
18 × 27 cm
The Getty Center for the History of Art and the Humanities
Santa Monica, California, U.S.A.
Inv. 93.R.3

188. L. Falconett
"Mexico. Femmes du Peuple, La cebollera. Marchande d'Oignons. Indiennes", in *Album of Mexico*
1865
20 × 30 cm
The Getty Center for the History of Art and the Humanities
Santa Monica, California, U.S.A.
Inv. 93.R.20

189. Anonymous
"Maison de [...] Bazaine. plazuela Buenavista",
from the album *Souvenirs de Mexique*
ca. 1863
24 × 31 cm
The Getty Center for the History of Art and
the Humanities
Santa Monica, California, U.S.A.
Inv. 90.R.74

190. Anonymous
"École des Mines (Mexico)", from the album
Souvenirs de Mexique
ca. 1863
24 × 31 cm
The Getty Center for the History of Art and
the Humanities
Santa Monica, California, U.S.A.
Inv. 90.R.74

191. André-Toussaint Petitjean
*"Mes Impressions de Voyage. Durango. 29
decembre, 1862"*, in *Album of Sketches,
Watercolors, Clichés-verre and Photographs of
Mexico*
1864-1866
18 × 27 cm
The Getty Center for the History of Art and
the Humanities
Santa Monica, California, U.S.A.
Inv. 93.R.3

192. Pedro Gualdi
View of Mexico City
1842
oil on canvas
149 × 100 cm
Collection of Alejandro y Germaine Burillo
Mexico City

193. Phillipe Ronde
San Juan de Ulúa and Veracruz (detail)
1851
ink on paper
24 × 33.8 cm
Bibliothèque Nationale de France
Paris, France
Inv. 198b-d/III-43

194. Eugenio Landesio
On the Way to Santa María Regla
1855-1877
oil on canvas
44.5 × 72 cm
Private collection
Mexico City

195. Paul Fischer
Study of Plants (detail)
late 19th century
pencil and watercolor on paper
16.5 × 25 cm
Private collection
Mexico City

196. Eugenio Landesio
On the Way to Omitlán, Hidalgo
1857
oil on canvas
45.5 × 63 cm
Musée du Louvre
Paris, France
Inv. MNR 341

197. Juan Patricio Morlete Ruiz
*View of the Main Plaza of Mexico City and the
Royal Palace* (detail)
ca. 1770-1772
oil on canvas
99 × 156 cm
National Museum of Fine Arts
Valetta, Malta
Inv. 8419

198. Eugenio Landesio
Hacienda de Colón
oil on canvas
83 × 117 cm
Collection of the Montiel Saucedo Family
Mexico City

199. Jean-Frédéric Waldeck
Landscape with Mountains in Chiapas (detail)
ca. 1832-1836
oil on wood
30 × 39 cm
Private collection
Mexico City

200. Hubert Sattler
Tulum
1866
oil on canvas
101 × 123.5 cm
Salzburger Museum Carolino Augusteum
Salzburg, Austria
Inv. 7142/49

201. Daniel Thomas Egerton
Valley of Mexico
ca. 1837
oil on canvas
105 × 143 cm
Collection of Banco Nacional de México, S.A.
Mexico City

pp. 256-257. EUGENIO LANDESIO
ON THE WAY TO OMITLÁN, HIDALGO [196]

CREDITS

General Coordination	Cándida Fernández de Calderón
	Alberto Sarmiento
Research and Curatorship	Pablo Diener
Consultation	Juana Gutiérrez Haces
Organization and Investigative Support	Melinda Cásares Gil
	Maricarmen Martuscelli González
Support in Photographic Research	Jacques Paire
Coordination of Curatorship and Mounting	Cándida Fernández de Calderón
	Leticia Gámez Ludgar
Curatorial Direction	Pablo Diener
	Juana Gutiérrez Haces
Mounting	Arturo Hernández Morales
	Antonio Alonso Alcalá
	José Germán Pérez García
	Jesús Reséndiz
Panorama: Research and Execution Historical Consultation	Dante Escalante
	Juana Gutiérrez Haces
Documentary Video	Aurelio de los Reyes
Conservation and Technical Consultation	José Sol Rosales
Transportation Logistics	Alfart, S.A.

EUGENIO LANDESIO
HACIENDA DE COLÓN [198]

Coordination of the Catalog	Cándida Fernández de Calderón
	Alberto Sarmiento
	Pablo Diener
*Translations**	Jeffrey Seefeldt
	Peter Billaudelle
	Pablo Diener
Design	Daniela Rocha / Ediciones del Equilibrista, S.A. de C.V.
Editorial Coordination	Carlos Miranda / Ediciones del Equilibrista, S.A. de C.V.
Editorial Production	Ediciones del Equilibrista, S.A. de C.V.
Photography	Pablo Diener
	Jorge Contreras
	Jörg P. Sanders
	Sdmeider-Schmilz
	Elke Walford. Fotowerkstatt
	Enrique Salazar
	Rafael Doniz
	Beppo Laudano
	Gonzalo de la Serna
Support by the Delegation of the European Community Commission in Mexico	Federico Bonilla
Administration	Ángeles González
	Ernesto Ochoa
Educational Services	Mónica Ponce
Librarian	Lilia Delgado

* The translator wishes to note that because various authors consulted Spanish translations in their research, several quotations and titles of works were not available in the original French, German or English and were, therefore, translated from the Spanish.

ACKNOWLEDGMENTS

Banco Nacional de México, S.A. through *Fomento Cultural Banamex, A.C.,* greatly acknowledges the institutions, museums, galleries and individuals whose valuable collaboration made this exhibition possible.

Delegation of the European Community Commission in Mexico
EMB. JACQUES LECOMTE

Ibero Cermex, S. A.
VALENTÍN DÍEZ MORODO
ALFONSO F. MORODO

Aeroméxico
JEAN BERTHELOT

Casa de América, Madrid, Spain
EDUARDO GARRÍGUEZ
RAMÓN GANDARIAS ALONSO DE CELIS
ROSA REGÁS

Instituto Goethe, A.C., Mexico City
HORST DEINWALLNER
GISELA LANG

Presidency of the Republic of Malta
DR. UGO MIFSUD BONNICI,
President

Mexican Department of State
General Office for Cultural Affairs
EMILIO CÁRDENAS
BEATRIZ MARGÁIN
JORGE LÓPEZ CASTRO

Embassy of Mexico in Germany
EMB. JUAN JOSÉ BREMER

Mexican Consulate in Berlin
ADRIANA VALADÉS

Embassy of Chile in Mexico
EDUARDO CRUZ

Embassy of Hungary in Mexico
SILVIA RAMÍREZ REYO

Embassy of Mexico in the United Kingdom
ALEJANDRA DE LA PAZ

Embassy of Germany in Mexico
GABRIELLE WEBER

Embassy of Austria in Mexico
EMB. KURT HENGL
JULIAN FRIEDRICH

JEAN-FRÉDÉRIC WALDECK
LANDSCAPE WITH MOUNTAINS IN CHIAPAS, (DETAIL) [199]

— Bristol Museums and Art Gallery; Bristol City Council; Bristol, England

— Deutsches Museum; Munich, Germany

— Graphische Sammlung Albertina; Vienna, Austria

— Hamburger Kunsthalle; Hamburg, Germany

— Kupferstichkabinett; Staatliche Museen zu Berlin; Preussischer Kulturbesitz; Berlin, Germany

— Louisiana State Museum; New Orleans, Louisiana, U.S.A.

— Musée du Louvre; Paris, France

— Musée Royal de l'Armée et D'Histoire Militaire; Brussels, Belgium

— Museo de América; Madrid, Spain

— Museo de Arte del Estado de Veracruz; Orizaba, Mexico

— Museo Franz Mayer; Mexico City

— Museo Nacional de Ciencias Naturales; Consejo Superior de Investigaciones Científicas; Madrid, Spain

— Museo Nacional de Historia (INAH); Mexico City

— Museo Naval; Madrid, Spain

— Museo Soumaya; Mexico City

— Museum Für Völkerkunde; Staatliche Museen Zu Berlin; Preussischer Kulturbesitz; Berlin, Germany

— National Maritime Museum; Greenwich, England

— National Museum of Fine Arts; Valletta, Malta

— National Museum of Natural History, Smithsonian Institution; Washington, D.C., U.S.A.

— Salzburger Museum Carolino Augusteum; Salzburg, Austria

— Staatliche Graphische Sammlung; Munich, Germany

— The British Museum, Department of Ethnography, Museum of Mankind; London, England

— Victoria and Albert Museum; London, England

— National Széchényi Library; Budapest, Hungary

— Österreichisches Staatsarchiv, Nachlässe und Sammlungen; Vienna, Austria

— Real Jardín Botánico, Consejo Superior de Investigaciones Científicas; Madrid, Spain

— The Getty Center of the History of Art and the Humanities, Santa Monica, California, U.S.A.

— Universidad Iberoamericana, A.C., Biblioteca Manuel Arango Arias; Mexico City

— Universidad de Sevilla, Facultad de Geografía e Historia, Departamento de Historia del Arte; Seville, Spain

— Universidad Nacional Autónoma de México, Facultad de Ingeniería; Mexico City

— Artis LTD.; British Virgin Islands

— Caylus Anticuario, S.A.; Madrid, Spain

— Galería A. Cristóbal; Mexico City

— Galería de Arte Jorge Carroza; Santiago, Chile

— Guillermo de Osma Galería; Madrid, Spain

— Deutsch-Südamerikanische Bank A.G.; Hamburg, Germany

— ING Baring Holdings, Limited; London, England

— Archivo General de la Nación; Mexico City

— Biblioteca Centro de Estudios de Historia de México, Condumex; Mexico City

— Biblioteca Nacional; Madrid, Spain

— Bibliothèque Nationale de France; Paris, France

— Filmoteca de la Universidad Nacional Autónoma de México; Mexico City

— Fototeca del Instituto Nacional de Antropología e Historia; Pachuca, Hidalgo, Mexico

— Ibero-Amerikanisches Institut, Preussischer Kulturbesitz; Berlin, Germany

— Mapoteca Orozco y Berra, Centro de Estadística Agropecuaria, SAGAR; Mexico City

Emilia Aglio Mayor

Donald Anderle

Josefina Barreiro

Anne Barz

Dean Baylis

Anja Bernhardt

Alan Borg

Richard Bösel

Gail Boyle

Dietrich Briesemeister

Peter Broucek

Patricia Burguete

Paz Cabello Carro

Elizabeth Carmichael

Jorge Carroza López

Miguel Ángel Corzo

Susan Crawford

Dominic Cutajar

Jean-Pierre Cuzin

Aurore de Laval

Alison Deeprose

Patty Eischen

Andrés Escalera Ureña

Jean Favier

Manuela Fischer

María Gaida

María Concepción García Sáiz

Enrique Hugo García Valencia

Sue Giles

Peter C. Glidewell

Catherine Goeres

Emilio Gómez Piñol

María González de Castejón

José Ignacio González-Aller Hierro

Piet de Gryse

Anthony Guy Visher

Kirsten Hammer

Robert Heitmeier

Klaus Helfrich

Christiane Hennet

María Dolores Higueras Rodríguez

Kustos Jenns Howoldt

Claudia Kheel-Cox

Jonathan King

Susan Lambert

Helmut R. Leppien

María Luisa Ferrer Garcés

Sarah McCormick

Brendan McCullagh

John Morgan

Isabel Morón

Barbara O'Connor

Konrad Oberhuber

John Orbell

Carlos Ortega

Peter Osborne

Guillermo de Osma

Gloria Pérez de Rada

Wolf Peter Fehlhammer

Géza Proprády

Andrée Pouderoux

Marcela Ramírez

Paula Richardson Fleming

Gottfried Riemann

María Edelmira Ríos-Samaniego

Concepción Romero

Nieves Sáenz

Fuensanta Salvador

María Pilar de San Pío

Araceli Sánchez-Piñol

Nikolaus Schaffer

Salomon & Brigitte Schärer

Gisela Scheffler

Max Seeberger

James F. Sefcik

Janet Skidmore

Dennis J. Stanford

George Syamken

David Taylor

Frances Tepak

Gabriel Terrades Pujol

Vyrtis Thomas

Eduardo Uhart

Rainer Ulrichs

Erich Urbanek

Elke Walford

Joanna Wallace

P. N. Wilson

Kurt Zeitler

José Ignacio Aldama

Lucía Alfaro

Guillermo Andrade

Dolores Béistegui de Robles

Antonio Bolívar

Ana María Buganza

Patricia Burguete

Alejandro y Germaine Burillo

Jorge Carretero Madrid

Gustavo Contreras

José Manuel Covarrubias Solís

Agustín Cristóbal

Ángel Cristóbal

Magdalena Cuevas de Carral

Miguel Ángel Fernández

Maricela Fonseca Larios

Claudia Fursagua

Juan Manuel Galarza y Mercado

Patricia Galeana

Pablo García y Colomé

Jesús González Vaquero

Lucía Gutiérrez

Víctor Hernández Ortiz

Enrique Hernández Pons

Olimpia de Hernández Pons

Lourdes Herrasti Maciá

Socorro Lagos de Minvielle

Jorge López Castro

Eleazar López Zamora

Beatriz Margáin

Roberto L. Mayer

Sergio Montiel

Luis Ortiz Macedo

Dolores Páez

Víctor Manuel Pérez Pineda

María Eugenia Ponce

Manuel Ramos Medina

Alma Ranfla

Dinorah Razo Veyro

Antonio Reyna Fischer

Héctor Rivero Borrell

Patricia Segués de Barrios Gómez

Soumaya Slim Domit

Ivan Trujillo

Dionisio Velasco Polo

Pilar Verdejo

Juan Pablo Villegas Pastor

Sandra Weisenthall

Rosa María Zaldívar Díaz López

Sergio Zaldívar

Benito Zamora

pp. 266-267. HUBERT SATTLER

TULUM [200]

DANIEL THOMAS EGERTON
VALLEY OF MEXICO [201]

The idea of organizing this exhibition, which brings together some of the works executed by the European "traveler-painters" in Mexico, emerged with the consciousness of the important presence of the European artists and the rich cultural contribution Europe made to Mexico. Conceiving this exhibition was relatively easy, but making it a reality was a totally different operation!

Without the involvement of Luis Guembe, of the Directorate General Audiovisual, Media, Information, Communication and Culture of the Commission in Brussels, who put me in contact with Alejandro Betancourt of Banamex, it would not have been possible to mount this exhibition.

Additionally, this initiative was brought to fruition thanks to the ever-generous help and support of Cándida Fernández de Calderón, Director of Fomento Cultural Banamex and that of her collaborator, Alberto Sarmiento; of the services of the Directorate General North-South Relations of the European Commission, most particularly the participation of Manel Camós and Imma Roca; as well as that of Federico Bonilla, from our Delegation in Mexico, who supported the idea and helped in obtaining its financing. To all of them, my special gratitude.

JACQUES LECOMTE
Head of the Delegation of the
European Community Commission in Mexico

EUROPEAN TRAVELER-ARTISTS
IN NINETEENTH-CENTURY MEXICO
was printed in August 1996 in the facilities of
Artes Gráficas Panorama. The typography
utilized in its composition were Adobe
Garamond and Caslon Open Face. The paper
utilized was 150-gram Magnostar. The
printing was supervised by Juan Carlos Burgoa.
1000 copies of the English edition were printed.